Endorsements:

"The phrase in Scripture... *"weary in well-doing"* is one that many of us are familiar with as we walk through each day. The demands on our time, and our abilities, seem to grow exponentially. As a result, productivity, impact and our spiritual well-being suffers. It is imperative that we do everything possible to ensure a life that is grounded in the Biblical principles of a successful Christian life. Timothy Barclay has given us a model...a how-to manual...on doing just that. I encourage you to read this book and allow it to help you get on the right path and stay there!"

Jonathan Falwell
Pastor, Thomas Road Baptist Church

Jonathan Falwell is the senior pastor of the 20,000 member Thomas Road Baptist Church (trbc.org) in Lynchburg, Virginia. He is the Executive Vice President of Spiritual Affairs at Liberty University, the largest evangelical university in the world. He has authored three books: InnovateChurch (Broadman & Holman), One Great Truth (Howard Publishers) and 1000 Days (Thomas Nelson Publishers).

"The trait of resilience has never been more important as people struggle to simply keep up with the daily demands of life. Christians are not an exception. However, there is a way to live effectively in the midst of difficult times and still have peace. This devotional is a ground-breaking & passionately written guide that uses current research on known factors that creates resilience; and applies them in a biblical fashion. Dr. Barclay provides the practical tools necessary to create spiritual resilience which will enable the reader to sustain a higher quality of life. I highly recommend this excellent resource."

Tim Clinton, Ed.D.
President, American Association of Christian Counselors
www.aacc.net

Dr. Tim Clinton is President of the nearly 50,000-member American Association of Christian Counselors (AACC), the largest and most diverse Christian counseling association in the world. He is Professor of Counseling and Pastoral Care, and Executive Director of the Center for Counseling and Family Studies at Liberty University. He is recognized as a world leader in faith and mental health issues and has authored 20 books including his latest, Breakthrough: When to Give In, When to Push Back.

"Dr. Barclay's highly innovative H-CAP approach to building spiritual growth, strength, and resilience is biblical, practical, and professionally competent. His emphasis on hope, commitment, accountability, and passion speaks to the deepest needs of our lives. Don't miss it!"

Ed Hindson, Th.D.
Distinguished Professor of Religion
Dean, Institute of Biblical Studies
Liberty University

Dr. Ed Hindson is the President of World Prophetic Ministry and Bible Teacher on The King Is Coming telecast. He is also the Assistant Chancellor and Dean of the Institute of Biblical Studies at Liberty University in Virginia. Ed has written over 20 books, including Final Signs; Approaching Armageddon; and Is the Antichrist Alive and Well? He has served as the editor of five major Study Bibles, including the Gold Medallion Award-winning Knowing Jesus Study Bible (Zondervan) and the best-selling King James Study Bible (Thomas Nelson). He is currently co-editing the new 16-volume Twenty-First Century Biblical Commentary series on the New Testament (AMG).

"I have known Dr. Barclay for over 20 years. Long before he had developed this devotional model, he was living it with passion, purpose and focus. His heart has always been committed to seeing others encounter Christ in a real and personal way. I'm so excited to see others experience this unique, powerful, approach to practical discipleship. I believe the H-CAP model will equip each believer with Biblical tools and tangible strategies for living a joyful & growing adventure with Christ. This approach is all about multiplication. Get it, read it, live it and repeat it!"

Pastor Chilly Chilton
Founder & Lead Pastor of Courage Church
A Multisite Faith Community in the heart of Detroit

Chilly Chilton is a youth specialist, church planter, lead pastor, mentor and blogger. His dynamic personality and bold message has touched the lives of people around the world for over 25 years. In the fall of 2004, Chilly planted Real Church in cultural center of Detroit. He now pastors two campuses that are radically impacting the communities of "America's Most Dangerous City."

High Capacity Living: A Practical Devotional to Building a Resilient Life

Tim Barclay, Ph.D.

Licensed Clinical Psychologist
Associate Professor, Liberty University

CROSSLINK
PUBLISHING

High Capacity Living: A Practical Devotional to Building a Resilient Life

Ⓓ CrossLink Publishing
Ⓒ www.crosslinkpublishing.com

ISBN 978-1-936746-55-2

Library of Congress Control Number: 2013937837

Acknowledgements

The model outlined in this devotional is taken from personal experience and research. It has taken many years of self-reflection and study to recognize these traits and to put them into operation. I live my life by these principles and my desire is to share them so others can live an abundant life without fear or regret. Of course, I must thank my lovely, beautiful, and committed wife Lynn, for 28 years of bliss, patience, and understanding. I would not be where I am or have the family I have without her. She has always been the glue that holds everything together (outside of God of course). I am also grateful to my kids, Stephanie Barclay Krop, Brittany Barclay Krop, and Tim Jr. I am so proud of all of you. You have provided me such inspiration to be the example I needed to be. I only hope that I've done a good job.

I would also thank those who have made a significant impact on my spiritual life, my good friend Pastor Alan "Chilly" Chilton, a true modern day apostle to the inner cities of America and the founder of Courage Church in the heart of Detroit; Pastor David Thomas, senior pastor of Victory Christian Center in Coitsville, OH.; Tom Sinclair who was the first person to witness to me and the one responsible for presenting the gospel to Lynn and me and brought us to church 28 years ago; and to my first pastor and teacher of the gospel, Pastor Vince Redhouse. You all share in the lives touched by this work due to your faithfulness. To my Mom and Dad, Don and Cathy Barclay; you always made me believe that I could accomplish anything.Thanks for pushing me and demanding excellence from me. I know there were times when it seemed like it wasn't sinking in, but it was.

The Development of the H-CAP Model and How to Use This Devotional

We truly don't realize what our potential is in being children of God. Sadly, we don't live up to our true abilities. What God sees in us and what we see in ourselves are diametrically opposite. Living the abundant life, the life we read about in Jesus as He walked the earth, the life of the apostles and prophets, and the amazing things God did through them is the same life God is calling you to. God wants to bring out your full potential. However, you must be a willing participant. My former pastor, David Thomas, from Victory Christian Center in Youngstown, OH always says, "Without God, we cannot, but without us, God will not." God will not force Himself on you. However, if you're tired of being normal, tired of feeling like you're running the "rat race" of life and aren't truly enjoying life, if you don't have a purpose to look forward to everyday and you're ready to change, this is your book. Living abundantly is about living a life of significance. If your goal is to live with a purpose and leave a lasting legacy, you need to keep reading.

The High Capacity Model of Well-being or H-CAP is a model that originated from my clinical work and research on resilience. People who are able to bounce back and adapt are less vulnerable to mental illness and have an overall better outlook on life. In researching the most effective ways to help patients overcome their symptoms of mental illness and to create and live a better quality of life, I discovered this necessitated four traits; these traits are Hope, Commitment, Accountability, and Passion (H-CAP). As I reflected on this through prayer, research, and practice, I discovered that people don't get better and in general are not able to create an effective lifestyle unless they have hope. Hope is defined as a state of mind that is characterized by desire, expectation, and belief that a desired outcome can be achieved in spite of current circumstances. They have to believe that something good can happen in their lives. This mindset is the exact opposite of what I'd see in my patients. Outside of my practice, I also became aware that many people even those who don't suffer from mental illness, Christian or not, also lack hope. Sure people say they believe things all the time, but seldom does the belief rise to the level of sustained intentional goal directed behavior. In cases where it does, it lasts only until they come across the first road block and then they give up.

I also discovered that people don't move forward in their life unless they're willing to commit to behaviors that will make their hope realized. Commitment is where you put feet to your hope. Commitment is defined as an obligation to act regardless of emotion. It's a state of mind that says "I'm willing to do whatever it takes to get there." Many people, Christians included, want certain things for their life but seldom are they willing to pay the price for it. In these cases, hope ends up being a pipedream, a false hope. They believe that the work and effort it will take to change their life just isn't worth it. People develop this mindset because they're willing to settle. They're comfortable in their misery. We make similar decisions all the time. God holds out His hands and tells us which one contains life and which one contains death. Why do so many choose death? Many are simply not willing to make the commitment.

The third trait is that of Accountability. Accountability is defined as the willingness to accept responsibility for ones actions. It involves relinquishing the right to assign blame. The acceptance of responsibility occurs at an individual level and incorporates relationships with others for support. There is no such thing as a self-made person. Sure some will tell you they achieved success from nothing and that they did it all by themselves. However, careful examination of these facts shows this to not be the case. While it is true that success can be obtained from meager beginnings, they had to learn from someone. Someone had to show them the ropes. The human brain was wired for relationships. The neurological wiring in our brains for emotional regulation begins early in the womb and continues throughout infancy. These connections are dependent on the nature and quality with the caregiver relationship. We see relationship in the Godhead as well. The Father, Son, and Holy Spirit each have their individual roles yet neither act without the other.

In helping people achieve their goals, it's important to create an environment for success. There are two aspects to accountability. The first is aligning yourself with like-minded people. For example, if your goal is to create a resilient spirit, you need to align yourself with people who have the same goal and also with people who are resilient (stronger than you). By hanging around these people, their state of mind (way of thinking and behaving) will rub off on you. It goes back to the old lesson that you become like those you hang around. The second part of accountability is giving trusted people the right to enter your space and hold you accountable when you're not doing the things you're supposed to without being defensive. It takes a humble spirit to listen to others about our behavior without trying to defend our wrong behavior. If it stings to hear such things, there's some truth in it. This is why the Bible stresses the need for fellowship and warns against being unequally yoked with the world.

The last trait is Passion. Passion is the motivation for what we do. Research shows that passions can be obsessive or harmonious. You can always tell what a person's passions are based on his or her behavior regardless of what they say. Obsessive passion flows from the outside in. This means that the behaviors one engages in are needed because it makes them feel good about themselves in some way. They need the behaviors to define who they are. When the ability to engage in these behaviors is not available or no longer possible, it affects their self-image in a negative way. Sin can operate on this level. Harmonious passions work in the opposite direction. This type of passion flows from the inside out. The behaviors that one engages in from this type of passion are a result of who they are. They don't need the behaviors to make them feel anything about themselves. They know who they are; they engage in behaviors on their terms, they control the behavior instead of the behavior controlling them. Think of Jesus in this example. He didn't heal people, raise people from the dead, or die on the cross because He needed to feel good about himself or to feel worthwhile. He did those things because it's who He is.

To get to where you want to go, in this case the development of spiritual resilience, you need to have all four of these traits in operation. If you take one out of the equation, you'll miss it. The good news is that everyone has these traits. We're given them in the creation process. Mankind is made in the image of God. Because we're made in His image, we have characteristics of God within us. Just as in the natural conception process, everyone has 50% of their mother's DNA and 50% of their father's DNA. So it is with God. These traits embody God's character. God is Hope, God is the definition of Commitment, God, is also Accountability, and God is also Passion. These are the very traits that cause us to seek God in the first place. If we already have these traits then, what's the problem? What happens that prevents people from seeing and using them? The answer is LIFE. Life happens. As people experience life, they begin to lose focus of these traits. They begin to focus on the circumstances which serve to erode hope. Once hope begins to diminish, our commitment to engage in goal seeking and obtaining behaviors subside. We start to think, "What's the use? It doesn't matter anyway." When this mindset sets in, relationships start to become fractured (accountability). People begin to withdraw and isolate themselves in their own world and begin to believe that no one understands. What relationships they do have serves mainly to reinforce this mindset. Birds of a feather flock together. As these things happen, passions become obsessive. Life feels like it's been sucked out of you. People in this state engage in erratic behaviors that serve only to dig the hole deeper.

Sadly, this is how most people in the world live, including Christians. It's just as the author Henry David Thoreau writes "The mass of men lead lives of quiet desperation. What is called resignation is confirmed desperation...." Life is meant to be lived, experienced. To experience life is to live it abundantly. Many Christians make the false assumption that living an abundant life means the absence of difficulty, turmoil, sickness, and death. Many assume that abundant living means wealth. No, abundant living is the ability to experience Hope, Commitment, Accountability, and Passion in the midst of any circumstance. This is living. This is what awaits you. In spite of living in our frail human bodies in a fallen world, we can still have Hope, we can Commit to right living, we can have Accountable relationships where we can receive love, comfort, and support, and we can have Passion (love) for people and for what we do. This is resilience!

How to Use This Tool

Each day, you will read a verse on a trait in the order of Hope, Commitment, Accountability, and Passion. You may also spend time reading the verses that come before and after to get a better understanding of the context. Many of the entries set the context but others may be more complex and due to space and time, it is generally directed to read the chapter. After reading the verse, read the Meditation and Action. After you read this, sit and meditate, contemplate on what is written and how it applies to your life. Each meditation ends with an explicit action point that you will need to engage in to cultivate that trait in you. These are small steps, nothing elaborate. Just do it. Each of the actions steps contained in each of the devotions is proven to work to create a given trait. Each day begins with a new trait. Once you go through each of the traits, the fifth day will be a reflective overview of the previous four days along with additional action points. This is where you will put all of the traits into operation at once. You will cycle through the model every five days which will give you constant and repetitive exposure to the model and action steps in their application. There are over 300 entries. If you apply them daily, this will give you enough exposure to right thoughts and behaviors that will create a resilient spirit. It will happen slowly and over time. You will see the changes and most importantly, others will as well. It's the continuous application of these simple steps that will change your life.

Accompanying this devotional is the H-CAP Questionnaire. The HCAP Questionnaire is a brief 30 item assessment that measures each of the traits, Hope, Commitment, Accountability, and Passion. After taking and scoring the assessment, you can evaluate your individual strengths and weaknesses. You may choose to focus on building the traits you are weak in by applying the strategies for that given trait. The assessment and devotional can also be used in a group Sunday school class format. See the H-CAP Questionnaire and instructions in the Appendix.

Hope

13 Brothers and sisters, we do not want you to be uninformed about those who sleep in death, so that you do not grieve like the rest of mankind, who have no hope. 14 For we believe that Jesus died and rose again, and so we believe that God will bring with Jesus those who have fallen asleep in him. 15 According to the Lord's word, we tell you that we who are still alive, who are left until the coming of the Lord, will certainly not precede those who have fallen asleep. 16 For the Lord himself will come down from heaven, with a loud command, with the voice of the archangel and with the trumpet call of God, and the dead in Christ will rise first. 17 After that, we who are still alive and are left will be caught up together with them in the clouds to meet the Lord in the air. And so we will be with the Lord forever. 18Therefore, encourage one another with these words.

—I Thessalonians 4:13-18 NIV

Meditation and Action

To hope is to look ahead and believe in something that is not yet here. This act provides encouragement to the soul and mind. It brings a sense of peace. If you have a goal, a dream, something that you want to achieve, if you look at it even though it remains in the future, it serves as a motivator. That desire to get there keeps you moving in that direction. So it is with our faith. Paul tells us to encourage one another with the hope of Christ's return. Notice how he spends time on describing the events that will take place. We believe that Jesus died and rose again, we believe that He'll bring those who have passed away back with Him in His return, and He'll literally descend from the clouds to which we'll also be caught up together with Him. Think about what is to come and encourage each other by reminding each other that the time is near. It's the looking forward that enables us to stick it out. What's standing in your way today? Why do you allow yourself to become overwhelmed? Your task for today; look ahead into the future and find the hope. Don't be side tracked by the current circumstance. There's always something to look forward to.

Commitment

Therefore, since we are surrounded by such a great cloud of witnesses, let us throw off everything that hinders and the sin that so easily entangles. And let us run with perseverance the race marked out for us.

—Hebrews 12:1 NIV

Meditation and Action

People are often confused when they come across difficult times as if they are the only one. We live in a generation of quitters. Paul tells us to run the race with perseverance. This statement alone is a clue that the life we need to live will not be easy. Perseverance takes commitment, dedication. This cannot be tested unless we are tired and worn; beat down. Until this point, it is not perseverance. How do we then keep going in the midst of difficult times? Ah, it's where you fix your eyes. If it is on the current circumstances, surely you will tire and give up. However, the key is to look ahead to what you are running toward. Christ endured the cross because He thought it worthwhile to endure present suffering for the grand prize before Him. The lesson is that we have not yet suffered to this point. Discipline here is not one of punishment but one of "training." The reason we experience life with all the good and bad is for training. It's about spiritual, emotional, and physical development. The message then is to endure hardship as a good soldier. The choice of success is up to YOU and no one else. Will you persevere? Others are watching and possibly waiting to see how you run the race. Your decision will not only affect you but those around you. Choose success!

Accountability

Do not be misled: "Bad company corrupts good character."
—I Corinthians 15:33 NIV

Meditation and Action

A common trait shared among those who achieve their goals is that of accountability. I've always found it amazing to see people who for all intent and purposes would be expected to fail due to their upbringing or environment. However, in spite of the most challenging of circumstances, they choose to live life to its fullest. One of the driving forces behind all of these stories is a relationship with someone who held them accountable and believed in them. These relationships are characterized by love, acceptance, encouragement, trust, and longsuffering. This is what makes the human spirit grow and rise to the occasion. The fact that we acquire the characteristics of those we associate with is not new. Paul reminds us of this same lesson in I Corinthians 15:33 that bad company corrupts good character. Human beings are created for relationships; we seek them out. We adopt the nature of the relationships we most identify with, good or bad. The nature of the relationships we cling to then will dictate the course of our lives. Want to change your marriage, befriend those with strong marriages. Want to change your attitude, hang with people who are positive. Want to become closer to God, spend more time with Him and others who do the same. Want to change the course of your life? Change your company. You have everything to gain and absolutely nothing to lose!

Passion

Fix our eyes on Jesus, the pioneer and perfecter of faith. For the joy set before him he endured the cross, scorning its shame, and sat down at the right hand of the throne of God.
—Hebrews 12:2 NIV

Meditation and Action

Comparing our actions or results with others takes away our individual focus to run our own race. When we compare ourselves to others, the questions we ask ourselves revolve around thoughts like "I want to do what they are doing," "I have to do_____ in order to get noticed," "I have to do_____ in order to be good enough." Such thoughts lead to obsessive type behaviors that actually work against us. Living a harmonious passion and life requires that you take the focus off of others and what they are doing and focus on your goals, what you are doing. Being distracted by others, and worrying if we're ahead of them or behind, leads us to engage in behaviors for the sake of "winning" or "to make us feel good." In other words, the behaviors no longer flow naturally from our being but the behaviors become necessary to create our being. This is backwards and the opposite of what Christ experienced. The joy comes from running your own race without the distraction of measuring up. Create a harmonious passion for yourself, run your own race.

H-CAP Recap

You've just completed the first round of the H-CAP model. For this day, review the scriptures and meditations you covered over the last four days. If you're using the H-CAP Scale, you can focus on the areas that need improvement. On the first day, we examined the concept of Hope and how hope can be created through the process of encouragement. This is the main process by which hope is created. The problem is we often times don't allow ourselves to receive this encouragement because we're too focused on the circumstance. Remember, hope comes from the ability to see beyond what's in front of you. You'll need to intentionally look ahead to greater things. Try this.

We also examined the concept of Commitment through the process of perseverance. To persevere requires a commitment to keep going even though you don't feel like it. One of the things you'll notice is that as you persevere, you will also be encouraged. You may feel like quitting, DON'T. You're right on the brink of success.

Accountability necessitates relationship. As the Bible verse for this lesson says, we become the company we keep. Maybe you need to commit to making a change in the people you chose to associate with. Having problems with being hopeful and perseverance? Create friendships with people who are hopeful and have spiritual stamina. By doing this, you'll also become more hopeful and develop perseverance. In this week's lesson on Passion, we see that Christ was at a crossroads. He could have chosen not to endure the cross. He's God. However, He also knew that without the shedding of blood, His blood, redemption for mankind would be impossible. He neither did it for himself nor to feel good or acceptable to the Father. Just the opposite; he did it because it's who He is. It's simply his nature. Don't be distracted by life and the other people in it trying to keep up. Run your own race. Allow your passions to reveal themselves and live them out harmoniously, not for the sake of "keeping up."

To build resilience, intentionally act on the following:

1. Be encouraged by your future. It's what you choose to see, not what you see.
2. Commit yourself to acting in ways that produce what you hope for.
3. Try to create at least one accountable relationship with someone who is where you want to be or exhibits the spiritual strength you desire.
4. Begin making steps to create a harmonious passion for your life. For many of you, this may be a radical step. Start by writing down some goal. What do you want to do with your life? It's never too late to change course. Create a road map for yourself and keep reading. Your future is waiting!

Hope

13So he sent two of his disciples, telling them, "Go into the city and a man carrying a jar of water will meet you. Follow him. 14Say to the owner of the house he enters, 'The Teacher asks: Where is my guest room, where I may eat the Passover with my disciples?' 15He will show you a large upper room, furnished and ready. Make preparations for us there." 16The disciples left, went into the city and found things just as Jesus had told them. So they prepared the Passover.

—Mark 14:13-16 NIV

Meditation and Action

This verse describes hope in action. Jesus tells two of his disciples to do something for Him in preparation for the last supper. Being God, He sees and foretells them exactly what will happen and what they need to say. The disciples had to believe that it would be just as Jesus had told them for them to act. What if the disciple had thought, "What if the man He talks about is not there and what if there's more than one person carrying a jar, what if it doesn't work out like as He says, how will we find this place?" It's possible, as it is human nature to doubt. However, they took Jesus at His word. They believed that it would work out as He had said and committed to action by going. As it happened, it worked out just as Jesus had told them. By believing and acting on their belief served to strengthen their hope in Jesus. Hope and action (commitment) work together. You can't have one without the other as they work to fulfill each other. Being hopeful is the foundation to spiritual resilience. God has called you to great things. You must believe them to be true and that He will fulfill them in you. However, you must act in your belief in order for them to be fulfilled. This will always be accompanied with the opportunity to doubt, this is normal. Look beyond the doubt and believe what He says. What has God called in you to do? Look past current circumstances and live for what's ahead, put action to this hope and be amazed at its fulfillment.

Commitment

Commit everything you do to the LORD. Trust him, and he will help you.
—Psalm 37:5 NLT

Meditation and Action

Spiritual resilience requires nothing less than a total commitment. Commitment implies an obligation to act regardless of emotion. You're either in or you're out. Just as when the Bible says that He would have us either be hot or cold than to be lukewarm. However, to be committed to something also requires the ability and willingness to trust. It's trusting the one to whom we're making the commitment to that they will make good on their promise to us. The relationship between commitment and trust is true in all aspects of our lives. Think about your level of commitment to God. Do you really trust Him for your present and future circumstances or are you hedging? What's keeping you from complete trust; fear? Fear is a normal emotion when confronted with the unknown. Take a moment and think deeply about your level of commitment to God and the things that get in your way. When people fail to trust it's usually because of fear, fear that things won't work out as planned, fear, they it will take longer than expected. These fears keep us from doing. However, this is not faith. Just because things don't work out as we want, is this a reason to not serve God? Don't fear the fear but act rightly through it. A strange thing will happen as you do. This is where you'll find yourself walking on water. Miracles won't happen unless you're willing to go all the way.

Accountability

23Let us hold unswervingly to the hope we profess, for he who promised is faithful. 24 And let us consider how we may spur one another on toward love and good deeds. 25 Let us not give up meeting together as some are in the habit of doing, but let us encourage one another and all the more as you see the day approaching.

—Hebrews 10: 23-25; NIV

Meditation and Action

Paul exhorts us to persevere. Living out our faith is tough in a world that is full of temptation. This is no different today than in biblical times. Sure, we have many more things that compete for our attention than in biblical times, however, the message is the same. It doesn't matter how many things are out there that compete for our attention, the skills to combat this are the same. The key message in this passage is that we can't make it alone. Many people think they are self-sufficient, impendent, and think that they don't need others. This is exactly the opposite of what the Bible teaches though. In order to be spiritually strong, we need each other. The verse says *Let us consider how we may spur one another on* and *let us not give up meeting together as some are in the habit of doing.* This means that our spiritual development and resilience is contingent upon our interaction with other like-minded people. We grow from this. This is how we can hold onto our hope, unswervingly. We were created for relationships; iron sharpens iron. If your goal is to become spiritually resilient, you must commit to fostering relationships with like-minded people so their states of mind will rub off on you. Do you have others you can hang around who are strong believers? If so, make a commitment to keep these relationships current. If not, seek out people of faith and create these relationships. You're spiritual growth is dependent on this.

Passion

"For God so loved the world that he gave his one and only Son, that whoever believes in him shall not perish but have eternal life.

—John 3:16 NIV

Meditation and Action

God is the definition of passion. There is no greater love than the creator of love. The key in this verse for the development of passion is the word "gave." God gave something of Himself to us in our need. The act of giving to others is an act of love and demonstrates passion. You can tell where a person's passion lay based upon their committed behaviors. Is it harmonious or obsessive? God's love is always harmonious meaning that it flows out of His being. Love isn't something He does to make Him feel or think something about Himself. It's who He is. God's committed behaviors revolve around benevolence and holiness. This is the example that we are to follow in our lives. You can transform your heart (state of mind) by giving to others in need. However, don't do it to fill a void in yourself, do it because it's just the right thing to do. It's not about you; it's about others. To create harmonious passion in your life, begin by doing for others. This can take many forms, giving a compliment, encouragement, time, etc. As you get in the habit of giving and doing for others, the strange thing that happens is that you begin to not focus on the negative things in life. Giving changes your outlook. Do your obsessions have you running the rat race and make you feel like you're chasing your own tail? Give to others. Do one of these tasks today and every day and you'll be on your way to renewing your heart and mind.

H-CAP Recap

Reflecting on your progress is important. We need to always stop and reflect how we're doing. Have you been applying the principles of Hope, Commitment, Accountability, and Passion? To recap the skills you need to be engaging in, hope and action work together. Hope also requires an element of trust. To hope means that we are trusting that we will obtain what we are seeking. However, this doesn't mean that things will always work out as we want them to. Just because we can't control everything and things don't work out in our time table doesn't mean that we won't get what we hope for. We need to break the spoiled child syndrome that says if you love me, you won't hurt me or do things I don't like. As you apply these strategies, trust that God will do as He says. Don't allow your circumstances to dictate your hope and trust. Hope goes beyond circumstances

Remember that commitment is an obligation to act in spite of emotion (feeling). This means that regardless of what our circumstances may be, we need to commit to right behaviors. Everyone has good times and bad times; that's life. No one is exempt. Will you be so shallow to only engage in right behaviors when things go good and according to your plans? Maturity is defined by doing rightly in spite of circumstances. Don't allow your fear of what may or may not happen to dictate right behavior. Do it anyway. This is what resilient people do and if this is your goal, you need to imitate that behavior.

In working on the strategies we just discussed, you will need to have a support system that you can count on to keep you grounded and encouraged. Creating this requires intentional effort. Resilient people hang around resilient people. Properly utilized supports will provided much needed encouragement which keeps hope alive. Create and maintain these relationships.

The practice of giving and doing for others creates harmonious passion because these acts take the focus off of us and our circumstances. Acts of giving have a way of renewing our spirit. These acts also serve to reinforce accountability. In fact, these traits overlap in such a way that working on one can influence the others.

Intentionally implement the following:

1. Don't allow your circumstances to dictate your hope and trust. Hope goes beyond circumstances.
2. Don't allow your fear of what may or may not happen to dictate right behavior. Do it anyway.
3. Create and maintain accountable relationships as a source of encouragement to build hope and commitment.

4. A great way to create harmonious passion is to practice giving of yourself to others in various ways. This will take your mind off your circumstances and will not only grow your passion but hope and commitment as well.

Hope

Everything is possible for him who believes.
—Mark 9:23 NIV

Meditation and Action

Seriously meditate and consider this verse. Everything is possible! The key word though is to believe. True belief leads to action. The question is if the action is in the right direction, meaning does the action (committed behavior) get you what you want or not? You will always live out your belief. You can say you believe in one thing but your behavior may actually show that you believe in another. You will always go in the direction you're looking. This is a neurological principle but it also applies to your state of mind. People often say they believe in God and that He has called them to specific things. However, their behavior doesn't reveal the stated belief. This is the difference between mere words and action. This is what James talks about in James 2:18. Do your behaviors truly match what you say you believe? You can align hope and action simply by being vigilant in reminding yourself about what you're hoping for. This is absolutely essential. You can't state a belief and just think that it will just remain there floating around in the recesses of your mind. This doesn't produce action. This is just wearing a label. You need to keep it active in the forefront of your mind. This is done by always reflecting on it.

This act in and of itself is hope in action and serves to keep it alive which results in committed behavior. Yes, everything is possible for those who believe. Live it!

Commitment

> For God so loved the world that he gave his one and only Son, that whoever believes in him shall not perish but have eternal life.
>
> —John 3:16 NIV

Meditation and Action

God is the definition of commitment. Recall that commitment is an obligation to act regardless of emotion. God was so committed to our redemption that He gave everything. God, the Father, gave the life of His son, Jesus, who willingly laid down his life. This was the only way for mankind to be redeemed. It required the perfect sacrifice and no one else could fulfill that obligation other than God Himself. Recall that in the garden prior to His arrest, Jesus prayed to God to be spared if there was another way. However, knowing the Father's will, He accepted it out of the obligation to love and to be obedient. Take a moment and think about the magnitude of this act and allow it to really sink in. Can we dare to give to God anything less than our best after such a sacrifice? There is no greater form or level of commitment than when one is willing to lay down their life for another. God knew that this level of sacrifice was the only way to redeem mankind and so was committed to making the way possible for us. You see His commitment to us; where is your commitment to Him and how do you show that commitment? Resilience demands nothing less. Begin by making a commitment to spending time with God on a regular basis. You don't have to have an agenda, just sit in quiet reflection and let Him speak to you. Commit yourself to doing for others which is allowing Him to live through you.

Accountability

1 Dear friends, this is now my second letter to you. I have written both of them as reminders to stimulate you to wholesome thinking. 2 I want you to recall the words spoken in the past by the holy prophets and the command given by our Lord and Savior through the apostles.

—2 Peter 3:1-2; NIV

Meditation and Action

The book of 2 Peter addresses the dangers of false teachers that threatened to corrupt their faith. Conforming to spiritual truth is the best defense against false teachers and doctrines. Paul was obligated to the church to keep this in the forefront of their mind. As an apostle and leader of the church, he was accountable for the spiritual development of his disciples. Paul was in the habit of reminding his disciples for the purpose of *stimulating them to wholesome thinking so they would remember.* We need to be mindful and be responsible for what we let into our mind. We are the gatekeepers to our mind. You can choose to listen to people who serve only to bring you down and believe the lies that serve to hinder your faith or you can listen to truth. Wholesome thinking is the key. Many people struggle with this because they either go it alone or surround themselves with the wrong people as in the case outlined in 2 Peter. What you choose to dwell on is an individual responsibility but aligning yourself with the right people and creating accountability, we can make this task much easier. Don't be deceived. Make it a point today and every day to think on things that are pure, right, excellent, and worthy of praise. Intentionally surround yourself with like-minded people who can pour these thoughts into you but also act by stimulating right thinking in others.

Passion

8Study this Book of Instruction continually. Meditate on it day and night so you will be sure to obey everything written in it. Only then will you prosper and succeed in all you do. 9This is my command—be strong and courageous! Do not be afraid or discouraged. For the LORD your God is with you wherever you go."

—Joshua 1:8-9 NLT

Meditation and Action

Where do we get courage from in light of problems? It comes from our confidence that we can make it, we can overcome, past and current knowledge, hope in the future. In matters of our faith, this comes from studying God's word. This verse tells us to study it continually, meditating on it day and night. We can always carry God's word in our heart when we meditate on the Bible and biblical principles. It's only as we meditate on these things will they get into our heart and mind for transformation to take place. This transformation leads to the creation of a harmonious passion. As we create and feed a harmonious passion, we become strong, courageous, and fearless. If you find yourself struggling, getting run down, becoming fearful, meditate on God's word. You can tell what a person dwells on through how they behave and act out their passions. When they are obsessive, these thoughts and subsequent behaviors will become self-serving. You need to dwell on the right things. Studying these devotions and applying them to your life, is a great way to accomplish this task. Engagement of these strategies and making them part of your everyday life will automatically cause you think about Godly things. Your task for today is to take what you've learned so far and make an intentional effort to think about them throughout your day and every day.

H-CAP Recap

R ead over the verses for Hope, Commitment, Accountability, and Passion. Your behaviors are reflective of what you truly believe regardless of what you say you believe in. The object in building spiritual resilience is to get the two to match up. Continued reflection on what you hope for is a great way to keep the hope active. This keeps hope in the forefront of your mind. You will really need to reflect on the goal when confronted with difficult times. It's during times of trouble when people generally retreat with thoughts of giving up and thinking there is no use. This is the opposite of what you need to be doing in those moments. Encourage yourself by looking through circumstances to what you're hoping for. This will keep it alive.

Resilience by definition requires 100% commitment. God doesn't want 50%-60% of you; He wants and demands all or nothing. If you're married, think about your relationship with your spouse, do you want only a partial commitment? Is it okay for them to be faithful 10, 20, or 60% of the time? This may sound ridiculous; however, God demands the same. He's 100% committed to us and He's already demonstrated that to us. Where do your commitments lay?

It's often said that the mind is the battleground for the soul. The things you dwell on, the things that dominate your thinking will reveal themselves in behaviors. It's important to train yourself in thinking on the right things to keep you moving in the right direction. This takes a considerable amount of training and requires accountability. Remember, birds of a feather flock together.

Passion is enhanced when our thoughts reflect right thinking. As in this week's action point on Accountability, dwelling on biblical principles and godly things influence our behavior in a positive way. The same is true in the opposite direction. If you want to go in the right direction and build resilience, you need to train your mind to think like strong godly people think. Applying the strategies outlined in this devotional is a great way to train your mind. Keep moving forward.

Intentionally implement the following:

1. Create a habit of encouraging yourself by looking through circumstances to what you're hoping for.
2. Evaluate your commitment to God. Are you giving 100% or do you split your loyalties? Spend more time in quiet reflection and doing things for others. Allow God to be seen through your actions.
3. Train your mind to think on godly principles. You can do this by not only making intentional efforts to apply these strategies to your

life but also creating accountable relationships where encouragement is reciprocal.

4. Passion is not only enhanced by right thinking but intentionally meeting needs of others is like adding fuel to a burning fire. Keep each of these strategies working in your life. You just need to apply one from each trait and work them each day.

Hope

18 Zechariah asked the angel, "How can I be sure of this? I am an old man and my wife is well along in years." 19 The angel answered, "I am Gabriel. I stand in the presence of God, and I have been sent to speak to you and to tell you this good news. 20 And now you will be silent and not able to speak until the day this happens, because you did not believe my words, which will come true at their proper time."
—Luke 1:18-20 NIV

Meditation and Action

You may need to read this verse a few times for the message to sink in. Zechariah is confronted by a heavenly being, not just an angel but the Archangel, Gabriel. A passive reading may seem like an average conversation between two people. Perhaps Zechariah took it this way given his response. It would stand to reason that if an Archangel appeared to someone, this alone would cause one to believe. However, we know this to not be the case as many people were witness to the miracles of Jesus but still didn't believe. As if having a heavenly being appearing to you and giving you good news isn't enough, Zechariah asks "how can I know for sure?" Really! What more could he ask for? The problem was his lack of belief. If he didn't take the presence of the angel as being enough and the fact that Gabriel told him that he was sent by God himself, what more could there be? There comes a point where you just have to believe for the sake of belief. The hope

Gabriel was offering to Zachariah was the hope of a child, something to look forward to and prepare for. It was a done deal. You may not have a visit from Gabriel but you do have the word of God. Its promises are still valid and apply to you. He offers abundant life to all who believe. Don't ask, "How can I know this for sure?" Believe to the point of action and you will see for yourself. Believe to the point of action!

Commitment

28"Lord, if it's you", Peter replied, "tell me to come to you on the water."29 "Come", he said. Then Peter got down out of the boat, walked on the water and came toward Jesus.30But when he saw the wind, he was afraid and, beginning to sink, cried out, "Lord, save me!"31Immediately Jesus reached out his hand and caught him. "You of little faith," he said, "why did you doubt?"
—Mathew 14:28-31 NIV

Meditation and Action

What a great example of commitment this is. Peter is so committed to his belief in what he was seeing that he challenges Jesus to bid him to come out and meet Him on the water. Jesus then puts the challenge back onto Peter and tells him to put his faith where his mouth is. Peter defies nature by stepping out of the boat and walks on water. However, as he realized he was committing an unnatural act, his attention went to the wind and waves that challenged his commitment. Taking his eyes off of his savior and focusing on the storm caused him to sink. How many times do we do this very thing? God calls us to the impossible, however, in order to do it we need to stay committed to going where we're looking. A process I call *mental optometry.* We need to stay focused on Him and not our circumstances no matter how difficult they may appear. God's challenge to you is the same He gave to Peter. He bids you to step out of the boat, your comfort zone, and meet Him. Yes, it may appear to be impossible, however, being committed to making your hope realized allows miracles to happen. Going through a rough time? If you focus on the circumstances, your emotions and behaviors will follow; focus on Christ and he'll keep you from sinking. Stay committed to looking where you want to go.

Accountability

Go, gather together all the Jews that are present in Shushan, and fast ye for me, and neither eat nor drink three days, night or day: I also and my maidens will fast likewise; and so will I go in unto the king, which [is] not according to the law: and if I perish, I perish.

—Esther 4:16 KJV

Meditation and Action

The story of Esther, Mordecai, and Haman is one that demonstrates God's provision when all appears to be hopeless. In order to save the Jews, Mordecai asked Esther to go before her husband the King and plead for the lives of the Jewish people against Haman's order. Haman wanted to destroy the Jews and devised a scheme to eliminate the Jewish customs and to adopt the customs of the land under penalty of death. Haman presented this in a way to the King and tricked him in giving his permission. Esther makes a bold decision to risk her own life and present herself to the King without his permission which would mean death, even for her. Esther knows that she needs support and asks that the Jewish people gather together and commit to praying for her with fasting for 3 days and nights. In order for the plan to be successful, she needed the commitment and support of other people to pray on her behalf. As result, God came through. We know how the story ends with the exposure and death of Haman with the gallows he had built for Mordecai. Haman fell victim to his own plan. However, what made this work was the support Esther had. We need others to support us not only in times of trouble but in good times as well. Support keeps us grounded and serves to keep us moving in the right direction. Do you need support for something you're facing or do you know of someone who needs support? Make an intentional decision to seek out support and or give support to someone. This will help keep you on the right track but also encourage you.

Passion

Those who live according to the sinful nature have their minds set on what that nature desires; but those who live in accordance with the Spirit have their minds set on what the Spirit desires.

—Romans 8:5 NIV

Meditation and Action

The mind that's set on sinful desires becomes an obsessive passion. In this case, behaviors work to fill a void and we begin to engage in behaviors to satisfy the craving that void creates. Following obsessive passions leads to feeling burned out. It leaves people with a sense of being lost, a "what's the use" attitude. Such living leaves people hopeless with a routine of simply going through the motions. If this sounds familiar, that's because the majority of the world's population lives this way. They live life on life's terms instead of living life on their terms, or in this case, God's. The counter to this form of passion is to refocus your mind's eye where you really want to go, which is the goal of creating high capacity living. How do you set your mind on what the Spirit desires? You accomplish this by meditating on the word of God. By prayerfully meditating on godly principles and applying them which is what you're doing by going through this devotional, you're actually transforming your mind. Over time, this transformation will work itself into having more spiritual desires as opposed to worldly desires. Look to your future and be hopeful. Commit yourself to engaging in behaviors that will get you what you want, spiritual resilience. Surround yourself with other like-minded people of faith. These things will create a passion (desire) for things of the Spirit. Follow it.

H-CAP Recap

Read over the verses for Hope, Commitment, Accountability, and Passion. We have something that Zachariah didn't have and something better than a visit from Gabriel. We have the inspired word of God. You won't get anything better than this. We can choose to believe it or doubt it. The outcome depends on which choice you make. Take it for what it is. Believe it and allow your belief to propel you to right action. This will grow a hopeful attitude.

Making your hope realized depends on the level of commitment your willing to engage in. Peter displays an excellent example of putting his money where his mouth is. The fact that he was able to walk on water is an example of the level of faith he had. The example also demonstrates that even though we may be capable of such feats, if we don't stay focused, we can sink. You will always go where you're looking. Keep your eyes on Jesus, not the circumstance.

Going through difficult times can be tough when facing them alone. The Bible tells us to bare each other's burdens. This means we're not supposed to go it alone. Do you have others you can count on for support and encouragement when hit with troubled times? If so, use those resources. If not, work at creating and maintaining a proper support system. Remember, strength comes in numbers.

In the recap on Passion, your behaviors will reflect what your mind is focused on thus revealing your passions. Do your passions control you or do you control them? If you make it a habit to set your mind on spiritual things, this will come out through harmonious passion. A sure way to make this happen is to remain committed to building these strategies. Don't give up!

Intentionally implement the following:

1. To hope and believe is a choice. Sometimes you have to make that choice simply because it's the right thing to do or that's all you have. Choose to believe and don't give up. Don't allow circumstances to dictate whether you believe or not. This is a mistake many people make. Hope has nothing to do with current circumstances; hope is in spite of circumstances.
2. Commit to backing up your faith with right action. Don't simply state your beliefs or make cognitive assertions. What you truly believe in is reflected in your actions. Step out in faith. Miracles won't happen until you take the step out of the boat. Make sure you're looking in the right direction, toward your hope and not the circumstance.
3. As we go through difficult times, having others around us that we can count on and trust in important to getting us through. We're not made to do it alone. We grow in the context of relationships. When you're struggling and your natural inclination is to

withdraw, don't. Create a support system, reach out to them and regain your strength. The process works by you also being there for them. Remember, iron sharpens iron.

4. This training process is about strengthening your mind. Training yourself to be mindful of spiritual things is the foundation for developing harmonious passion. Remember, your passions will always be revealed through behavior and they will be either obsessive or harmonious. If you flood your mind with spiritual things, meaning being vigilant about living out the strategies you're learning and being mindful and serving others, you will achieve this goal.

Hope

24 For in this hope we were saved. But hope that is seen is no hope at all. Who hopes for what he already has? 25But if we hope for what we do not yet have, we wait for it patiently.
—Romans 8:24-25 NIV

Meditation and Action

This verse gives the definition of what hope/faith is. By its nature, hope is something that is yet to happen. We want and anticipate something to materialize in the near or distant future. To hope in something requires three things, an object of our hope, waiting, and patience. Hope has to have an object, the "thing" we want to happen. If we already have what we hope for, it's not hope because the anticipation is gone. Because we don't yet have what we hope for, we must also wait for it to become reality. Note the ending of being patient. Waiting requires patience. Although Paul is referring to the object of our hope being Christ and our waiting and being patient for Him to fulfill His purpose within us, the same rules apply to anything we hope for in our lives. The strategies remain the same although the object of what we hope for may change. We need to make sure that our hopes are grounded in a harmonious passion and not an obsessive one. We can and should always have goals that we aim for in life, however, we need to keep in mind that as we hope, we're living out God's plan for our life at that point in time. As we reach one goal, we create another. The concept of hope then is always moving forward. Living a hopeful life is a journey and not a sprint to the finish. It will also accompany various roadblocks. Remaining hopeful in spite of these roadblocks is what builds resilience. What are you hoping for in your life? Whatever it is, make sure it comes from a harmonious passion. Hold on to your hope and wait, be patient, and live it out as if it is on the horizon.

Commitment

You rely on your sword, you do detestable things, and each of you defiles his neighbor's wife. Should you then possess the land?
—Ezekiel 33:26 NIV

Meditation and Action

Commitment is necessary to building success; however, commitment needs to be to the right things. Ezekiel was a prophet during the Babylonian exile. The chapter deals with his message regarding the sins of the nation and how the people had no right to call God unfair when they were guilty. They were merely reaping what they had sown through their disobedience. Read through it. Our behavior reveals what we're committed to. If we say that we're committed to God and building our faith, our behaviors should reflect this. If we make this claim but our behaviors neglect our spiritual development and reflect what the rest of the world is doing, we deceive ourselves. You can't blame God for the outcome. You created it. However, this is exactly what many people do. You cannot inherit the things God has promised while living like the world that rejects God. It's a simple life law that in choosing the behavior, you also choose the consequences. The fact that you haven't stopped to reflect on those consequences before your choice to act is no excuse. Your task for today is to reflect on your behaviors. What do they reveal about your commitment? Do they reflect godly or worldly pursuits? If you really want to possess the land, be committed to the right behaviors!

Accountability

> Then Sarai said to Abram, "You are responsible for the wrong I am suffering. I put my servant in your arms, and now that she knows she is pregnant, she despises me. May the LORD judge between you and me."
> —Genesis 16:5; NIV

Meditation and Action

Recall the story of the promise made to Abram that God would give him a son though his wife, Sarai. A long time had passed and they were getting impatient. They began to doubt that God would actually provide as described because Sarai was beyond childbearing years. As a result, Sarai came up with a plan for Abram to have a child through her maidservant, Hargar. It sounded like a good plan in their mind. Maybe this was the way God meant for this to work. Sarai was the one who brought up the idea and she and Abram rationalized the idea until it made sense to them. This turned out to be a tragic mistake as this was not God's plan. Sarai soon became jealous because her relationship with Hagar had now changed. Hagar was the one who was now carrying Abram's child. However, notice Sarai's response. She blames Abram for this but it was her suggestion to begin with. Not that Abram was without fault, he chose to listen to her and follow through with it but Sarai shows a complete lack of responsibility for her behavior. Find someone or something to blame is always our first reaction when things go wrong. It's human nature. However, it's also self-defeating and wrong and serves only to make things worse. Do you have a tendency to shift blame? Are you currently facing a situation where you're not taking responsibility for your part in something? Make it a point today to face the music and start a course for making it right.

Passion

11Never be lacking in zeal, but keep your spiritual fervor, serving the Lord. 12Be joyful in hope, patient in affliction, faithful in prayer. 13Share with God's people who are in need. Practice hospitality.

—Romans 12:11-13 NIV

Meditation and Action

Paul tells us that passion (zeal, fervor) is something that we should always have. Not only this but the ability to be joyful in difficult times. This is the goal; this is what the world is looking and longing for but how is this possible? Paul gives us the answer in the next verse, passion creates itself through doing for others, in this case, it's sharing with people who are in need and practicing hospitality. When we make this a habit, neuroscience research actually shows that it changes the function and structure of the brain. So, the transforming of the mind that the Bible speaks of is literal. Although, Paul knew nothing of how the brain works, he was aware of the changes in attitude and mind. The goal for us is to keep the passion alive; however, the passion we create needs to be harmonious and not obsessive. To create and maintain a harmonious passion, continue your efforts in doing for others. Don't let one day pass where you can't say that you've made a difference in someone's life today. Take some time and think deeply about this

41

verse and what it means to be that passionate about life. Then, put it into action by making a difference in someone's life.

H-CAP Recap

R eview the verses for Hope, Commitment, Accountability, and Passion. Hope is something we can't see in the moment but something we're waiting for. It resides in the future. Because of this, we must wait for what we hope for. This requires patience. However, it's not just waiting but keeping busy with the right committed behaviors to keep hope alive while we wait. What are you doing with your time as you wait?

Commitment is an obligation to act. If you choose the behavior, you also choose the consequences. If your style of life reflects the rest of the world that doesn't believe and accept God, you can't expect to inherit the promises of God. Consider what your behaviors reveal about your commitment to God. Make the necessary changes. Applying these strategies is the way to do that.

In considering accountability, when things don't go as planned, it's natural and usually our first response to blame. Recall Adam and Eve. However, just because this response may come naturally doesn't mean it's the right response. Take responsibility for your actions even when wrong but then do what it takes to make it right.

Passion is the motivation for doing what we do. The week's verse on Passion tells us that it's up to us to maintain our zeal for God. We are to be joyful in hope, patient in affliction, and faithful in prayer. Keeping harmonious passion alive is about serving God and others. The verse tells us to practice hospitality. Go out of your way to be kind to others.

Intentionally implement the following:

1. Practice patience in waiting. Hope is not about instant gratification.
2. Keep you commitments aligned with your hope. This is the only way to make your hope realized.
3. Take responsibility for your behavior. If you do wrong, make it right. Don't play the blame game. Remember, you choose the behavior, you choose the consequences that go along with it.
4. Go out of your way to be kind to others. Making this a daily habit will create and keep harmonious passion alive.

Hope

And we know that in all things God works for the good of those who love him, who have been called according to his purpose.

—Romans 8:28 NIV

Meditation and Action

Paul gives this message because the belief in it creates hope. The hope is the assurance that all things will eventually work out for our good. Imagine your state of mind going into a situation regardless of how it turns out that God works for our good if we love Him and are called according to His purpose. If you're a Christian, this is you. You have been called; you do end up winning in the end. The ultimate end, being death, has no hold on us. Some may take this verse out of context and believe that every situation in which we find ourselves, God should work out in our favor. This is not what this means. God can certainly do so if doing so is according to His will. However, it's not always about the current situation. This also ties into Philippians 4:6 and being anxious for nothing. If you truly believe these statements to be true they will change behavior. The key is getting yourself to believe them when circumstances are not working out for you. Although circumstances may not work according to your plan and this will happen at times, the belief that ultimately things will work themselves out can save yourself a lot of emotional turmoil. Remember, you can only control what's in your ability to control and nothing more. It's when you try to exert control over things beyond yourself that causes problems. Don't mistake roadblocks for things not working out. God sees things that you do not. Have hope and believe in the fact that He's in control and will work things out whatever that is for your situation. The only thing you need to focus on is serving and living rightly. He'll do the rest.

Commitment

[12]Therefore, dear brothers and sisters, you have no obligation to do what your sinful nature urges you to do.[13]For if you live by its dictates, you will die. But if through the power of the Spirit you put to death the deeds of your sinful nature, you will live.

—Romans 8:12-13 NLT

Meditation and Action

At times it can feel like we don't have any control over what we do. Bad behaviors can be automatic, impulsive, and habitual. However, we'll always engage in the behaviors we're committed to, good or bad. If we're committed to reform and changing bad habits, being committed to vigilance and being mindful of our behaviors will result in change. However, if we don't commit to being vigilant of what we need to change, we'll keep on doing the same things over and over.

Paul makes it very clear; we have no obligation to do what our sinful nature urges us to do. You say "I can't help myself." That's a copout. What sinful urges do you struggle with? Commit yourself at this moment to be hyper vigilant about monitoring your behaviors. It will take some time to catch on. Don't beat yourself up during the process; you will have times of failure. God forgives you as you stay the course. It's the process of being mindful of your behaviors that will give you the power to put those desires to death. I challenge you to commit to this process for 30 days and see what happens. Be empowered by the Spirit.

Accountability

Learn to do right! Seek justice, encourage the oppressed. Defend the cause of the fatherless, plead the case of the widow.

—Isaiah 1:17; NIV

Meditation and Action

Isaiah was a prophet in the land of Judah 700 years before the time of Christ. Although the nation appeared to be successful and prosperous, they were in spiritual decline and were likened to Sodom and Gomorrah. Isaiah tells the nation to LEARN to do right, SEEK justice, ENCOURAGE the oppressed, DEFEND the cause of the fatherless.

To learn, seek, encourage, and defend are all intentional acts to right a position and to move forward to where one should go. They are strategies to get to where you want and need to go. This is accountability at its core. Take responsibility for yourself, learn what you need to know and apply it. Seek out what is right to include relationships where you can be encouraged in the right paths and encourage others along the way. Defend the cause of people who struggle and falling behind. Hold yourself accountable to engage in these behaviors. God will certainly hold you accountable and ask you how well you did in doing His business. Unless you hold yourself accountable, you won't know what direction you're going. Where in your life can you apply these strategies today? Think about it and apply them and you'll be on your way to spiritual success.

Passion

If I gave everything I have to the poor and even sacrificed my body, I could boast about it; but if I didn't love others, I would have gained nothing.
—I Corinthians 13:3 NLT

Meditation and Action

This verse talks about obsessive passion, doing for the sake of doing. The act of giving should be done with the giver in mind, not the receiver. According to Paul, we can have the appearance of being a giver, being a Christian, being holy; however, when we engage in these behaviors without love, we're really doing it because it fills a void. People often times get into a pattern of behavior where they're always doing for others out of fear. In other words they need to "do" because it makes them feel like they're worth something. This is the void they're trying to fill; it's misdirected giving. This type of giving is really about them and what they don't have as opposed what they have and who they are. People who boast about what they do for others do so to not just inform others how good they are but more importantly to tell and remind themselves. This kind of giving gains nothing as far as eternity is concerned. In creating passion, giving is important. However, give with the right heart. Give to meet the needs of another, not your own and don't broadcast your giving. To help create and maintain passion, take on this task by giving to others who need something that you can provide and leave it at that. Make the gift about the receiver. Remember, it's not about you!

H-CAP Recap

Review the verses for Hope, Commitment, Accountability, and Passion. People often mistake a roadblock or a perceived delay in what they hope for as a mistake. When things don't work out as we expect we become frustrated which can lead to doubt or giving up. Paul reminds us that all things work together for our good. We need to remind ourselves that we can't control everything and at times, we'll need to take detours. What sense does it make to get discouraged, frustrated, angry, etc… These behaviors lead to nothing good. Look to the future; this is where hope is. God has it under control; just roll with it.

Commitment to do the right thing requires an intentional act. Sometimes, the commitment comes easy. Other times, it can be difficult when confronted with temptation. Success will depend on not only your level of commitment but your hope and accountability system. Everyone has times when they struggle and we will make mistakes. Your willingness and commitment to applying these strategies will strengthen your mind and put to death the deeds of the sinful nature. Commit to being vigilant in monitoring your thoughts and behaviors and act rightly through them.

Being accountable begins with you taking responsibility for yourself. We can have individual goals for ourselves but we also need to keep in mind that ultimately, mankind is our business. Learning to do right, seeking justice, encouraging the oppressed, defending the cause of the fatherless, and pleading the case of the widow is our business.

In applying the previously examined strategies, you will create a harmonious passion in your life. In this week's verse, Paul tells us that we can do all the right outward behaviors, however, if we don't have love, it's all meaningless. In other words, it becomes obsessive. Many people do the right things on the outside but for the wrong reasons. This is why it's important to apply all the strategies and not just a few. It's your heart and mind that need to change.

Intentionally implement the following:

1. Convince yourself that God has it under control. Don't focus on circumstance but the big picture.
2. Commit to being vigilant in monitoring your thoughts and behaviors and act rightly through them.
3. Take responsibility for yourself. Applying these strategies is learning to do right. Giving them to others is encouraging.
4. Do for others not for self-gain but out of love. Applying these strategies will build this type of love. It comes through doing.

Hope

So faith comes from hearing, and hearing through the word
of Christ.

—Romans 10:17 ESV

Meditation and Action

Hope comes from being encouraged that something can happen. It's the ability to believe that you can have an effect on something. In matters of faith, it's a belief that God will work out His plan in you and will give you the strength to do it. Simply put, hope comes from encouragement. As the verse says, it comes through hearing. We become more hopeful when we receive encouragement from others; the same is true when we encourage others. This is a necessary component to early human development. In healthy environments, children are encouraged and rewarded with praise and this contributes to their self-worth. It puts into place the belief that they can achieve their goals in spite of obstacles and creates resilience to not give up. The same thing applies to matters of faith. Hopelessness and pessimism is created by doing the opposite. Be encouraged by others but you can also encourage yourself as David did in the wilderness as he was being pursued by Saul. Research reveals an interesting thing about the spoken word of encouragement. When we verbally talk to ourselves, the brain doesn't distinguish between our own voice and that of another. The brain simply responds to the spoken word. Get into the habit of encouraging yourself in all matters but equally be an encourager of others. There is no single thing that you can do to create hope than being encouraged.

Commitment

36"Teacher, which is the greatest commandment in the Law?"37Jesus replied: "Love the Lord your God with all your heart and with all your soul and with all your mind."38This is the first and greatest commandment.39And the second is like it: 'Love your neighbor as yourself.'
—Matthew 22:36-39 NIV

Meditation and Action

The key to spiritual resilience is love; the ability to give it and receive it. To love is an intentional act. It's a commitment we need to make; to love others. This can be a hard thing to do. However, we can't give to someone something we don't have for ourselves. Many people have a very negative view of themselves due to past hurts. They believe that they are worthless and have nothing to give. They find it extremely difficult to look in the mirror without condemning themselves and will avoid mirrors for this very reason. People in this mind set may often engage in acts of kindness to others but these actions mainly serve to make themselves feel better, to fill a void, and can become obsessive. In order to love others, we need to have a healthy love for ourselves.

I'm not referring to a selfish and prideful sense of self but we do need to view ourselves through the lens in which God views us. He paid the ultimate price for our salvation; He gave his life. This act reveals our value. Our value isn't determined by our past and the bad things we did or even of what happened to us. Commit yourself to searching the scripture to see the view God has of you. Allow yourself to accept His love for you and as you do, learn to love yourself.

Accountability

Do not be yoked together with unbelievers. For what do righteousness and wickedness have in common? Or what fellowship can light have with darkness?
—2 Corinthians 6:14 NIV

Meditation and Action

The apostle Paul writes this letter to the church in Corinth. Paul provides a steep warning to the church. Paul was known for his abrupt and get to the point style. The believers in Corinth needed to consecrate themselves, set themselves apart, and cling to the way of life that God had prescribed. The requirements for this is very clear, Do not be yoked together with unbelievers. This doesn't mean that they can't be in the company of unbelievers as that would be impossible. However, to be yoked is to become part of. It's a joining. They were associating with non-believers to the point that it was having a negative influence on them. Paul follows this up with the examples of comparing righteousness and wickedness, light and darkness. These comparisons reveal the general law of physics that two things cannot occupy the same space at the same time. You will either be associating with righteousness or wickedness or light or darkness. Which one are you associating with? The point Paul was making is that you need to be ALL IN. To build accountability requires a decision. Separate yourself from the yoke of unbelievers and yoke yourself with like-minded people who have a heart and passion for the things of God. This is your task. If you do this, you will be blessed beyond measure.

Passion

2 Be shepherds of God's flock that is under your care, serving as overseers--not because you must, but because you are willing, as God wants you to be; not greedy for money, but eager to serve; 3 not lording it over those entrusted to you, but being examples to the flock.

—I Peter 5:2-3 NIV

Meditation and Action

Those that "do" (behave) out of greed and those that lord their authority over others do so because it fills a void. People who lord authority over others are not leaders and engage in this type of behavior because they're really weak and insecure. The over reactive behaviors serve to bolster self-worth but in a negative way. This produces conflict within the person that engages in the behavior as it creates an endless cycle for the need to aggress their position over others as the need for self-gratification and worth has an insatiable appetite. This is the opposite of how God requires us to lead and care for others. Paul says to be shepherds. This means to guide and be watchful. Shepherds carefully and vigilantly watch over their flock to guard against danger. The attitude is not one of greed but of serving. A good leader serves others and pours their abundance of life into others by offering encouragement and protection. It's leading by example and treating others as you expect to be treated. This is the example Jesus left for us and is the example we are to aspire to. Notice that this type of leadership comes from the inside out. What kind of example are you giving to your family and others under your responsibility? Are you a "do as I say and not as I do" type of leader? Begin the transformation process by serving those under your care; they are not there to serve you.

H-CAP Recap

Review the verses for Hope, Commitment, Accountability, and Passion. The main source of hope is through being encouraged. You can encourage yourself, receive it from others, and give it to others. All will be a source of encouragement to you. Don't be stingy in dispensing encouragement even to yourself. It creates hope.

To love others effectively requires us to have a healthy love of ourselves. The Bible tells us to love our neighbor as ourselves so without a proper view of this concept will influence how we love others. We can't give something we don't have. We are valuable in the sight of God; He paid a heavy price for our salvation. God finds you a worthwhile investment. Commit to seeing yourself in the same light and then pass it on.

Trying to build a resilient spirit will require you to hang around people who are resilient. The Bible is clear that we should not be unequally yoked with non-believers. The point isn't that we can't hang around or associate with non-believers. This would be impossible. However, these relationships can't be as such to negatively influence us. Your primary relationships need to be with likeminded believers.

God wants us to serve others with a harmonious passion. Great leadership is done by example but the example needs to right. Great leaders inspire others to service. Great leaders give hope and encourage commitment and accountability. What type of leader are you? Great leaders serve, they aren't served.

Intentionally implement the following:

1. Be generous in giving encouragement to others. This will serve to be encouraging to you and will grow your hope.
2. Commit to being kind to yourself and seeing yourself through God's eyes. You are valuable, important, and special. You do matter. As you gain confidence in this, give it to others.
3. If resilience is your goal, your primary relationships need to be with likeminded people. Create and maintain the right relationships.
4. Lead by example by serving others. Don't expect others to serve you.

Hope

11Never be lazy, but work hard and serve the Lord enthusiastically. 12Rejoice in our confident hope. Be patient in trouble, and keep on praying. 13When God's people are in need, be ready to help them. Always be eager to practice hospitality.

—Romans 12:11-13 NLT

Meditation and Action

Creating and maintaining hope is an ongoing process. It's not something that you acquire once and leave it alone and expecting it to be there when you need it. It needs to be cultivated to work, if not, hopelessness takes over. Paul tells us to never be lazy but work enthusiastically. We see here that hope is tied to our passion and when these traits are in alignment, it creates right action. We should also be confident in our hope but also patient. By definition, the object of our hope is in the future that has not yet materialized so we need to wait and be patient, particularly when confronted with roadblocks. This is what life is. Cultivating and maintaining hope requires us to be encouraged. We can encourage ourselves but also receive encouragement from others. We can be encouraged by serving others as well. Putting others first and meeting the needs of others creates hope within us. You can achieve this by routinely engaging in random acts of kindness by giving words of encouragement to others. This is the practice of hospitality that Paul speaks of. Keeping hope alive is an individual responsibility. Life will always throw you doubts, but don't be lazy, be diligent in serving others and offering words of encouragement and allow this to encourage you. Resilience begins with hope.

Commitment

> That is why the LORD says, "Turn to me now, while there is time. Give me your hearts. Come with fasting, weeping, and mourning."
>
> —Joel 2:12 NLT

Meditation and Action

Commitment to spiritual things entails intentional action on our part. Joel was a prophet in Judah during a time of drought and plague which was also a picture of the nation's spiritual condition. Give the chapter a read through. In this verse, he gives instruction to the nation and tells them that the present disasters should be used to awaken them from their spiritual decline. This message also applies to us. The reason we as a nation are in spiritual decline is because there's a breakdown in individual spiritual growth. Will you hear and heed this warning and get back on track or keep going in the same direction? To strengthen your spirit and faith requires you to exercise it. At times, this may require fasting, weeping, and mourning. These behaviors have a way of refocusing our attention to the things of God and off of our circumstances. Recall that our behaviors reveal our true commitments. Where do yours lay? Are you too busy trying to *keep up with the Jones'* and spending too much time feeding the desires of the flesh? Just like a commitment to going to the gym on a regular basis serves to strengthen the body, we also need to be committed to going to the spiritual gym. This requires us to turn to God and the giving of our hearts through prayer and fasting. This is an exercise in breaking down the flesh and strengthening the spirit. Your task is to set a regular time to go to your spiritual gym and get your workout on!

Accountability

If we claim to have fellowship with him yet walk in the darkness, we lie and do not live by the truth.
—I John 1:6 NIV

Meditation and Action

We can't claim fellowship or a relationship with God and walk in darkness or live as the world does at the same time. Doing so is not walking in truth. We become like those we hang around with. If we have fellowship with God and godly people, we become godlier. If you hang around people who are in darkness, you will also walk in darkness with them. It's a simple yet profound principle. Because we're designed for relationships, who we hang around is very important. Who we hang around with is also a choice we make. If your goal is spiritual resilience, you need to develop friendships and hang around people who are spiritually resilient. Exposing yourself to such an influence will develop a like state of mind. Notice that this also takes a commitment on your part to act. You need to create these accountable relationships. You have to create your own success. Don't deceive yourself. You're either walking with Him or you're not. Are you walking the fence? What changes do you need to make in order to walk the walk; eliminate some unhealthy relationships, creating or strengthening more godly relationships? Make the right choice and live it out. In doing so, you'll find that you will be more hopeful, have more commitment, and experience more of a harmonious passion for actually living life as it was intended. Try it!

Passion

Do not conform any longer to the pattern of this world, but be transformed by the renewing of your mind. Then you will be able to test and approve what God's will is--his good, pleasing and perfect will.

—Romans 12:2 NIV

Meditation and Action

What you conform to reveals where your passion lay. The patterns of this world have a very powerful stronghold and lead to obsessive passions that consume us and rob us of our witness and ability to live an abundant life. The Bible tells us that although we live in the world, we are not to be of the world. Remember, we're just passengers, sojourners, passing through. Falling into this trap is as old as time and can be seen throughout the Bible. Look at the history of Israel. When they served God, they were blessed. As they became acculturated to their surroundings and accepted the behaviors and customs of others, they suffered loss and fell under the rule of their enemies. This happens today when Christians become tuned into the culture of the world and allow their senses to slowly become dulled. They soon find themselves accepting sinful ways of life and principles erasing the distinct difference in the way of life of the Christian and the non-believer. When the world looks at the believer, they should see differences in how we live our life, the way we speak (the language we use) and how we behave. This transformation is made by the renewing of our mind. Renew your mind by meditating and applying the word of God to your life. As you work through this devotional, you're doing just that. As you apply these strategies, your mind will be renewed resulting in changed thought, emotion, and behavior. Renew your mind and come out of the world.

H-CAP Recap

Review the verses for Hope, Commitment, Accountability, and Passion. Hope isn't something you have and just leave it alone and expect it to be there when you need it. Like anything else, it needs to be tended to in order for it to grow. Hope is a living thing that needs to be fed and stretched for it to expand and get us through difficult times. Paul gives us the workout routine to make this happen, be patient, pray, and practice hospitality.

There are times in your spiritual journey when you need to really get tough. In addition to our normal service, we may need to resort to more drastic measures to break through. As Joel describes, these times call for weeping, fasting, and mourning. These behaviors require additional commitment to action but also get the job done. Are you ready to take it to the next level?

We need to be responsible and accountable for the things we allow to influence us. As this week's verse in accountability states, we can't claim to walk with God yet be influenced by the world. The only way to combat this is to create and maintain relationships that reinforce godly principles in your life. Walk with those who walk with God.

The purpose of you taking on the task of applying these strategies to your life is about transforming your mind. If you transform your mind, you transform your life. It all begins with your state of mind. Committing yourself to building these traits in your life will create a new passion in your life which will lead to experiencing and living life abundantly.

Intentionally implement the following:

1. Hope begins with shifting your focus in that direction. Practice being hospitable, pray, and be patient. This is the workout routine to build your hope.
2. If you're ready to get serious, set aside a time for fasting. Start small, even a meal and pray instead.
3. If you claim to walk with God, you need to have accountable relationships with others who walk with God. If you don't have solid relationships in this area, you're on the line of walking in darkness. Walk with those who walk with God.
4. Resilience and living abundantly begins with transforming your mind. Applying these strategies will do just that and will create a harmonious passion for godly things.

Hope

17You may say to yourselves, "These nations are stronger than we are. How can we drive them out?" 18But do not be afraid of them; remember well what the LORD your God did to Pharaoh and to all Egypt.

—Deuteronomy 7:17-18 NIV

Meditation and Action

Being hopeful requires us to not only look ahead toward our goal and what we're hoping for but to also have the ability to look back. Looking back to times as reminders of how and when God came through as He promised serves to keep our eyes in the direction we want to go. The problem is that when people look back in the rear view mirror of their life, they tend to see the failures as Israel did many times. Give the chapter and book of Deuteronomy a read. They refused to acknowledge God and take Him at his word and to be hopeful that He would bring them through. Instead, they chose to focus on the unfairness of walking through the desert and complained at every corner to Moses that God lead them out there only to destroy them. They failed to recall all the miracles God did for them in Egypt to free them.We do no different today. The God of today is the same God of yesterday. He still makes a way for His people. Do you tend to be like Israel complaining about your circumstances? Remember, you will always go in the direction you're looking. Look to the great things

God has done in light of your own goals. He can still part seas. If you're facing difficult times or when you face difficult times, believe, have hope, and remember that God still does miracles. Remind yourself of all the things He's done in your life and what you've seen Him do in the lives of others. Look in this direction.

Commitment

Therefore, my dear brothers, stand firm. Let nothing move you. Always give yourselves fully to the work of the Lord, because you know that your labor in the Lord is not in vain.
—I Corinthians 15:58 NIV

Meditation and Action

If you examine the life of successful people, one of the things you'll find they have in common is their determination. In spite of difficulties, they are committed to doing whatever it takes to get the job done. This is a necessary trait to succeed in all things, particularly when it comes to spirituality as this has eternal consequences. As Christians, we need to take nothing less than the same attitude when it applies to our faith. We put more effort into other areas of our life that have no eternal meaning yet when it comes to investing in our faith, we approach it casually. As Paul tells the Corinthian believers to give themselves fully to the work of God, stand firm, let nothing move you, we need to do the same. This is commitment. How different would your life be if you committed yourself at this level? Examine your life and the things you devote time and resources to and compare it to your relationship with God. Do you need to reallocate some time and resources? By making time to read, meditate, and take action with this devotional is a big step in the right direction. Keep taking the action steps you've been applying and you'll be immovable. The key is to keep doing it, it's a lifestyle not a once and a while activity.

Accountability

They devoted themselves to the apostles' teaching and to the fellowship, to the breaking of bread and to prayer.
—Acts 2:42 NIV

Meditation and Action

Acts 2 talks about the coming of the Holy Spirit. The key thing to remember in this verse is that they devoted themselves to the apostles' teaching. In other words, they were committed to listening and adhering to what they were teaching but also to the gathering together. This wasn't an individual thing. Yes, their salvation was individual; however, individual strength comes from the collective gathering and encouragement of like-minded others. This is what you have going on here. The devotion to teaching, fellowship, and breaking of bread are all separate things and in chronological order. First, they made a commitment to be devoted to spiritual instruction. Second, they committed themselves to meeting together and establish relationships. Lastly, they were committed to the breaking of bread and prayer. Breaking bread with others is a sign of connection and oneness. It's aligning one with the other for a mutual purpose. In this case, prayer and fellowship which in turn produces hope. Devoting yourself to these things will require you to form relationships with like-minded others where mutual encouragement can occur. Your task for today is to commit yourself to finding someone to align yourself with and have a time of prayer together. Optimally, make a regular commitment to do this even if it's once a week. Add this to your behaviors and watch your spirit soar!

Passion

Be on your guard; standfirm in the faith; be men of courage; be strong.

—I Corinthians 16:13 NIV

Meditation and Action

We can increase passion by doing (committed behaviors). As you work through this devotional, you'll quickly notice that each of the traits, Hope, Commitment, Accountability, and Passion, overlap. This is because they are reciprocal, meaning they need each other to create each other. Paul tells us to be on guard and to stand firm in our faith, let nothing move us. This means our circumstances, good or bad. God's existence and our faith in Him are not and should not be dependent on our circumstances. We have a bad habit of serving God and praising Him when things are going good for us, however, when things go wrong, we become disgruntled, let our faith wane and become complacent in our serving Him. We do this because we're hurt and angry. It serves as a passive aggressive attempt at "getting even." However, this is counter to what Paul says to be. "Let nothing move you. Always give yourselves fully to the work of the Lord." When we look only to our circumstances, we can't give ourselves fully to the work of the Lord. We need to look to and focus on the right thing to keep our passion for God alive. We need to keep in mind that our labor is not in vain even though it may "feel" like it at the time. To give ourselves fully means to always do this regardless. If you're going through a difficult time, continue to give yourself to the things of God. This is what resilience is made of.

H-CAP Recap

R eview the verses for Hope, Commitment, Accountability, and Passion. When going through rough times, it's easy to focus on circumstances and complain. This takes no energy to do this and we often do it automatically without thinking. However, it does suck the energy from us. Get into the habit of reminding yourself and looking at what God has done for you and others. Remember, this is all part of the process of growth.

Serving God and creating spiritual resilience is a fulltime job. It's not a hobby and there is no such thing as being a part-time Christian. You either are or you're not. God demands nothing less than all you can give. It takes commitment to stand firm in the midst of difficult times. It's what you do during those times is what matters and is where your strength will come from. Give yourself to the work of God.

Commitment to the things of God will require the forming of quality relationships. Spiritual growth depends on the relationship you have with others striving for the same goal. Devote yourself to learning the word of God; don't underestimate the process of fellowship (accountability) and prayer with and for each other (breaking bread). Remember, strength comes in numbers.

We need to guard our passion and commitment to God and stand firm in our faith. Of course to use this state of mind will require difficult times as this advice is not needed when things are going good. Remember, growth doesn't come without conflict. Don't be surprised when difficult times hit you. Stand firm and stay committed to applying these principles.

Intentionally implement the following:

1. During difficult times, reflect on how God brought you through. He hasn't left and He will do it again. To do this will require a commitment to action. If you're not reflecting on God's goodness and transferring that into hope for you now and the future, you're going backwards.
2. Stand firm. To help you in this process, commit to seeking God and rally around your accountability system. Strength will renew.
3. Your hope and faith require careful guarding against worldly intrusions. Standing firm and staying committed to applying these principles during these times will renew your passion. It doesn't happen on its own or by mistake. Stand!

Hope

18I pray also that the eyes of your heart may be enlightened in order that you may know the hope to which he has called you, the riches of his glorious inheritance in the saints, 19and his incomparably great power for us who believe. That power is like the working of his mighty strength, 20which he exerted in Christ when he raised him from the dead and seated him at his right hand in the heavenly realms.

—Ephesians 1:18-19 NIV

Meditation and Action

Hope comes through being enlightened. How and from where then does enlightenment come? It comes from being hopeful, hopeful toward God's riches and power to work in your life. This is the same power that raised Christ from the dead. This power can only be experienced and lived out through hope. Belief/faith is the only mechanism that can move God's hand. The enlightenment that Paul speaks of is the knowledge and acknowledgement of this fact. There is no secret to it. This is the place where many people fail because they get too caught up in their circumstances which at times may appear hopeless because you can't control everything. This can cause us to take our eyes off of God and look only to the natural where discouragement sets in. Remember, hope is in spite of circumstances. Look beyond yourself and the circumstance and live/behave through your hope in the future, what your goals are, and not current circumstances. Are you struggling to see though your circumstances? Do you tend to see only what's in front of you and allow yourself to be controlled by the feelings of the moment? The challenge is to look through circumstances toward what you hope for and allow what you see to dictate your behavior. This is where the power is.

Commitment

> Those who live according to the sinful nature have their minds set on what that nature desires; but those who live in accordance with the Spirit have their minds set on what the Spirit desires.
> —Romans 8:5 NIV

Meditation and Action

This verse is the foundation of a principle I call *mental optometry.* You will always go in the direction you're looking. You've experienced this if you've driven a car. While trying to keep the wheel straight and in the direction you want to go but then casually look in another direction. Regardless of how hard you try to keep the wheel straight, eventually, you will begin to veer in the direction you're looking. This is because it's a neurological principle that we will go and orientate ourselves to our vision. The same law applies to our mind's eye. Regardless of our intentions, we'll eventually go where our desires lead us. These desires can be of our sinful nature or our spiritual nature. Whatever your mind is set on, you're thoughts, emotions, and behaviors will follow. Anyone who's had to wear corrective lenses knows that it's necessary to get adjustments on a regular basis. The Bible is that correction for our mind's eye. To make the necessary corrections, you need to meditate on it, study it, and apply it. As you diligently contemplate and apply these strategies, you're doing just that. What is your mind's eye focused on? Do you find yourself looking at life through your circumstances and getting discouraged? Do you feel like giving up? Do you need an adjustment by having a new lens in which to view life? Set your mind on the things of the spirit and keep your focus there. It will result in developing a desire for those things making your faith stronger.

Accountability

Blessed is the man who does not walk in the counsel of the wicked or stand in the way of sinners or sit in the seat of mockers.
—Psalm 1:1 NIV

Meditation and Action

Receiving advice and direction from others is part of life and relationships. We do it all the time. One thing we always need to balance is emotion versus investment. Immediate gratification or delayed gratification. Where we receive "counsel" direction, advice is very important to the direction we take. The psalmist cautions us where to not get our advice. There's plenty of opportunity to gain counsel from ungodly people. However, obtaining counsel from godly people requires right relationships. One of the key strategies in building accountability is seeking advice and direction from people who know. Be careful who you align yourself with. Don't take advice from a fool and don't be trapped into the false belief of instant gratification. Take counsel from others more experienced than you and who have traveled that road before. Adherence to such advice is the mark of a wise person. Are you seeking direction for something? Make sure the direction you seek comes from godly sources, even if it's something you don't want to hear. Notice that accountability at this level also requires commitment because if you don't have these relationships, you need to commit to action to create them and maintain them. As you maintain these relationships, it will also influence your passion. Create accountability; do this and you'll make it through and be there for someone else.

Passion

Little children, let us not love in word or talk but indeed and
in truth.

—I John 3:18 ESV

Meditation and Action

John continues in the same theme of passion through "doing." It's easy
to talk the talk. In fact this is what people are good at, particularly
when it comes to Christian living. People can be quick to judge yet
live the same style of life of those they condemn. As Christians, it's
imperative to walk our talk. At the height of this is the act of loving
and caring for others. It's simply not enough to say that we love
people; we must show our love to others through our actions. Again,
this is a mindset that we continue in and must not be dependent upon
circumstances or feeling. Examine your behaviors in light of this verse
and the others you've been exposed to thus far. Can it be said of you
through your behaviors (not words) that you love and care for others?
If this is not evident in your life, it's time to change. The change
comes in the form of "doing." Loving others can include simple
behaviors such as giving a kind word, meeting a need for someone.
The act of caring for others makes us feel good. This feeling is the
passion you're trying to create. Seek opportunities to grow it. Meditate

on this and ask God to show you someone today for you to put this trait into action.

H-CAP Recap

Review the verses for Hope, Commitment, Accountability, and Passion. Hope comes through being enlightened. This mind transformation comes from the knowledge of the hope to which we're called. If we really knew and understood the power of the resurrection and the love of God, our lives would be dramatically different. Being enlightened comes from letting this sink in. Spend some time contemplating this.

Give yourself a mind's eye checkup. You go where you're looking. The key is to look in the right direction. What you see with your natural eye and your mind's eye are two different things. Set your mind's eye on spiritual things, meaning occupy your mind with hopeful thoughts of God's plan for your life. This has staying power and will change your attitude.

Getting advice and direction from others is important as it provides encouragement. However, you need to be careful from whom you get this direction. A wise person creates and surrounds themselves with people who are where they are trying to go. This assures success. Don't be a fool. Take care in creating relationships with the right people and dissolve relationships that are not good for you. You create your own success. God's already given you the tools; it's up to you to use them.

Our passion is ultimately revealed through our actions regardless of what we say. Creating harmonious passion begins with action. Doing for others, meeting needs of others, has a way of inspiring us to do more of it. It creates a positive motivation for serving. It's as easy as giving a kind word and making others feel valued. Make someone feel important every day.

Intentionally implement the following:

1. Remind yourself to spend time reflecting on how God has come through for you and others. Allow this to encourage you to stand as you remain hopeful. This is an intentional act.
2. Occupy your mind with things that are hopeful. Remember, you go where you're looking. If you don't like where you are, look beyond circumstance by using #1. These strategies work together.
3. When seeking direction, make sure you get it from the right people. Seek out people who are already where you want to go. They've been there before and you can learn from them.
4. To create and maintain harmonious passion, do things for others. It doesn't have to be big. Just make it a habit to do something kind for someone every day.

Hope

16 Now may our Lord Jesus Christ himself, and God our Father, who loved us and gave us eternal comfort and good hope through grace, 17 comfort your hearts and establish them in every good work and word.
—2 Thessalonians 2:16-17 RSV

Meditation and Action

God is the definition and source of hope. Through hope comes comfort and peace. Paul tells us how hope can be created and established though doing good work and word. Hope then comes through doing. It requires action. Hope is not something that is attained at a single moment such as a material possession. While it is something we have in various degrees, it must be cultivated in order for it to be there as we need it. It can be created by doing good works. It can also be created through the words we use. Through the use of words, comes encouragement, encouragement builds hope. If you find that you struggle with being hopeful, do things for other people; speak words of encouragement not only to yourself but to others. Doing these things takes the focus off of you and current circumstances and on to others. It's through this giving process that we in turn receive from God. If you've been struggling in this area, try this experiment. Commit to seek out someone each day and do something kind for them. Speak words of encouragement to people. As you do this, notice what changes in your mood and attitude. Although your circumstances may still be the same, you will not. The reason for this change of attitude is that the works you do and the words you use provide encouragement which creates hope. Not doing these behaviors leads to discouragement and hopelessness.

Commitment

But now is the time to get rid of anger, rage, malicious behavior, slander, and dirty language.
—Colossians 3:8 NLT

Meditation and Action

Change is hard. Why? Because, it takes real commitment to make it happen. This means we need to always be vigilant of what's going on around us and its effect on us. This is how we gain control. However, many times we give control to the circumstances in our lives which results in us becoming the emotion and acting it out in the form of anger, rage, malicious behavior, and filthy language. Have you ever allowed yourself to be overcome by your circumstances? The problem isn't the circumstances. Everyone has difficult circumstances to deal with, that's life. Being a Christian doesn't exempt us from life's problems. However, it's our response to the twists and turns of life that sets us apart. If you allow negative events to shape the lens in which you view the world, you become reactive to life instead of responsive. The difference is reaction is a knee jerk impulsive action which usually ends up in the expression of anger, rage, bad behavior, and inappropriate language. Responding requires thought. What does life bring out in you; anger, rage, malicious behavior, filthy language? If so, you're reacting instead of responding. Spiritual success is not about getting rid of difficult times but responding to them. Remember, it's not the circumstance, it's you. Commit yourself to responding, not reacting.

Accountability

But they soon forgot what he had done and did not wait for his counsel.
—Psalm 106:13 NIV

Meditation and Action

This psalm depicts the goodness of God to Israel. However, in spite of God's goodness to them, they continued to rebel and disappoint God which brought more hardship to Israel. They brought this upon themselves. They would continually go back and forth from times of repentance, worship, and prosperity to complacency, sin, and hardship. Why? Just as the verse says, they soon forgot and did not wait for counsel. We do this too but this is also why we have the Bible, to learn from the mistakes of others. Sometimes, we need to be patient and wait for the right answer to come. We need to learn to wait on God. This goes against our very nature of wanting it NOW. Godly counsel is priceless and when we adhere to it, can save much heartache. To live under the umbrella of God's blessing will require us to seek godly counsel but at times, waiting. Resist moving without clear and godly direction. A successful person, who manages their affairs wisely, waits for the right time to take action. Learn from the mistakes of others but also learn from their successes. This is what makes them prosperous. Are you facing something and have a tendency to "jump the gun?" Wait, seek godly advice, then wait for God to give the go ahead.

Passion

But your assistant, Joshua son of Nun, will enter it. Encourage him, because he will lead Israel to inherit it.
—Deuteronomy 1:38 NIV

Meditation and Action

You are most likely aware of the story of Joshua and Caleb in their spying out the Promise Land and being the only two out of 10 spies that came back with a good report. The remaining 10 spies spread fear into the nation that they couldn't fulfill what God had promised. Here, Moses gives the reminder that because of his faith, it will be Joshua who will lead Israel into the land God had promised them so many years ago. However, the key word in this verse is "encourage.' Encouragement is needed to build hope, commitment, accountability, and passion. Moses understood the need for encouragement and what it can do. We see Joshua as a giant in the faith; however, he also needed to be encouraged. This served to keep his passion alive and focused on the right things. The fact that Moses mentions the need for encouragement speaks to the fact that discouragement is always standing at the door. Nobody ever outgrows the need to be encouraged or to provide encouragement. Moses knew Joshua would be challenged which is why he told them to encourage him. This served to keep his mind's eye on the prize. We all face a future filled with the blessings of God, just as Israel faced entering the Promise Land. What is the land God has given you to possess (goals)? Encourage yourself but also give encouragement to others in their pursuits. Doing so will keep your passions alive and give you the strength you need to achieve your goals.

H-CAP Recap

Review the verses for Hope, Commitment, Accountability, and Passion. Hope is not something that remains static. It must be tended and cultivated. In other words it must be kept alive and in order for it to live requires it to be fed. We feed hope by our actions. As Paul tells us in this week's verse, hope is created and maintained through our work and word. This means doing for others and speaking words of peace and kindness to others. Make these daily habits and your hope will thrive.

There's a big difference between a response and a reaction. When caught off guard in a bad situation, it can be easy to act out in anger and the use of inappropriate language. However, it's up to us to control these reactions. It's not the fault of the circumstance but your lack of coping with it. This may be a hard thing for you to accept but it won't change unless you accept it. Commit to responding by not allowing yourself to get carried away in the heat of the moment. Respond, don't react.

Surrounding ourselves with wise counsel is important and will save a lot of unnecessary heartache. We neglect this area of our life because we soon forget the goodness of God just as Israel did. They had a cycle of serving God, rebelling, consequences, and repentance. This is the cycle we're trying to avoid but to do so, we need to adhere to counsel and wait. This is accountability.

Encouragement is linked to Hope, Commitment, Accountability, and Passion. It's the fuel that keeps them moving forward. Just because God has called you to something, you can't assume that there's nothing left for you to do. You will encounter road blocks and it's these road blocks that can suck the life from you. Encourage yourself and be a source of encouragement to others. You can't make it through and maintain your passion without it.

Intentionally implement the following:

1. Keep hope alive by doing for others and speaking words of peace and kindness to others.
2. Respond, don't react. Commit to responding by not allowing yourself to get carried away in the heat of the moment.
3. Don't fall into a negative cycle. Surround yourself with wise counsel and wait on God.
4. Don't assume you have all the passion you need to make it through. It needs to be fed to keep it alive. Life has a way of sucking away passion. Encourage yourself and others to keep passion alive.

Hope

But Christ, as the Son, is in charge of God's entire house.
And we are God's house, if we keep our courage and remain
confident in our hope in Christ
—Hebrews 3:6 NLT

Meditation and Action

As you consider this verse for today, notice the part where it says that if we keep our courage and remain confident in our hope. Paul is saying that maintaining courage, confidence, and hope is our responsibility. It's something that must be tended to. Hope then is not a possession that is acquired at a moment in time and used as needed. It must be tended to on a regular basis. You've heard the expression before "if you don't use it, you lose it." Hope is attached to confidence and courage. When we hope, we have a certain confidence in what we hope for which also brings a boldness to act on it. Why do we need to be confident and courageous in our hope? Confidence and courage are not needed unless you face opposition to something. Without something opposing you, confidence and courage serve no purpose. The opposition for us is "life." Life can be hard and the world around us can be a mean and nasty place and will beat you to your knees if you let it. This is where hope comes in. Hope gives us the ability to stand up to life in confidence and courage. Courage comes through encouragement which creates hope. Encourage yourself and others around you. Doing so will give you the strength to face life and live it boldly without fear.

Commitment

For I can testify about them that they are zealous for God, but their zeal is not based on knowledge.
—Romans 10:2 NIV

Meditation and Action

This verse is where commitment and hope come together. However, we need to make sure that our commitment to right behaviors is rightly aligned with what we hope for. We can be hopeful that something can happen but if we're not committed to putting feet to our hope, our hope is nothing more than a pipe dream. Conversely, as in this verse, we can have a lot of committed type behaviors, but if they are not rightly directed by hope founded in knowledge, we end up with misdirected zeal. Many people follow the road of wanting something for themselves and pursue it with an obsessive passion. However, when the passion isn't based on correct knowledge, it ends up being a train wreck. Once the crash happens, blame sets in. To strengthen your spiritual resolve, examine your behaviors. What do they reveal about your goals? Are your goals misdirected? Take some time and make sure that the goals you set for yourself are founded in knowledge; not only practical knowledge based on your experience but also with the word of God. Then, examine your behaviors. Do the two line up? If not, which one of these need adjusted, your goals or behaviors? Be committed to the right things.

Accountability

> You will be made rich in every way so that you can be generous on every occasion, and through us your generosity will result in thanksgiving to God.
> —2 Corinthians 9:11

Meditation and Action

One of the key strategies in creating accountability is the act of giving to others. Intentional giving to others in need takes the focus off of us and allows us to become "others" centered. Paul tells us that this is the key to prosperity. This is one of the most important distinguishing features of well-being and prosperity. Just the fact of having wealth in no way equates to happiness. There are countless wealthy people in the world who are miserable. There are also countless non-wealthy people who are extremely happy. Why? It's because of their generosity. As Christians, we have a responsibility (accountability) for mankind. It's not about the accumulation of the most money and stuff. You can't take any of it with you. It'll be left behind for others to consume. You won't be remembered for how much money you left but for what you did for others. This is what the Bible calls storing up treasure in heaven. Mankind is the business of Christianity. Make yourself accountable to tend to mankind. To build this trait, make it a point to be generous to at least one person a day. Your generosity doesn't have to be money. If you have it to give, then give. However, you can also be generous with your time and words. Try it.

Passion

They encourage each other to do evil and plan how to set their traps in secret. "Who will ever notice?" they ask.
—Psalm 64:5 NLT

Meditation and Action

Encouragement can serve harmonious or obsessive passions. This is an example how encouragement can serve in an obsessive manner. Encouragement is a vital human emotion and state of mind. However, like all things of God, it can be corrupted and used in a negative way as seen here. It's important that you encourage yourself, accept encouragement, and give encouragement to others in the right direction. A key to distinguishing the difference is the secrecy. People who plot to do wrong things spend a lot of time scheming to not get caught. They also falsely assume and convince themselves that they won't get caught. Obsessive passions also create difficulties in other areas of our life. If you find yourself engaging in this type of behavior, this is a sign that you're going in the wrong direction. You're being led by a negative passion (desire) that breeds sin and the consequences of your actions are not too far off. Obsessive passions have a way of deceiving us because it feeds into a sinful desire. We've all experienced these times. The question for you is what have you learned from them? If you carefully review these times, you can make yourself mindful of and sensitive to the Spirit who will lead you out of this. This is where the trait of Accountability can help build Passion. To keep harmonious passion alive, it's important to keep yourself surrounded by accountable relationships for proper checks and balance. What changes do you need to make in your accountability system to keep you encouraged in the right direction?

H-CAP Recap

Review the verses for Hope, Commitment, Accountability, and Passion. To keep hope alive, it's important to keep your courage and confidence up. Without courage and confidence, hope cannot exist. The fact that the Bible tells us that we need these things is an indication that we'll face difficult times. Be encouraged by the fact that God is with you and that you don't walk alone. Encouragement creates courage and confidence.

Resilience is based on being committed to the right things in life. It's easy to get caught up in endless pursuits of goals that lead to nowhere. This is because these types of goals and passions are not based on knowledge but feeling. This is a one way path to destruction. Make sure your goals have a foundation of knowledge of practicality and of the word of God. Commit yourself to the right things.

Christianity is being in the business of mankind. We need to be accountable to each other by taking care of each other's needs. It not the business of the government to do these things, it's us. Be generous in giving to others. Your giving doesn't necessarily have to be about money, it can be anything. Hold yourself accountable.

Everyone has passion which leads to goal directed behavior. The question is whether the passion is obsessive or harmonious. People can be determined to pursue an obsessive passion which they know leads to negative consequences because it's all they know. They don't know how to stop it. Cultivating harmonious passions will require you to align yourself with the right people who follow harmonious passions. Find them.

Intentionally implement the following:

1. Keep your courage and confidence alive. Life has a unique way of eroding them if we're not vigilant. Get in the habit of encouraging yourself and encouraging others. These acts bring encouragement.
2. Examine your goals. Make sure they are based on knowledge and can be supported by that knowledge. Once you know you're in the right, pursue it vigorously.
3. Remember, we're in the business of mankind. Accountability means helping others. What can you do for someone today?
4. Keeping your harmonious passion alive will require you to use the other traits. Align yourself with like-minded people with similar goals. Doing so creates a support system of accountability, where hope and commitment thrive. This equates to passion.

Hope

And without faith it is impossible to please God, because anyone who comes to him must believe that he exists and that he rewards those who earnestly seek him.

—Hebrews 11:6 NIV

Meditation and Action

Because God is the definition and ultimate source of hope, it is the only vehicle that moves His hand. God only operates through the activation of hope/faith. Hope is believing that something can happen in spite of current circumstances. It's the ability to look beyond yourself and circumstances to something better. This creates a motivation to work toward what we hope for. This motivation is the passion that ultimately dictates our committed behaviors. Whatever goals you set for yourself spiritually, personally, or professionally it is impossible for them to materialize unless you hope that they are attainable and you're willing to commit to the behaviors necessary to make them happen. Without this, it is impossible to please God. What is God calling you to? What do you want for your relationships and life in general? Believe that it can be done and take intentional action in that direction and God will reward you. Just understand that your hope will be challenged along the way. Don't be discouraged by this; expect it. As you're confronted with obstacles, be others focused, be an encourager of others. This will encourage you during these times and keep hope alive which will create confidence. This is the reward Paul speaks of. If you happen to be struggling to maintain hope and find that your mind's eye is becoming shortsighted and can only see your current circumstances, seek out people that you can bless. This will correct your vision.

Commitment

> We demolish arguments and every pretension that sets itself up against the knowledge of God, and we take captive every thought to make it obedient to Christ.
>
> —2 Corinthians 10:5 NIV

Meditation and Action

To strengthen your spirit requires vigilance. What Paul says to the Corinthians, he says to us as well. We need to demolish arguments (thoughts, positions, states of mind) that creep into our thought processes that serve to misguide us. Demolish them, not just pass them by but obliterate them. How do we do this, by taking our thoughts captive? The battle for the soul begins with the mind. Everyone has random and automatic thoughts. Some are positive and some are negative. It's the nature of the human brain. The thoughts in and of themselves aren't the problem. It's when we give them a foothold. We give them a foothold when we begin to dialogue with them. We often do this automatically and are unaware of it. We're constantly dialoguing with your thoughts. This is called self-talk. We need to develop an awareness of the nature of our dialogue in order to correct it. What do you do when you have a tempting, captivating thought? Do you engage it, converse with it? If so, you're really feeding it. Remember, the thought is normal, what you do with it from there is the problem. Take every thought captive. Commit to refuse to engage and dialogue with these types of thoughts. Don't chase them away; this will serve to make them stronger. Simply acknowledge them, observe that they are there and shift your focus back to more productive thoughts. Do it every time without fail. This is how you get your control back. It's an active process.

Accountability

No one serving as a soldier gets involved in civilian affairs--
he wants to please his commanding officer.
—2 Tim 2:4 NIV

Meditation and Action

This is a good example of accountability. A soldier needs to have a certain mindset in order to function under stress. They need to be able to act without thought and obey commands. They are trained to think and act like soldiers. They don't bog themselves down with civilian matters because they don't apply to them. In order to please their commanding officer, they need to be liked minded and committed to the same mission. In other words, each one needs the assurance that they will act accordingly, do what they are told, and have each other's back. They need to be counted on. However, success in other areas of life is created the same. It's a state of mind. You can't achieve your goals when you're being distracted by other things. In keeping with developing spiritual resilience, your mind needs to be focused on godly things. You can't allow yourself to be mired in the trappings of the world. This is displeasing to God, our commanding officer, and will take us from our primary mission. Do you have a goal that you're striving for? Make sure you create an environment that's conducive to obtaining your goal. Don't be distracted by other things. It's up to you to create and maintain an environment that leads you to success. What changes do you need to make in your environment to keep you focused? You task is to make those changes. It's a right step toward accountability.

Passion

Live in harmony with each other. Don't be too proud to enjoy the company of ordinary people. And don't think you know it all!

—Romans 12:16 NLT

Meditation and Action

Living an abundant (blessed) life with a strong faith can breed a sense of pride if we're not careful. This attitude can also create a sense of being above others who may not have and act in the level of faith you do. As you begin to become resilient in your faith, becoming stronger, and living in God's blessing, this will usually be your first hurdle and one that will continually knock on the door of your mind and heart. You must acknowledge this and don't fool yourself that this won't happen and are above this from happening. If this is your mindset, surprise, it's already taken you over. People overcome with this attitude also have a belief that they have all the answers and find it difficult to accept being wrong. A good way to keep this attitude at bay is to learn to enjoy the company of all kinds of people, not just the company in which you're most comfortable. Everyone has the same basic needs of feeling loved, needed, etc. Get in the habit of meeting these needs in ALL people. Accept the fact that you can and are wrong at times and acknowledge when you are. The act of doing this serves to keep us humble and authentic. This also creates harmony and feeds into right passions for serving God and others building our faith. As you continue in the task of meeting at least one need a day for someone, add a deed to others not generally in your circle.

H-CAP Recap

Review the verses for Hope, Commitment, Accountability, and Passion. Hope is believing but hope also comes with believing. We cannot please God and serve God without having hope/faith. How do you get it then? It's a choice to believe. It's not a feeling. You will begin to see hope as you allow yourself to become encouraged by the word of God and others.

Practice taking your thoughts captive. Self-control begins with controlling your mind. You choose what you dwell on and what thoughts you dialogue with. Be aware of how you engage in this process and don't waste time dialoging with negative anxiety provoking thoughts. This does nothing more than add fuel to that fire. Change your internal dialogue.

This week's verse on accountability uses a military theme. Accountability requires us to maintain our focus and not allow ourselves to become distracted. When we allow ourselves to be bogged down by worldly concerns, we lose sight of our mission. Soldiers rely on each other. It's called the buddy system. Keep mission focused.

While it's important to keep an accountability circle around us, we cannot be so far removed from others that we don't notice other's needs, hurting people around us. Living a resilience and abundant life can also create a false sense of pride. Never think it beneath you to walk along side and help those less fortunate than yourself. You can avoid this by making a habit out of serving others.

Intentionally implement the following:

1. Creating hope begins with a choice; a choice to believe. It's only when you choose to believe in something does encouragement begin to grow.
2. Don't allow yourself to be controlled by negative internal dialogue. You choose what to captivate your mind. Take charge, refuse to entertain self-defeating thoughts.
3. Stay mission focused. Refuse to allow yourself to be bogged down with worldly concerns. This step works directly with step #3.
4. Serve others with a humble attitude. Never think of yourself as being better than.....

Hope

6But when he asks, he must believe and not doubt, because he who doubts is like a wave of the sea, blown and tossed by the wind. 7That man should not think he will receive anything from the Lord; 8 he is a double-minded man, unstable in all he does.
—James 1:6-8 NIV

Meditation and Action

Doubt brings indecision. It can paralyze you from taking action. Indecision is also fence riding. These are cognitive processes which can lead to discouragement and once discouragement sets in, it robs us of hope. This is the danger that James speaks of. It's important to understand that these times come to everyone, it's simply a part of human nature and life. Things will always surface that have the potential to cause us to doubt. It's not a bad thing in and of itself. At times we need to be cautious and thoughtful as we consider options. However, as we consider choices, we need to keep in mind the goals that God has called us to. This is an individual thing. Consider the goals you have for yourself spiritually, personally, and professionally. Allow the hope you have for these goals to dictate the decisions you make. Let hope and belief be your guide as you consider your circumstances and take intentional action. It's only as we waiver in our hope that it can happen and end up wallowing in indecision. As James describes it, this literally feels like we're being tossed about like a wave on the ocean. The process of avoiding this is to keep your goals and the hope of achieving them alive and active. Keep looking ahead and move in that direction serving the needs and encouraging of others. God will make the way for you, just act through your hope.

Commitment

11Never be lacking in zeal, but keep your spiritual fervor, serving the Lord.12Be joyful in hope, patient in affliction, faithful in prayer.13Share with God's people who are in need. Practice hospitality.

—Romans 12:11-13 NIV

Meditation and Action

These verses bring together all of the traits in the H-CAP model. Our passion, zeal for God, is dependent on our hopefulness. However, these things can only work together as we commit ourselves to seeking them. In this case, Paul tells us to be faithful in prayer, share and give to people in need, particularly other believers (accountability), and being hospitable. These are the actions we need to be committed to. A strange thing happens when we really make the choice to focus on and do these very things; we begin to become others focused and not self-focused. It takes our mind off of our circumstances by meeting the needs of others. When we do this, it energizes our spirit; it renews our spirit which feeds back into itself. Our needs also get met in the process. That's how giving and doing work. By giving; we get. However, notice how these acts are intentional. It's not about feeling like it. These are directives, instructions for right behaviors. Engaging in these behaviors transforms and renews your mind and creates harmonious passion. Do you feel that you're losing your zeal for God? Commit to prayer and serving others. You can do no other thing that will make it return any quicker. Commit!

Accountability

> You must worship no other gods, for the LORD, whose very name is Jealous, is a God who is jealous about his relationship with you.
> —Exodus 34:14 NLT

Meditation and Action

Accountability is about relationship(s). God makes it very clear that He will not share Himself with you with anyone or anything else. It's all or nothing. To get to where you want and need to be spiritually, you need to guard this relationship and keep in sacred. Relationship also bears the connotation of being with; knowing. You can only know someone by being with them. It's being with God that makes us more like God and transforms our minds and behaviors to be godlier. This is what relationships do. They rub off on us. We become like those we hang around. This is why the Bible is very clear on not being unequally yoked with non-believers and emphasizes the need for fellowship among believers. If you want to be stronger in your faith, you need to hang around others who have more faith than you. What better person than God Himself. Spend more time with Him but get in the habit of just sitting and listening. Let Him do the talking. Prayer isn't about you doing the talking. With that said, have you taken an inventory of your relationships lately? What changes do you need to make? Perhaps you need to create and or increase time with others who are more in line with spiritual things and or are in line with your other goals such as career, family, etc… Make sure your goals and relationships actually match up. If not, make the necessary changes. You won't get there any other way.

Passion

Put to death therefore what is earthly in you: sexual immorality, impurity, passion, evil desire, and covetousness, which is idolatry.

—Colossians 3:5 ESV

Meditation and Action

Paul's letter to the Church at Colosse was a warning because they were in the habit of entertaining false doctrines. They were mixing Christian truth with other doctrines of the day to make them more acceptable. This is still happening today throughout the world. Each person has an individual responsibility for their faith and the development (growth) of their faith. Paul tells us to put to death earthly desires (obsessive passions) which include sexual immorality, impurity of all kinds, evil desires, and greed. These traits are innate within mankind due to the fall. However, we mistakenly assume that it's God responsibility to take these desires away from us. This is not the case. We will always wrestle with these things as long as we are in human flesh, Christian or not. This is our battle and one we must fight and win daily. It's part of the growth and development of our faith and is what creates resilience. Resilience can't come without battling against something and making difficult decisions. In other words, this is life and God does not spare us from life just because we're Christians. This is the purpose of this devotional, to give you the tools necessary to be successful in this battle. You'll take some hits and bruises and get scars you may carry with you for the rest of your life, however, if you apply these principles, you will make it and be better and stronger for it. This is the definition of resilience. Take responsibility for your own faith and put to death earthly desires!

H-CAP Recap

Review the verses for Hope, Commitment, Accountability, and Passion. Hope requires us to take committed action. This is particularly true when struck by doubt. Doubt is normal. Get in the habit of acting through it. Don't allow yourself to be paralyzed. The more you sit in fear, the less likely you will live out your hope.

Commitment is an obligation to act regardless of feeling. Paul tells us to never lack in zeal (passion). Commitment to hope, patience, prayer, and serving others will create and maintain all of these traits. It takes an intentional decision to act to make it happen. Commit to doing these things.

If our goal is to be more like Jesus, we need to hang around Him more often. We develop the mind set of those we hang around with. If creating spiritual resilience is your goal, spend more time with others who are more resilient than you. Let these relationships rub off on you. What better example is the Father Himself. Spend more time sitting and listening to what He has to say to you. Prayer isn't about you setting aside a routine time and going through a list. It's more about sitting and saying nothing. Listen.

God doesn't spare us from life to include desires (obsessive passions) that can derail us. He doesn't create them, they are just there. It's our responsibility to control these distractions, not God's. He's given us everything we need and it's our responsibility through the choices we make to control them instead of the obsessive desires controlling us. Take responsibility for your own faith and put to death earthly desires!

Intentionally implement the following:

1. Doubt is a normal occurrence; it's what you do when hit by it that matters. Get in the habit of acting through it. Look to your hope, encourage yourself, and keep moving in that direction.

2. Commitment is an obligation to act. It's only in our action is hope fulfilled. As we act, it also builds passion. Act on prayer, practice waiting, serve others. All of these things will keep your eyes on the road, the road to abundant living.

3. You will only be as strong as who you follow, who you hang around. This is why it's important to select who we allow to influence us carefully. Follow Jesus; spend time with Him and other like-minded people. Be accountable. Make whatever adjustments you need. Note how this also takes commitment to act.

4. There are many things that can distract us from serving God. If you stop long enough and reflect, you'll find that most of these things are driven by obsessive passions and have little to no value in the end. The point is for you to see this now before you get to the end

and look back with regret. It's your responsibility to make the right choices. If you've made wrong choices, and we all have, make them right. With God, there's always a repair cycle. This will create and maintain harmonious passion and make life fun and worth living.

Hope

13But Moses told the people, "Don't be afraid. Just stand still and watch the LORD rescue you today. The Egyptians you see today will never be seen again.14The LORD himself will fight for you. Just stay calm."15Then the LORD said to Moses, "Why are you crying out to me? Tell the people to get moving! 16 Pick up your staff and raise your hand over the sea. Divide the water so the Israelites can walk through the middle of the sea on dry ground.

—Exodus 14:13-16 NLT

Meditation and Action

Recall and consider the state of mind of the people of Israel as they approached the Red Sea as they were being chased by Pharaoh's army. Remember, Israel had witnessed direct miracles of God as they were finally set free from slavery. God had made a way for them to escape. Yet, as they're being pursued they suddenly forgot about God's ability to make a way for them and in choosing to look and focus on their current circumstances, they complained and were gripped in fear. God has given everyone the ability to hope. It's what you do with it. If God has called you to something, you must keep the hope alive by recalling past experiences where it's been fulfilled and then act on that hope. We see an example of this as God asks Moses why he's crying to Him about it, just keep moving. This is what we do when we're faced with the challenges of life. Life can seemingly chase us down to a point where it appears there's nowhere to go. It's at these times when we need to recognize that we already have everything we need to be spiritually strong. God has already given mankind everything we need to live an abundant life. There's nothing more He can or will do. This is the message He tried to get across to Moses and Israel, just keep moving. Don't look at the circumstance, look toward your hope and act. It's only as we act in faith do the waters part. Are you being chased by life and fear being destroyed?

Commitment

So I tell you this, and insist on it in the Lord, that you must no longer live as the Gentiles do, in the futility of their thinking.
—Ephesians 4:17 NIV

Meditation and Action

The battleground for the soul is the mind. Paul is very emphatic in his statement by using the word "insist." What is it about the Gentiles? It's their useless thinking. The Gentiles believed many different things and had many different customs compared to the Jewish faith. Jewish traditions were structured and regimented designed around a specific purpose of the law. The Gentile mind was susceptible to go in whatever direction the wind takes it. We experience this today. We become captivated by random thoughts and are too easily swept away by the emotions these thoughts stir up. Remember, you always go in the direction you're looking; this includes what you're looking at with your mind's eye as well. Take control of your mind. It's not that the random thoughts and impulses are bad in and of themselves. You can't stop the mind from thinking. That's a neurological impossibility. However, you can control whether you engage (dialogue) with certain thoughts or emotions. Take control. Don't engage in futile thoughts. The key is to first notice that you're being distracted. You can't redirect your thoughts unless you notice the distraction. Once you notice the distraction, simply observe the thought/emotion and without engaging (dialoging) with it, redirect your attention back to right thinking. We call this skill mindfulness. Be mindful of where your mind is and be intentional on what you allow it to focus on.

Accountability

The disciple is not above his master, nor the servant above his lord.

—Matthew 10:24 KJV

Meditation and Action

The term disciple means "pupil." It's being a student of one with greater knowledge than you. The goal is to obtain the knowledge of the teacher and become more like them in the talent or skill they possess. We find this relationship in all aspects of business, personal life, and spiritual life. We also call it mentoring. Behind every successful person was a mentor, a teacher who showed them how to negotiate whatever path they were on. The most basic form of this relationship is a parent and developing child. Children naturally look up to their parent(s) and through the process of being with them; we pick up their mannerisms and ways of reacting and responding. We also see this in sports with the relationship between players and a coach. These relationships mold us into the person we need to be in order to be successful at that task. The same applies when it comes to our relationship with God. If your goal is to grow spiritually, we need to have a spiritual mentor. Don't fool yourself; you can't make it to the level of rising above circumstances on your own. You need other people around you to emulate and provide the right example. Accountability is also about when you're not doing these things, you need to give these people the right to check you without being defensive toward their observations. Do you want to truly live an abundant spiritual life? Begin the developmental process by finding someone stronger than you in faith and learn from them. Do this today.

Passion

Finally, all of you, live in harmony with one another; be sympathetic, love as brothers, be compassionate and humble.
—I Peter 3:8 NIV

Meditation and Action

The theme of I Peter is the grace of God and how to live as Christians in a world that's hostile to Christian belief. Hostility toward Christ and the way of life that Christianity demands is something that has always been under attack and always will be. Peter tells us that we need to live by example. It's not that we become doormats and never stick up for ourselves but we also need to be sympathetic and compassionate to those within and outside of the church. We forget that it's through acts of kindness and understanding that bring people to Christ, not vengeance or excuse making. Common courtesy and empathy is something that is lacking in the world today. We must choose our battles wisely and recognize that some just aren't worth the fight in the long run. If it's a matter of violating a principle of life and or sin, yes, you must take a stand. However, many problems we struggle with don't rise to this level but really may be because we want our way. Developing empathy, sympathy, compassion, and humility comes from loving others though acts of kindness. If you make these behaviors a daily priority, you will be well on your way in creating a passion for godly things that will make your spirit strong and harmonious. Create a habit of engaging in these tasks daily. Doing this will change your attitude.

H-CAP Recap

Review the verses for Hope, Commitment, Accountability, and Passion. The Bible tells us that God has given everyone a measure of faith, the ability to hope. It's what you do with it. When faced with challenges, it's human nature to stop, rethink, and second guess ourselves (doubt). When these times hit, stay calm, reflect on God's goodness and of times when God has come through for you and others. Then, keep moving in the direction of your hope. Move; don't stop in fear because the world is chasing you.

Right living is a commitment. This begins with controlling your mind which builds resilience. Get in the habit of observing your thoughts and emotions without allowing yourself to become them (engage/dialogue with them). When you notice your mind going to a place you don't want to go, observe it and let it go by gently redirecting your attention to where you want to go. You may do this countless times throughout the day. This is taking control.

Becoming a master at what you do and how you live requires an accountable relationship with a teacher. In order to learn from this person(s) you need to model their behaviors and learn to think like they think. This can only happen over time and depends on the amount of time you spend with them. The more time spent in their presence, the more they will influence your thoughts and actions. Jesus is the ultimate example but you also need others around you to serve in this role. Find them.

Living in a culture that is hostile to Christianity can be difficult. It's full of temptations that can serve to draw us away from what God has for us. We soon exchange our pursuit of holiness for the pursuit of obsessive passions. Harmonious passions are rooted in a peaceful state of mind. It's the ability to live in harmony with our circumstances and with others without allowing difficult circumstances or people to influence that state of mind. Developing empathy, sympathy, compassion, and humility comes from loving others though acts of kindness.

Intentionally implement the following:

1. When trouble hits, do your best to remain calm. Remember the big picture (where you're going). Maintain your hope and act through the difficulty. Don't stand in fear and do nothing. Keep moving in faith in the direction you need to go.
2. Don't allow circumstances, thoughts, or emotions to control you. Practice being observant, aware of your thoughts and feelings and see how they move you to action. It's not the thoughts or feelings that are wrong but what you do with them. Don't engage and dialogue with negative/obsessive thoughts or feelings. Acknowledge their presence

and direct your focus back to your task. You'll go through this process hundreds if not thousands of times a day.

3. Who are you accountable to? Who do you look up to in the faith? You should be following someone's example. Find people who are stronger then you and learn from them. Allow their relationship to influence you toward growth. Do the same for others. This is accountability.

4. Harmonious passion can exist in any circumstance, even in a fallen world. It's your attitude. Cultivate this by developing empathy, sympathy, compassion, and humility from loving others though acts of kindness.

Hope

5I wait for the LORD, my soul waits, and in his word I hope;6 my soul waits for the LORD more than watchmen for the morning, more than watchmen for the morning.
—Psalm 130:5-6 RSV

Meditation and Action

Because hope is based on something that is yet to come, we must wait. Hope by its nature connotes having to wait. However, this is the most difficult thing for the human mind to engage in. It's our nature to want it now. The craving for instant gratification can be very strong. There are many stories throughout the Bible where people have made bad choices and suffered negative consequences because they refused to wait on God. They wanted to do it "now." Although waiting for something to materialize can be difficult, it's not that we're doing nothing. There's always something we can be doing even if it's making preparations. These preparations can vary depending on what you're waiting for. For example, if you're working toward something, although you may want it now, it may not be God's timing. There may be more preparation you need to do to get ready for what God has for you. In this case, as you wait, you need to continue in your committed behaviors slowly working toward your hope. As you work, you need to be vigilant for opportunities God sends your way. Don't allow yourself to become frustrated in the waiting. Your preparation is all part of the journey that will enable you to truly enjoy the end result. Allow your journey to remake your attitude and outlook. This process is called transformation and only comes through hope. As you wait, stay committed to your work.

Commitment

May the God of hope fill you with all joy and peace as you trust in him, so that you may overflow with hope by the power of the Holy Spirit.

—Romans 15:13 NIV

Meditation and Action

Commitment is an obligation. Obligation also includes an element of trust, and trust is linked to hopefulness. Trust and hopefulness are also connected to accountability as you need to be accountable to what you're hoping and trusting in. This begins with a commitment to hope, accountability, and trust. Joy, peace, and power of the Holy Spirit, will only come to the degree of your commitment to these things. In other words, your benefit of hope, peace, and power will reflect the amount of your commitment. Make an intentional decision to be hopeful. Look to the positive side of things. I'm not simply referring to "positive thinking" but it is true that you go where you're looking. When confronted with obstacles, you need to find the opportunity. Without a positive outlook, you won't find the opportunity. It's been said that trouble is often opportunity in disguise. Trust in the fact that things will always work out for your benefit. God promises this. It may not be in that exact moment and God may not always do things the way you want them to be done. Trust that He knows best and will in time work things to the advantage of his children. This is the type of thinking you need to engage in when hit with the roadblocks of life. This takes an intentional commitment to action on your part. Your mind will automatically want to go in the other direction. Don't blame, get anxious, run away, doubt. Trust in God. Surrender to this, accept it and experience His peace.

Accountability

Plans go wrong for lack of advice; many advisers bring success.

—Proverbs 15:22 NLT

Meditation and Action

Living life brings with it many decisions. These decisions can be tough to say the least. A single decision can change the course of your life and bring with it great benefits or disaster. What's the best way to go about making these decisions? As Proverbs states, it's important to get advice but we need to get the *right advice* even if it's something we don't want to hear or do. Successful people surround themselves with people they can trust to give them right direction. They don't simply surround themselves with people who tell them what they want to hear to make them feel good. This leads to destruction. Are you going through a tough time? You may not at the moment but you will meet these crossroads in the future. Seek out people whom you can trust and obtain advice from them. Note that the key word here is *many*. Get the opinions of many people before you commit to a decision. However, the people you seek advice from needs to be those who have the actual knowledge to help you, have been where you are, and have navigated these decisions before. Whether you're facing a decision currently or not, create for yourself a group of people you can count on for right direction and feed those relationships. Turn to each other in times of need, count on each other, and learn from each other's successes and mistakes. This is accountability at its best.

Passion

47 If you do not serve the LORD your God with joy and
enthusiasm for the abundant benefits you have received, 48
you will serve your enemies whom the LORD will send
against you. You will be left hungry, thirsty, naked, and
lacking in everything. The LORD will put an iron yoke on
your neck, oppressing you harshly until he has destroyed you.
—Deuteronomy 28:47-48 NLT

Meditation and Action

As you think about this verse, consider the people you know,
particularly Christians. How many people do you know actually live
with enthusiasm? Note that serving with enthusiasm is a requirement.
It says that if service is not done with enthusiasm, you will be
overtaken by the enemy and placed in bondage. You may be thinking,
how do I get enthusiasm then? The answer lies in looking to the
abundant benefits we've received through our salvation and knowing
God. Remember, you go where you're looking. If you look to hope
and blessing, it will change your outlook on life and give you purpose.
If you keep your eye on circumstances, you'll become disgruntled and
hopeless. This is how most people live, disgruntled. Is it any wonder
then that mankind wears an iron yoke, oppressed with doom? This is
because this is how they see the world and God's creation. They don't
open their eyes to what's really around them and the opportunities that
exist for blessing. Resilience brings enthusiasm because resilient

people are able to look beyond themselves to opportunity. To add enthusiasm to your life, count your blessings. Focus on them and be a blessing to others around you. Do this and you will quickly begin to notice a level of excitement enter into your life. This is your purpose. Live it. Never waste a day not doing the things you love.

H-CAP Recap

Review the verses for Hope, Commitment, Accountability, and Passion. Waiting is the hardest thing to do. What makes it so difficult is the anticipation. If you're not careful, it can get the best of you and cause you to take shortcuts. There is no instant gratification when it comes to building resilience. It takes time. It's the journey and experience that creates resilience. You can't have resilience without creating the mind for it. The key is to stay committed to the behaviors necessary that make your hope fulfilled. Occupy yourself in these things to include prayer and fellowship with other like-minded people. Accountability will keep you grounded.

The act of commitment includes an element of trust. At some level we need to trust that what we are committed to will ultimately bring our hope to life. Trust can be thwarted when confronted with the realities of life. These times have a way of sucking the life out of us. However, it's during these times that trust and commitment are tested. Direct your mind to believing that God will work it out. Just stay committed to the right behaviors in the process.

Life cannot be successfully navigated alone. We need each other. The Bible is clear that success depends on the quality of direction we get from others. The key point is where the advice coming from. Good advice doesn't mean you have to like it. Things are not as they often appear, at least to us. It's important to get the perspective of others who have been there before and learn from them. Seek and heed advice from people more knowledgeable than you. Such relationships are priceless.

God demands all or nothing. He's looking for people to pour out his passion on who are willing to live an abundant life. The problem is many just won't accept it. It's difficult to understand why anyone would turn down such a gift, but they do. Perhaps you're one of them. Choosing to not live enthusiastically gives us the alternative being stress, succumbing to pressure, chaos, controlled by circumstances. This is how the world lives. Break the cycle.

Intentionally implement the following:

1. There is no instant gratification when it comes to building resilience. Occupy yourself in your committed behaviors that work toward your hope while you're waiting.
2. As you're waiting, occupy your mind with the belief that God will work it all out. Trust in this; make yourself believe it by constantly looking in that direction.
3. Relationships, relationships, relationships. You can't get to where you want to go without them. The most important decision is who these relationships are with. Choose wisely. Your future depends

on it. Seek advice from people who have more experience in what you're trying to obtain. Don't be a fool.

4. Living the abundant life is a blessing from God who wants everyone to have it. Create, maintain, and follow a harmonious passion by serving and meeting needs of others. This is where you'll find it.

Hope

'Where can we go up? Our brethren have discouraged our hearts, saying, "The people [are] greater and taller than we; the cities [are] great and fortified up to heaven; moreover we have seen the sons of the Anakim there."
—Deuteronomy 1:28 NKJV

Meditation and Action

The book of Deuteronomy chronicles the expedition of the Promised Land. Recall that of the 12 spies that were sent, 10 came back with a bad and negative report that they can't do it. In spite of what God had told them, they chose to see only with their natural eye and became discouraged. Discouragement breeds hopelessness which is what we see here. On their return, the 10 spies spread their discouragement to the rest of the nation which resulted in Israel wondering around for 40 years. Only two of the 12 were encouraged by what they saw, Joshua and Caleb. However, their words of encouragement were not powerful enough to convince the whole nation. This is because hopelessness and discouragement requires no effort. It's always the path of least resistance. Discouragement comes naturally and won't take any effort. You simply need to focus your natural and mind's eye on your current circumstances and human nature does the rest. On the other hand, encouragement and hopefulness takes effort. It requires you to look beyond what your natural eye sees and to see the promise through your mind's eye. Remember, you will always go where you're looking. What has God called for you in life? Don't simply look at your circumstances and allow them to dictate what your future will be. This breeds discouragement. Encouragement comes from looking into the future, what can be. This is hope in action.

Commitment

31Get rid of all bitterness, rage and anger, brawling and slander, along with every form of malice.32 Be kind and compassionate to one another, forgiving each other, just as in Christ God forgave you.

—Ephesians 4:31-32 NIV

Meditation and Action

In this verse, Paul is talking about the unity of the body of Christ. There are a lot of things to consider within a single sentence. Getting rid of all bitterness, anger, brawling, slander, malice, being kind to others, and forgiving others is quite a list. As Christians, these are the acts we need to be committed to. Some are internal and toward ourselves, such as getting rid of bitterness, anger, rage, and slander. These things are within us. We can't blame these on others although this is always our first reaction. We can often point to these faults in others but rarely do we see them in ourselves. Kindness and forgiving others are outward acts toward others. Being kind toward others and choosing to forgive are outward acts that will help you rid yourself of bitterness, rage, anger, etc. It's the unwillingness to be compassionate and forgiving toward others (being others focused) that allows bitterness to fester which turns into anger and malice. The very thing many people resist is the thing that will set them free. Blaming and holding grudges keeps people from looking at themselves and having to take responsibility. As you read and ponder on the acts in this verse, consider where your commitment to these things lie. What do you need to improve on? Change will only come to the degree you're willing to commit to them.

Accountability

> God gave Solomon very great wisdom and understanding, and knowledge as vast as the sands of the seashore.
> —1 Kings 4:29

Meditation and Action

Solomon is noted as being the wisest man who ever lived. The question is how did he acquire such knowledge? Of course it was a gift from God. However, this gift of insight came from his relationship with God and his willingness to obey. It was only as he committed himself to living rightly and seeking God's direction for his life did God grant him this insight. The point of this is that we too can gain increased insight and wisdom. As we seek God and become closer to

Him we become more spiritually minded. As we become spiritually minded we begin to see things differently and through this insight we are able to apply knowledge. This is what wisdom is. Don't simply be amazed at the wisdom of others. Join their ranks. Spiritual insight, discernment, and wisdom are natural byproducts of our relationship with God and the people of God. You become like those you hang around. If you spend more time in God's presence and train your mind by applying these strategies, God will give you the mind of the Holy Spirit. You will gain discernment. However, this only comes through the accountable relationship, not only with God but with other like-minded people. Your task for today and for the future is to spend more time getting to know God. Read and study the Bible, fellowship with other Christians and let your mind grow.

Passion

> Enthusiasm without knowledge is no good; haste makes mistakes.
>
> —Proverbs 19:2 NLT

Meditation and Action

Enthusiasm without knowledge leads to misdirected behavior. The successful achievement of any goal requires a hopeful attitude accompanied with a commitment to goal seeking and obtaining behavior. The two work together along with accountability and passion. If we take out the passion (enthusiasm) our goal becomes nothing more than a pipedream and the work we do to seek our goal becomes laborious. Notice that people who limit themselves to passion alone end up making hasty decisions which end up with negative and often disastrous consequences. This is also what is called an obsessive passion. Our zeal and passion needs to be accompanied with the proper knowledge. By having knowledge, our passion works for us, not against us. It's knowledge that drives passion and along with hope, commitment, and accountability, creates opportunity. By committing yourself to working through this devotional, you're adding knowledge and creating passion. The goal is to keep them moving. These traits that create resilience are always in motion, growing, and moving forward. They don't stay static. However, it's your responsibility to keep them going in the right direction. This takes attention and vigilance to these tasks every day. Your faith must be fed. Take time daily to meditate on these precepts and keep your passion and knowledge alive.

H-CAP Recap

Review the verses for Hope, Commitment, Accountability, and Passion. To see and believe what God has for your life requires hope. It's a choice to look in that direction. It takes no effort to be discouraged. You need only to look at your circumstances and the world around you and it's easy to get discouraged. Creating hope will require you to look beyond those things and see what God says about the possibilities. Look to where you want to go, not where you are.

Change is hard and it's just easier to blame others for our moods. However, the Bible is clear that getting rid of anger, malice, rage, etc... is our responsibility. These are character flaws that you allowed yourself to develop. What's the remedy? Engage in acts of kindness. Commit to doing good to others. Make it a habit and those flaws will disappear.

Knowledge and wisdom come with experience and through right relationships. It's an act of wisdom and commitment to create these relationships. God's desire is for all to have the mind of the Spirit, to have discernment but you need to walk with the right people to acquire it. Are you in the company of wise people or fools?

Passion without knowledge leads to bad decisions and disaster. Passion in anything we do is important and living an abundant life requires passion. However, to keep passion from becoming obsessive, it must be backed by knowledge. In other words, you can't make it on emotion alone. Many people make decisions based on emotions in the moment because they overly identify with the "feeling." Don't live by feeling but by knowledge and faith.

Intentionally implement the following:

1. Keep your eyes on the road. Hope is a choice to look into the future which impacts how you live your life and the decisions you make for today. Choose to live out your hope.

2. Everyone has the propensity to develop anger and bitterness. You need only to focus on the negative things you experience in life. Your attitude is a choice. Making a commitment to doing good deeds for others is the only way to take responsibility to change it.

3. Common sense and wisdom is a lost commodity. God freely gives it to those who seek it. It only comes through having the right relationships where that state of mind rubs off on you. Hang around God and let Him speak to you and hang around wise people. Allow these relationships to influence you.

4. Passion without knowledge leads to obsessive passion and burnout. You can't live on emotion alone. Allow your hope to fuel your

passion and know what it is you're striving for. Allow your passion to develop from who you are, not to define who you are.

Hope

6"Be strong and courageous, for you are the one who will lead these people to possess all the land I swore to their ancestors I would give them. 7Be strong and very courageous. Be careful to obey all the instructions Moses gave you. Do not deviate from them, turning either to the right or to the left. Then you will be successful in everything you do.

—Joshua 1:6-7 NLT

Meditation and Action

The highlight of the book of Joshua is the possession of the Promised Land. After 40 years of wandering in the desert due to their lack of hope, they were now ready. However, notice the command and reminder given to Joshua. If you recall, 40 years prior, Joshua and Caleb were the only 2 of the 12 spies that were hopeful and believed that they could possess the land. Why did God have to remind Him to be strong and courageous and to be careful to obey the instructions given to him by Moses? The answer is that God wanted Joshua to be prepared. He wanted to remind Joshua that what his natural eye and his mind's eye saw would be two different things. As he did 40 years ago, he needed to see beyond current circumstances and see the hope that God promised. The way to do this is to not deviate from the task at hand. Don't turn to the right or left, set your eyes on the hope laid before you and go in that direction without being distracted. If you do this, success is promised. Where are your passions calling you? Don't be surprised at the many things along the way to possess what God has called you to that can serve as distractions, giants, and fears of failure. Don't deviate from right behaviors, don't allow yourself to be tempted to look in other directions. Be strong and courageous as you enter, don't fear taking some hits along the way, and you will succeed.

Commitment

13Brothers, I do not consider myself yet to have taken hold of it. But one thing I do: Forgetting what is behind and straining toward what is ahead, 14I press on toward the goal to win the prize for which God has called me heavenward in Christ Jesus.
—Philippians 3:13-14 NIV

Meditation and Action

Successful and resilient people don't spend time looking in the rear view mirror of life. Remember, you go where you're looking. You can't move ahead while looking and living in the past. We all make mistakes. Paul addresses this when he says that he has not yet arrived but he doesn't allow himself to be bogged down by the past. He continues to look and move forward. If anyone has a right to hold on to and get stuck in the past it's Paul. He was the number one terrorist of his time traveling around and killing believers of Christ. People were still fearful after his conversion and it took time to change people's minds and see that he was genuine. However, he did not allow himself to be troubled by his past. He found comfort in God's forgiveness and from then on, ran his race. Are you plagued by your past? Have you made some serious mistakes or perhaps you've been led to believe that you're not good enough? Whatever is in your past is just that, in the past. Do not allow your past to define you in the present or your future. Forget the past. You can't change it, why do you keep reliving it? Learn to accept it and keep your mind's eye focused on what's ahead. You can only change what is now! Make a commitment to live with the mindset to live in the here and now. Make right decisions for today and prepare your future. Press on toward the prize to which God has called you.

Accountability

So then everyone of us shall give account of himself to God.
—Romans 14:12 KJV

Meditation and Action

A very small and simple verse but it has a great impact. The bottom line is that we're all accountable to someone. It doesn't matter where you are on the ladder; you have to answer to someone. Even the highest ranking CEO is accountable to others. Problems arise when we have the attitude that we answer to no one. This brings with it a sense of entitlement and thoughts of being above others. When we operate in this manner we become more self-centered and less centered on others. This leads to obsessive passions and will ultimately lead to your destruction. Is a lack of accountability a problem for you? Take a moment to take an inventory of what you are accountable for and to whom in the different areas of your life. In what areas do you need to be more accountable? Your task for today is to make an accountability plan. In whatever areas you need more accountability, your marriage, relationship with God, work, etc., create relationships with people and tell them your goals. Ask them to help keep you on track and when they point things out to you, you must also give up the right to blame and be defensive. Part of being accountable is knowing how to receive direction and criticism. If you dare to do this, you'll be amazed at the results.

Passion

Then the LORD saw that the wickedness of man was great in the earth, and that every intent of the thoughts of his heart was only evil continually.

—Genesis 6:5 KJV

Meditation and Action

Due to the fall, obsessive passions come naturally. Harmonious passions need to be cultivated. In other words, they take work, a commitment to create them. Take a moment and consider how mankind doesn't need to be taught how to lie, cheat, steal, etc. Recall your own childhood. As parents, we teach our children how to behave properly. Doing the right thing doesn't always come naturally. We need to be taught to put others first, to delay gratification, plan for the future and not the moment. This encompasses the wickedness that God speaks of in this verse. These traits stay with us forever and are constantly at war within us to do good. This is what Paul spoke of in Romans 7:19. If we do not take hold of this, it can turn into an obsessive passion leading us to engage in various behaviors that become detrimental to our well-being and tear down resilience. Are you caught in a cycle of obsessive passions? Change comes from looking in the direction you want to go. This verse provides the answer "every intent of the thoughts of his heart." Passions are created by what we choose to focus on. Take your thoughts captive; focus your thoughts on doing for others. Never let a day go by where you don't make an impact on someone's life. Make this a daily mission. Doing this will create harmonious passion in your life. However, to keep it, you need to continue your efforts to keep it alive.

H-CAP Recap

R eview the verses for Hope, Commitment, Accountability, and Passion. Be courageous, expect challenges. In living out your hope, you will be confronted with many road blocks along the way. Don't be surprised and don't allow fear to keep you from fulfilling what you hope for. You must choose to allow hope to direct your behavior and not the fear of what you see.

Don't allow yourself to get bogged down in your past by reliving past mistakes. Refuse to allow yourself to be defined by a negative past. This is your choice. Take Paul's advice, forget what is behind and keep moving forward. You can't go forward looking in the rear view mirror.

People who live unaccountable lives are reckless and irresponsible. Everyone needs to be accountable to someone. There is no such thing as a self-made person. Success is created through quality relationships where there is accountability. If you want your hopes to be fulfilled, you need to surround yourself with the right people.

The heart of man is wicked. This is an unfortunate trait we inherited as a result of the fall. It's wickedness that comes natural to us which is why we continue to battle against sin. This penchant to sin leads to the fulfilling of obsessive passions which takes us further from the truth, well-being, peace of mind, and salvation. The good news is that we can change this by allowing God to live through us. Don't be self-centered; be others centered.

Intentionally implement the following:

1. Life is tough. Be courageous. Don't be surprised when confronted with obstacles. If you know to expect them, you can plan your response now. Keep your faith, keep looking to your hope and remain encouraged and committed to the right behaviors during tough times. This is what builds resilience.

2. Refuse to allow past mistakes to dictate your future. The past is done and can't be changed. The only thing that can be changed is the future because it hasn't been lived yet. If you enter the here and now and future by looking in the rear view mirror, you're destined to repeat your mistakes. Look ahead.

3. If you want to fulfill your goals in life, you need to be accountable. A lack of accountability leads to impulsive and reckless behavior. Learn to receive instruction and trust wise counsel.

4. Peace of mind comes only with harmonious passion. Chaos comes from obsessive passion. You have one or the other. There is no middle. Creating harmonious passion begins with taking you from the center and putting others first. Remember, the biblical model of receiving is through giving.

Hope

Why am I discouraged? Why is my heart so sad? I will put my hope in God! I will praise him again— my Savior and my God!

—Psalm 43:5 NLT

Meditation and Action

Everyone has moments when they feel down and discouraged. Even Jesus had these moments; it's part of our human nature. However, if we're not careful, this mood can over take us and alter our vision and take us places we don't want to go. The psalmist gives us the antidote for this state of mind: put your hope in God and praise Him. The reason this simple solution works is because it takes the focus off of you and your circumstances and directs your attention to someone else. It's about being others focused instead of being self-focused. When it's about you, this will always lead to an obsessive passion of chasing things which ultimately lead to discouragement. When you take that energy and put it to use for others, it renews hope, courage, and confidence. It's just the opposite of what you would think but it works. This is why it's so difficult, because it's so simple and contrary to human nature. This is also why it requires intention (commitment). Are you discouraged? The problem is what you're looking at and what you're doing, or in this case, what you're not doing. As God tells Moses in Exodus 14:13-16, why are you crying to me, tell the people to just go! If this is you, don't cry

to God, He's already given everything you need. Just use it. Put your
hope in Him and go forward! As you move, hope and confidence will be
renewed. I dare you to move!

Commitment

1Since, then, you have been raised with Christ, set your
hearts on things above, where Christ is seated at the right
hand of God. 2Set your minds on things above, not on
earthly things.

—Colossians 3:1-2 NIV

Meditation and Action

Since we've been raised with Christ, since we have such great a salvation,
we need to be committed to it. It's a lifestyle, not a title. Paul tells us that
since Christ has done these things for us, we're obligated to set our hearts
and minds on things above and not on earthly things. The Bible speaks
endlessly about the mind and what we need to think on in order to live an
effective Christian life. However, to set your mind takes an intentional
act. You have to commit to resetting your mental vision or your mind's
eye to spiritual things; not on earthly things. Don't be confused, we are in
the world so we need to focus on the here and now but we need to do so
through our faith. It's far too easy for us to get bogged down with earthly
matters and we place too much emotional energy into too many things
that in the long run, don't really matter. How much calmer and peaceful

would life be if we didn't allow ourselves to get so caught up in the emotions of our circumstances? It's possible; just set your mind on things above. Be anxious for nothing. It's where you're directing your mental vision. A term I refer to as *mental optometry.* As in yesterday's strategy on Hope, when you see you're going off course, intentionally redirect your thoughts on heavenly things, the goodness of God, serving others, etc... Commit to adopting this state of mind for yourself. It's an ongoing work, so be patient. It's the journey. Just look where you're going and not so much where you are.

Accountability

For there are three that bear witness in heaven: the Father, the Word, and the Holy Spirit; and these three are one.
—I John 5:7 NKJV

Meditation and Action

We were created for relationships. Through this verse we see that accountability was created from the beginning. The Godhead consists of three persons being the Father, the Son (Word), and the Holy Spirit. They are separate and have distinctly different roles yet none of them act in isolation without the other knowing. The Father is the creator, the Son is the redeemer, and the Holy Spirit is our guide. Although the trinity can be difficult to understand in the human mind, three beings, yet one, the point is not how three can be one but the accountability each has with the other to achieve a common goal. Because we are created in the image of God, we have the same need for affiliation and accountability. Although it comes naturally to us we can attach ourselves to the wrong people. If your goal is to obtain spiritual resilience, you need to create and maintain relationships with other like-minded people. Over time, these relationships will influence your state of mind which will produce the outcome of your goal. Think about your relationships in relation to your goals. Are your relationships helping you or hurting/hindering you? If you find that they are hindering you, dissolve those relationships and create relationships with others who can help you grow in the right direction. This can be a difficult decision. Be accountable. Commit to making right relationships today and feed those relationships.

Passion

But 200 of the men were too exhausted to cross the brook, so David continued the pursuit with 400 men.
—I Samuel 30:10 NLT

Meditation and Action

This chapter in I Samuel outlines David's return from battle to Ziklag only to find the village ransacked and its inhabitants kidnapped by the Amalekites. David and his men were plunged into great sorrow by what they had found. However, unlike many of David's men who looked to blame, David focused on solving the problem. It's often said that a crisis doesn't make the man; it shows what the man is made of. David rises to the occasion by assembling a group of men to pursue the Amalekites and take back what was taken. However, note that David goes with 200 less people. I'm sure that everyone was exhausted, yet David and 400 others looked beyond themselves and were energized by their passion. David's passion and heart for God inspired his men and relentlessly pursued the enemy. Outnumbered and energized completely on their passion, David and his men fought the Amalekites from dusk until the evening of the next day. God gave them the victory and they recovered everything that was taken from them and also took the spoils left behind. David even shared with those of his men left behind. A couple things to note here is the fact that even though David and his men had God on their side, they had to engage in battle and they fought for over 24 hours. Just because God calls us to something, doesn't mean that it will always be easy. However, passion can carry us forward and as we commit to the process, passion continues to grow. It's about keeping the faith.

H-CAP Recap

Review the verses for Hope, Commitment, Accountability, and Passion. Everyone has times when they experience discouragement for whatever reason. Allowing yourself to stay in that mood will ultimately change your attitude and discouragement will turn into hopelessness. Recognize when discouragement hits and take intentional action to remind yourself of the goodness or God and begin to praise Him. Remember, you go where you're looking.

The Bible frequently discusses the need to control the mind. This is the battleground. Our minds our constantly bombarded with information all which compete for the place of attention. Although this is a normal brain activity, it's our responsibility to what thoughts we give attention to. Commit to setting your mind on things above. As you go throughout your day, intentionally keep this mindset. Guard your heart.

Everyone needs relationships. It's through the nature and quality of relationships that the brain makes neurological connections that serve as the foundation for emotional regulation and states of mind. Make sure your relationships line up with your goals. Cut what you need to cut and add what you need to add.

Many people have the false belief that just because God has called them to something, the process will be easy; not so. God's way is not necessarily made easy. If it were, there would be no need for hope. Hope is refined through the trial. This is the process that creates resilience. Growth never comes without conflict. Allow your passion for your goal to carry you through difficult times.

Intentionally implement the following:

1. Don't allow yourself to get stuck in negative thoughts of discouragement. Remind yourself of who you are in Christ and of God's goodness.
2. Commit to guarding your mind. The onslaught of thoughts vying for attention is normal. You choose which thoughts and emotions to engage. Choose to think on heavenly things.
3. Achieving your goals will require you to have relationships with like-minded people. You won't make it alone. Do your relationships line up with your goals? Make whatever changes are necessary.
4. Don't be surprised at the work it takes to achieve your goals. Nothing worth having comes easy. Growth never comes without conflict. Allow the passion of your goal to fill your heart. You can access this by looking at the goal and reminding yourself of your mission. It will get you through tough times.

Hope

When I am afraid, I will trust in you.

—Psalm 56:3 NIV

Meditation and Action

Today's verse on hope is short yet powerful. It provides explicit instruction on what to do in times of fear and discouragement; trust in God. Although it may sound simple, there are some behind the scenes things that need to be understood. The first is that trust implies an object to hope in. The second is that trust also implies a commitment to follow through with right behaviors that serve to fulfill our hope that things will work out. Thirdly, trust also implies accountability. Holding ourselves accountable to another requires a sense of trust that the person will not violate that trust and hurt us. God does not intentionally inflict hurt upon His children for the sake of hurt. Although He allows us to suffer the consequences of our behavior and disciplines us, it is in love. Recall your own experiences as a child and the discipline given to you by your parents. Although you may have resented it at the time, in hindsight, you can look back and see that it was good. How much easier life would be if we learned to trust God with our lives and to not live in fear? This is God's purpose for you. When in those difficult times, just purposely remind yourself that God will come through, He hasn't left your side; keep looking ahead through your circumstances. Will you trust Him with your life, your goals, and dreams? If you're ready, step out and start living. Hope begins with trust, commitment, and accountability.

Commitment

7Have nothing to do with godless myths and old wives' tales; rather, train yourself to be godly. 8For physical training is of some value, but godliness has value for all things, holding promise for both the present life and the life to come.

—I Timothy 4:7-8 NIV

Meditation and Action

Being a godly person requires training. Being a Christian is not just a title. It's a lifestyle that identifies us with the risen Christ. However, in order to live an effective Christian life our faith requires training. You're just not endowed with these abilities at salvation. Just as the body grows through its various physical and developmental changes, so does our spirit. Just as an athlete trains their body to perform at its optimal level, so must we train our spirit. Where is this training ground? It's life. Life's experiences, it's up and downs are the training grounds that perfect our spiritual nature. We must be committed to training the sprit just as an athlete needs to be totally committed to the process of training the physical body. However, we seem to place more emphasis on physical training as opposed to spiritual training. As

Paul says, physical training has some value, but how much more valuable is spiritual training. Spiritual training has eternal consequences, physical training does not. Spiritual training requires you to exercise and stretch your hope, strengthen your commitment to right action that builds hope, and invest in and strengthen your accountability. All these things will grow into harmonious passion which equates to living an abundant resilient life. Commit yourself to training for eternity. Reading and applying the action steps in this devotional is a great start. Apply them daily!

Accountability

The person who strays from common sense will end up in the company of the dead.
—Proverbs 21:16 NLT

Meditation and Action

Common sense seems to be a lost commodity. What should be common often times are not because we have a habit of complicating things and the "commonness" of sense eludes us. However, we need to be mindful of the fact that the lack of common sense leads to only one place, the company of the dead. It places us with the rest of the world who have no sense. These negative relationships begin to take hold and grow because they confirm that state of mind, similar to an earlier devotion of bad company corrupting good character (1 Cor 15:33). You may be going through a rough time right now, if not now, one is around the corner. It happens to all of us. The point is, don't stray from common sense during times of stress. These are the times when you need to stick close to your relationships to help guide your common sense of direction. When going through difficult times our tendency is to allow our decision making to become emotional which overrides common sense. This is why right relationships are so important. They can keep us grounded. Make sure you invest in these relationships. Don't make it harder than it has to be. Your task for today is to keep good company that will enable you to use your common sense and stay the course. Do this intentionally every day.

Passion

I know what enthusiasm they have for God, but it is misdirected zeal.
—Romans 10:2 NLT

Meditation and Action

Misdirected passion leads to obsessive passion. Enthusiasm is good but misdirected enthusiasm can lead down the wrong road. Consider the things that turn you on. Are they good for you in that they enhance your relationships, broaden your knowledge of God and increase your faith, do they promote the welfare of others or are they self-serving? It's not that we can't or shouldn't have hobbies that we spend time alone or even with others. However, where does serving God rate on your scale? Passion without knowledge leads to disaster. It's important to gain knowledge before putting things into practice. Living a Christian life and abundant life will require you to spend time acquiring knowledge. This knowledge is obtained by spending time reading and meditating on the Bible, which you're doing here, involvement in fellowshipping with other like-minded people, and applying this knowledge to your daily life by serving others. Passion is linked to accountability. It's an ongoing process that feeds into itself. When stopped, passion can wane and or become obsessive. Do you find yourself lacking passion for God? If so, you're on the right track by applying these devotions. Add to this an accountability system of like-minded people you can fellowship with. This will increase your faith and passion for serving which will ultimately end in a resilient faith.

H-CAP Recap

Review the verses for Hope, Commitment, Accountability, and Passion. Hope embodies the willingness to trust which also encompasses the traits of commitment, and accountability. When fear sets in, it's an automatic reaction to withdraw. God has not given us a spirit of fear. When you've done all you can do to stand, the Bible tell us to just stand. Purposely acknowledge that God is with you and don't focus on the emotion of fear but look toward your hope.

Just as we train the body and subject it to stressful exercise, so must we strengthen our spirit. Growth doesn't come without conflict, no pain; no gain. We accept this when it comes to physical exercise but complain and avoid when it comes to the spirit. Why, because the gym for the spirit is daily living. As your personal trainer would tell you "suck it up", "keep going", "you have one more left in you", "you can make it; you're doing great." So it is with the spirit. You can make it.

Difficult times have a way of bringing out our emotions which tend to lead to knee jerk reactions that override common sense. This is where accountability comes in and can save you from additional heartache. Lean on and draw from these relationships and take direction from these relationships and stay the course.

Enthusiasm without knowledge is a train wreck waiting to happen. Enthusiasm is good but without knowledge it becomes obsessive and misdirected. Knowledge is acquired through time and experience. Just plain enthusiasm says "I want it now though, I don't want to go through the experience; it takes too long." Remind yourself that it's the journey that brings the experience.

Intentionally implement the following:

1. Fear is a natural response. When it hits you, don't be taken by surprise, assess the situation and take action. Just keep looking in the direction of your hope and continue to act (commit) though it.
2. As noted in the previous point, you can see how these traits build on each other. This is exercising your spirit and mind. Encourage yourself through it, you can make it.
3. Seek common sense, particularly when experiencing difficult times. Don't rush to judgment. Assess and seek advice from your accountability system, pray, and then take action.
4. Knowledge is power and is the life blood to harmonious passion. Without it, your passions are misdirected and you're really using them to fill an unmet need. As you immerse yourself in cultivating these traits, you will increase your knowledge.

Hope

May the God of hope fill you with all joy and peace as you
trust in him, so that you may overflow with hope by the
power of the Holy Spirit.

—Romans 15:13 NIV

Meditation and Action

This passage reflects Paul's prayer and blessing to be filled with joy and

peace. However, note that this only comes through our willingness to

trust our future to God. To place trust in someone or something implies

that hope in whatever has been entrusted will be revealed at some point in

time. In the case of spiritual resilience, it's placing trust in God to direct

your path. Peace of mind is the one thing that everyone in the world is

seeking. However, it can't be found in the business of life. People look

for peace in all the wrong places which leads only to fulfilling obsessive

passions which cause deeper turmoil. When you truly trust that God will

work out His passion within you, there is nothing to fear regardless of

what circumstances you find yourself. Hope and trust lead to fearless

living and without fear; the only thing that can be left is peace and joy. If

you're tired of running the rat race, stop. Trust in God. Live out your trust

by committing to behaviors that will encourage your hope in things to

come. The level of peace you experience will be commensurate to the

degree of hope and trust you place in Him. Remember, it's not about your

circumstance; it's about hoping and trusting Him to bring you through them. Don't allow negative circumstances to take your eyes from what you expect to come to pass. Keep believing and behaving as if.... This is the path to peace.

Commitment

> Finally, brothers, whatever is true, whatever is noble, whatever is right, whatever is pure, whatever is lovely, whatever is admirable--if anything is excellent or praiseworthy--think about such things.
>
> —Philippians 4:8 NIV

Meditation and Action

Paul lays out the exercise regimen here for spiritual training and growth. Again, the Bible speaks much about our minds and where we should be looking. Have you ever noticed that you never need to teach someone how to lie or commit other wrong behaviors? We do this naturally because it's our fallen nature. However, doing rightly requires training and commitment to the right things. Paul tells us what these things are here in this verse. The answer lies in the training and renewing of your mind. It's done by thinking on things that are noble, right, pure, lovely, admirable, excellent, and praiseworthy. Thoughts of these things will not come naturally. It takes practice. Notice your own thoughts and how easy it is to think of the negative, to catastrophize and make things worse than they really are, to think the worst of people and circumstances. This has a direct effect on our emotional state and behavior. If this is you, and to some degree it is in all of us, commit to training your mind to think on the things Paul tells us. As you do this, you'll begin to see that it requires more work than you originally thought. It requires you to always be mindful of what's going through your mind and whether to engage or disengage from certain thoughts and feelings. Commit yourself to excellence and think on those things. You take control of your mind.

Accountability

4Pay careful attention to your own work, for then you will get the satisfaction of a job well done, and you won't need to compare yourself to anyone else. 5For we are each responsible for our own conduct.
                                                   —Galatians 6:4-5 NLT

Meditation and Action

We are in the habit of comparing ourselves to others which is never a good measure. We run our own race. It's an individual competition. It's not about how good we are compared to others. Christ's example is the measuring stick, not the person next to you. If you do everything in the spirit of excellence, you should never need to compare what and how you're doing compared to another. The buck stops here. Part of accountability is taking responsibility for our own actions. We like to take credit when things go good because it makes us look good. However, when things don't work out as planned, we seek to find someone or something to blame. This is due to our fallen nature. Mankind doesn't need to be taught how to do this, it just comes naturally. This doesn't make it right and must be resisted. When things go right, humbly, accept responsibility but also acknowledge others who helped you and made it possible. When things go wrong, take responsibility. Doing so will earn the respect of others because they will see you as a person with integrity. Are there things in your life where you're shifting blame? Be accountable, take responsibility and make it right. Acknowledge to those who have been impacted by your decision(s) and put in place a plan of corrective action. By doing this you'll earn their trust and respect. This is how God would have us to live. Do it!

Passion

15While David was at Horesh in the Desert of Ziph, he learned that Saul had come out to take his life. 16And Saul's son Jonathan went to David at Horesh and helped him find strength in God. 17"Don't be afraid," he said. "My father Saul will not lay a hand on you. You will be king over Israel, and I will be second to you. Even my father Saul knows this."

—I Samuel 23:15-17 NIV

Meditation and Action

Passion needs encouragement. This is called accountability. Notice how each of the traits of Hope, Commitment, Accountability, and Passion are linked together. David knew God's hand was directing his life. However, this didn't stop David from experiencing the fear of death as Saul pursued him. This is a natural reaction. You may say that he lacked faith. However, experiencing emotions are normal but being dialed too much into emotion can derail our efforts. Remember, you go where you're looking. David's fear of Saul was overriding his assurance of God's plan for his life. This is where Jonathan comes in. This verse describes the result when passion meets accountability. We need other people in our lives that can pour into us and keep us on track. Jonathan was an excellent example of this for David. Verse 16 gives us the result that David found strength in God from Jonathan's encouragement. Jonathan helped David adjust his mental focus which got him back on track. You need to develop this habit for yourself. Encourage yourself, be encouraged by others, and encourage others. Today's lesson can be applied in two ways, 1. If you find yourself becoming discouraged, find someone and allow yourself to be encouraged. 2. Be a source of encouragement to someone going through a tough time. You will fall into one of these categories and possibly both. Act on them. You have nothing to lose and passion to gain.

H-CAP Recap

Review the verses for Hope, Commitment, Accountability, and Passion. Living out your hope requires you to trust God to carry out His part of the deal which is to give you peace and joy. However, because you don't experience these things doesn't mean that He's not keeping His side of the deal, it's you. Trust is demonstrated by your actions and peace and joy is not dependent on circumstances. Keep hope alive by trusting that God will work it out.

It's often been said that the mind is the battleground. You have to train it and make it strong to make your faith strong. Don't allow your mind to be captivated with the business of stuff. Paul tells you what kinds of things you need to think on. Make these things your focus and everything else will fall into place. It is a battle you must win. Train yourself to go in this direction.

Accountability is about taking responsibility. Comparing ourselves to another serves to create obsessive passions which will eventually derail you. Our journey is an individual thing. The competition is with yourself. It's striving to be a better person than you were yesterday through Christ. Take responsibility for your actions right or wrong. Acknowledge others who have helped you and make right wrong decisions.

Harmonious passion is always linked to Hope, Commitment, and Accountability. It's normal to feel down and discouraged. You haven't "fallen off the wagon." It's part of life. It's what you do in these circumstances. Passion is renewed through good accountable relationships where we can receive encouragement.

Intentionally implement the following:

1. Trust is backed up by behavior. In the face of adversity, keep moving forward trusting that God will bring you through. It's this belief alone that brings peace and joy regardless of circumstance.
2. Take yourself to the spiritual gym every day. Applying these strategies is certainly a way of doing that. Train your mind to recognize when you're getting off track and redirect your thinking to things that are true, noble, pure, excellent, and praiseworthy.
3. Run your own race. Take responsibility for your decisions and actions and stop comparing yourself to others. Christ is the only standard.
4. When discouragement sets in and you find your passion wearing thin, seek encouragement from others and be a source of encouragement for others. Doing so will reenergize your passion and get you back on track.

Hope

3All praise to God, the Father of our Lord Jesus Christ. It is by his great mercy that we have been born again, because God raised Jesus Christ from the dead. Now we live with great expectation,4 and we have a priceless inheritance—an inheritance that is kept in heaven for you, pure and undefiled, beyond the reach of change and decay.
—I Peter 1:3-4 NLT

Meditation and Action

The key word in this verse is expectation. To expect means that we anticipate something to happen. We have a certainty that whatever we are expecting to happen will happen. Expectation is to hope. However, notice how Peter describes this form of hope. He says that since we have been saved as a result of Christ being raised from the dead, we now live in great expectation. The operative word is live. To live in expectation adds action, committed behaviors, to what we expect and hope for. This form of expectation is not an intellectual belief. It goes beyond that. It is a hope and belief that something will definitely happen and as a result, it changes behavior. It brings a certainty to our hope and we are so sure of it that we live as if it's true. Do the things you hope in change your behavior? If not, sit and really consider this verse and recognize what it really means to have the priceless inheritance we have. This is our future regardless of what's happening now. Knowing what great benefits we have in store for us can provide hope and peace throughout the journey. It's a confidence of knowing that we win the war in the end and knowing this can provide strength to fight one more day. Sometimes we just need to be reminded of this fact. We need to remind ourselves for the sake of encouragement but we also need to be a source of encouragement to others. Live in expectation.

Commitment

15Be diligent in these matters; give yourself wholly to them, so that everyone may see your progress. 16Watch your life and doctrine closely. Persevere in them, because if you do, you will save both yourself and your hearers.
—I Timothy 4:15-16 NIV

Meditation and Action

In this chapter, Paul gives Timothy instructions for godly living and instructing others. Give it a read through and consider this meditation and action step. He tells Timothy to be diligent, give yourself wholly. In other words, be committed to doing these things. Persevere in living a godly life because people are watching. We always need to be careful to monitor and evaluate our lives and doctrine (the code we live by). We never know who may be watching but if we persevere in right living we save ourselves yet influence others who are watching us. It's about being a godly example. Be mindful everyday of your behaviors; think before you act. When you act unjustly or make a bad decision, make it right. Your behaviors speak louder than words; they are more visible. Our ability to be a godly example is dependent on our willingness to persevere. Perseverance means we need to come to the point of being tired and worn out and then continue. Until that point, it's not perseverance. However, it's only as we push through and go beyond ourselves do we increase our stamina. This applies to physical stamina as well as spiritual stamina. Life is our gym. This is perseverance. This is commitment. Are you up to it?

Accountability

14But each one is tempted when, by his own evil desire, he is dragged away and enticed. 15Then, after desire has conceived, it gives birth to sin; and sin, when it is full-grown, gives birth to death. 16Don't be deceived, my dear brothers.

—James 1:14-16 NIV

Meditation and Action

Accountability begins and ends with you. Sin begins from your own evil desires; God does not tempt you. We all have evil desires. It's our sin nature. We can't deny this and pretend it doesn't exist within each human being. This is part of the problem, a refusal to acknowledge that the mind and heart of mankind is inherently tarnished. We can't fix it unless we acknowledge it. Acceptance of responsibility is the beginning of corrective action. Evil desires are prone to take root when we subtly deny their power over us. Once the desire is conceived, the birth of sin is inevitable. You've reached the point of no return. It's just like biological conception. Once conception takes place, birth is inevitable. It's too late at that point to undo it. However, there is a window where evil desires can be cut off. It's in the temptation stage. This is where accountability begins and will allow you to make the right decision. Don't be deceived by the temptation. Acknowledge it as temptation to do wrong and hold yourself accountable for your actions. Are you playing with temptation and seeking to justify a wrong behavior? If you're not confronting this in the moment, think about the times when you've done this and recognize the breakdown in your accountability. Don't be deceived. Be accountable for what you're doing and back off. It'll be one of the best decisions you'll ever make. To think that you can manage it is a deception.

Passion

10 Although he had forbidden Solomon to follow other gods, Solomon did not keep the Lord's command. 11 So the Lord said to Solomon, "Since this is your attitude and you have not kept my covenant and my decrees, which I commanded you, I will most certainly tear the kingdom away from you and give it to one of your subordinates.

—I Kings 11:10-11 NIV

Meditation and Action

No one is too big to fall. We must be vigilant to keep passion alive. Solomon is an example of this. Solomon is credited with being the wisest man who ever lived. However, he was also human which means he was also fallible as we all are. This means we all struggle with the same things, being sin itself. Solomon allowed his once harmonious passion to become obsessive and misdirected from the negative influence of his wives. The question isn't that if Solomon could be sidetracked with a misdirected passion, what hope is there for me? Everyone faces the same challenges to their faith. It's the vigilance we apply to keep our passions going in the right direction. This doesn't take a genius or having to be the wisest person who ever lived to make this happen. Solomon put his pants on, or robes in this case, like everyone else. The keeping of our attitude is an individual thing and it must be kept in check because it's subject to being misled. These examples are given to us for our good so we can learn from them.

Learning from this and being proactive is putting wisdom into action which makes you wiser then Solomon. The question is will you heed this example? Be careful to keep the strategies in this book alive in your life. Doing so will keep you from falling into the trap Solomon found himself.

H-Cap Recap

Review the verses for Hope, Commitment, Accountability, and Passion. Part of prayer is reflection and meditation on the goodness of God and what He's done for us and the benefits we have as a result of His actions. Get into the habit of reflecting and reminding yourself of this and allow it to really sink in. We really do win; it really is possible to live an anxious free life. It begins and ends with hope.

Resilience is the ability to persevere. We're called to persevere but perseverance only comes when we arrive at the end of ourselves. Paul tells us to persevere in right living; monitor our behavior closely to make sure we're living the right way; be an example. Doing this saves ourselves and allows us to live an abundantly but also to impact those who are watching. Commit yourself to monitoring your behavior and choose to be a godly example.

Accountability begins with you. Don't be deceived in thinking that you can manage your temptations. You need to eradicate them from your life. Accountability begins with recognizing that the temptation comes from within you, not from God. The blame lies within you. Accepting this fact and not seeking to blame others is the first step.

When tempted, run in the other direction; don't give it a place in your mind.

Keeping vigilant in applying these strategies to your life will make you wise. Consider this week's verse on Passion. When not keeping guard of our heart and mind, it will make it easier to be influenced by negative and ungodly things. This will turn into a passion for the wrong things. Solomon's passion was to please his wives instead of God. You don't have to make the same mistake; this is why it was recorded.

Intentionally implement the following:

1. Make it a habit to just sit quietly and reflect on the goodness of God. Allow it to renew your commitment to hope.
2. Be vigilant in monitoring your behavior to make sure you're providing a good example. Like it or not, you're a role model and others are watching. Persevere in right living.
3. Temptation is nothing to fool with. We're all tempted. The problem is what you do with it. Do you dialogue with it? In doing this, you're actually feeding it.
4. Being wise is the ability to apply knowledge. Even though we're subject to temptation, we don't have to give into it. Don't allow your passion to be sidetracked. Remain vigilant. Seek to please God, not others or even yourself. If your response is to please God, you can never go wrong. Make pleasing Him your passion. This is wisdom in action.

Hope

Let us fix our eyes on Jesus, the author and perfecter of our faith, who for the joy set before him endured the cross, scorning its shame, and sat down at the right hand of the throne of God.

—Hebrews 12:2 NIV

Meditation and Action

We know that Jesus was God but He was also human. Being human, He was subject to all of the same thoughts and feelings we have, only without sin. Because he was without sin, doesn't mean that He didn't experience the type of tempting thoughts and emotions we have such as lust, envy, corruption, selfishness, etc. He did, being without sin means that He didn't surrender to them. The thoughts and feelings are normal; it's what you do with them that make the difference. For instance, we know that while Jesus was in the garden prior to his arrest and betrayal by Judas, he agonized in prayer asking God to take away having to die on the cross. It was a fearful anticipation that brought about normal human concerns and emotions. What allowed Him to overcome and not give in to these temptations of walking away and saving Himself was that He fixed His eyes on what was ahead. He had hope and knew that His father would not allow death to take Him. Because He was assured that death could not have power over Him, He endured the cross. It was His hope, His expectation that what His father told Him would in fact, come to pass. This expectation was carried out through committed behavior by fixing His eyes in the direction He wanted to go instead of the current circumstance. When faced with troubled times, what is your reaction? Do you look at the circumstance or do you look ahead? Fix your eyes your hope; allow this expectation to give you strength to endure. This is what resilience is.

Commitment

We do not want you to become lazy, but to imitate those who through faith and patience inherit what has been promised.
                                                    —Hebrews 6:12 NIV

Meditation and Action

The letters of Paul can really serve as a spiritual personal trainer. Laziness has no place in the commitment process or in living the Christian life. Training here consists of imitating faithful people, people who are stronger than we are. This also incorporates the trait of accountability. The commitment to align ourselves with other like-minded people for the purposes of learning what they know serves to mold us to their behaviors and style of life. This is why it's so important to hang around the right people. Influence can go both ways and have a positive or negative impact on your life. Choosing the right people to be a role model for us requires scrutiny and intentional action on our part. Being lazy will serve only to allow yourself to be influenced negatively. Take a moment and evaluate your own life. Having spiritual growth as your goal, who can you align yourself with and imitate and use as a role model? Don't just use the copout answer, "Jesus." This goes without saying but it's important to have an active flesh and blood relationship to foster accountability and commitment. If you're serious about creating resilience and strengthening your faith, you need to commit to the workout process of building faith and patience. Imitating these traits in others means you have to do them. It's the only way to inherit the promises of God.

Accountability

But Rehoboam rejected the advice of the older men and instead asked the opinion of the young men who had grown up with him and were now his advisers.
—I Kings 12:8 NLT

Meditation and Action

Rehoboam was the king of Judah, the southern kingdom of Israel after the nation split. Unlike his father before him, Rehoboam didn't seek direction from God in the decisions he made. Instead, he chose to surround himself with his friends who told him what he wanted to hear. He grew up the king's son and had a bad sense of entitlement. His heart and attitude was not to rule for the welfare of the nation but to serve himself. Things haven't changed much because we do this at times too. Judging rightly can be a difficult thing. Sometimes it goes against what we want to do. This is why it's so important to get wise counsel from those who know and have experience. Although we may be tempted to seek advice from our friends who may tend to tell us what we want to hear, at times we need someone to stand up and tell us things we may not want to hear. Doing right hurts sometimes; it doesn't always feel good. Right decisions and actions should not be based on feeling but the rightness of the behavior. This is the difference between mature adult thinking and childish selfish thinking. Who's in your inner circle? Do you surround yourself with people who tend to tell you what you want to hear? If so, begin to reach out to others wiser than you. Open your heart and mind to listening and heeding the advice of people more knowledgeable than you. Growth does not come without conflict and you need to be open and willing to take direction. Keep your ego out of it.

Passion

Then I pressed further, "What you are doing is not right!"
"Should you not walk in the fear of our God in order to
avoid being mocked by enemy nations?"
—Nehemiah 5:9 NLT

Meditation and Action

Misdirected passion can lead to disaster. Be vigilant to keep passion alive and don't allow it to become obsessive and look like the world. This was Nehemiah's message. As Christians we're called to be different in how we carry ourselves. This means differences in how we act (behavior) the words we use and how we use them, and loving people (compassion). It's easy to get caught up in the situation and lose your head but this can have bad consequences. When we act as the world does, we end up being mocked. Have you ever heard people say or perhaps you've said it yourself things to the effect of not wanting to be a Christian or not wanting to be in church because Christians are nothing but hypocrites. It's important to be consistent in our behavior and that our behavior is directed by a harmonious passion. Passion that is obsessive leads not only to legalism but also worldly lusts and desires. Passions that are harmonious are peaceful. Obsessive passions work from the outside in but harmonious passions work from the inside out. People are watching you whether you like it or not. It's important that you provide a right example.

What kind of example are you leaving? Do you give reason for others to criticize your behavior while you claim to be a Christian? If you're going to be mocked, let it be for doing good and be consistent. Be mindful of what passions direct your behavior and keep yourself from being mocked by the world.

H-CAP Recap

Review the verses for Hope, Commitment, Accountability, and Passion. Being committed to what you hope for and trusting that it will materialize has enormous staying power when faced with difficult times. However, you need to not only look toward it when times get tough but make the decision to trust it regardless of circumstance. Don't back down.

An attitude of laziness has no place in the mindset of those who seek excellence. This week's action point on Commitment tells us that the way to exercise our faith and patience is to imitate others who live it. To make this happen we need relationships with these people so we can receive instruction and encouragement much like you'd expect from a personal trainer. As you imitate the behavior, it transforms your lifestyle. What people can serve in this role for you? Don't be lazy, get busy!

Who you have in your inner circle and depend on for direction is crucial to your personal, professional, and spiritual welfare. Don't be a fool and surround yourself with people who tell you things you want to hear and don't challenge your way of thinking. This leads to destruction. Select trusted advisors wisely who are more knowledgeable and have more experience than you.

Harmonious passion works from the inside out as opposed to obsessive passions that work from the outside in. Not living a consistent life leaves you open to being mocked by the world. As a Christian, you're already labeled and being watched. What do others see in your behavior? Do you give reason for people to doubt the sincerity of your faith? Are your behaviors and what you claim to believe in alignment? Although Christians will always be mocked simply because we're counter to worldly culture, at least let it be because we love and serve others and not because we're self-serving.

Intentionally implement the following:

1. Hope is tested when times get tough. Look to the joy that is set before you and keep moving in that direction.
2. Resilience and laziness are direct opposites. To adopt the proper mindset you need to imitate those who are where you're trying to go. In order to do this, you need to know them, develop relationships with them. You need the details of how they approach life. Commit yourself to making this happen.
3. Accountability is about responsibility and relationships. Being responsible means that you'll have to do things that you don't like and take advice that may go against your self-serving ego. Are you big enough to handle this? What types of people are in your inner circle?

4. The world is always looking for ways to mock Christians. Sadly, much of the criticism is true because what people claim to believe and how they act are two different things. Do your passions serve to bring you acceptance from the world or from God? If from God, you need not fear the world's judgment because it's meaningless.

Hope

2Dear friends, we are already God's children, but he has not yet shown us what we will be like when Christ appears. But we do know that we will be like him, for we will see him as he really is. 3And all who have this eager expectation will keep themselves pure, just as he is pure.

—I John 3:2-3 NLT

Meditation and Action

In this verse, John describes how hoping (expectation) for something yet to come works to keep ourselves on track (pure). The things you hope for need to be real and meaningful to you. It has to be worth striving and waiting for. John uses the hope of our physical transformation in the example of spiritual and eternal benefits. He addresses this letter to believers. These people already know Christ. He's appealing to their desire to attain spiritual strength and allowing the hope of what we will be, what we will be transformed into, when Christ returns. For the believer, this is like the coronation, the receiving of our heavenly bodies. Although there is much theological speculation, the fact is that we have no idea what our new heavenly bodies will be. We do know that we will be like Christ. The eager expectation is the motivation (passion) to keep ourselves pure, in other words, living rightly. As you look at your life and the behaviors you engage in, what keeps you going in that direction? What are your expectations? The answer to these questions will reveal what your goals really are. Do they serve to keep yourself pure or do they lead you to fulfill obsessive passions? If your goals serve to feed your obsessive passions, you need to create new goals that feed into developing your spiritual nature. Keeping yourself pure is the objective.

Commitment

Reflect on what I am saying, for the Lord will give you insight into all this.

— 2 Timothy 2:7 NIV

Meditation and Action

Quiet reflection is a time of insight. Insight is when we get those *Ah Ha* moments which are important to our spiritual development. Spending time in quiet reflection is the best opportunity to make these happen. This is when God is talking to you and you not talking. Too often we think of prayer is our coming to God with an agenda while we do all the talking and petitioning. This is not real prayer. Prayer can be most effective just sitting in quiet reflection on God Himself. For most, this is the hardest thing for the brain to engage in because it's the nature of the brain to always seek some thought or emotion to attach itself to. These are called racing thoughts and they're normal. Training yourself to sit quietly is a task that takes effort. It is a training process that has been proven through brain imaging studies to have tremendous benefits to our overall well-being. Taking time out of your day for simple quite reflection is important for spiritual development. It's training for your mind. This is the best exercise you can do to strengthen the mind. How is your prayer life? Does your routine consist of the same tasks of reading and going through your check list, so to speak, of items? That's a one sided conversation. Commit to training your mind to sit and observe the things of God and let Him do the talking.

Accountability

If you ignore criticism, you will end in poverty and disgrace;
if you accept correction, you will be honored.
—Proverbs 13:18 NLT

Meditation and Action

The ability to accept criticism is a mark of a wise person. You've heard the expression, "the truth hurts." The problem is that when we hear things that are critical, our natural tendency is to defend. We either move against the person offering the criticism by giving it back to them or move away and withdraw from the relationship and or situation. None of these are good options. Growth cannot occur without conflict. It's possible that there may be truth in what others say, even if it's small. The reality is that if it hurts you, there must be some truth in it, otherwise, why would you care? Being accountable to others means that you heed instruction and allow others to check you without being defensive. Like the verse says, to ignore this will lead you into poverty. As you think about this passage and finding a way to cultivate the trait of accountability in your life, think about the times when you've been confronted with this and have reacted negatively out of your hurt and defensiveness. You can't make it right unless you're willing to examine this. If this has happened recently, accept that criticism but instead of being defensive, accept it and change it. Then, go to that person, thank them and tell them what you've done. This last part will often be the most difficult but it is what accountability is all about. This will build your integrity and others will see this and honor you for it.

Passion

> For I know your eagerness to help, and I have been boasting
> about it to the Macedonians, telling them that since last year
> you in Achaia were ready to give; and your enthusiasm has
> stirred most of them to action.
>
> —2 Corinthians 9:2 NIV

Meditation and Action

Enthusiasm is contagious but it has to be to the right thing. A harmonious passion can be inspiring to others which creates hopefulness. Inspiration comes from hope and passion. The inspiration you give to others will lead them to right action. Think about what has inspired you and how that inspiration produced action (committed behaviors). This is the positive influence we need to have on others. This is how the gospel is spread and this is also how our faith grows. However, inspiration needs to come from not only the right sources but it also needs to be continual. To get inspiration in spiritual resilience, it will be necessary for you to listen to and hang around other Christians so you can be in the position to be inspired. We can also receive inspiration by giving inspiration to and serving others. As we see in this verse, Paul is telling the church at Corinth that in telling the believers in Macedonia about their eagerness and willingness to give, it inspired the Macedonians. In relating this message, Paul was also an inspiration. It's a reciprocal process that feeds into each other to produce a common outcome which is motivation. Do you lack inspiration? Place yourself in an environment to be inspired and be an inspiration to others through your commitment to serve. If you commit to making this a priority, you can have only one outcome, passion and resilience!

H-CAP Recap

Review the verses for Hope, Commitment, Accountability, and Passion. What we hope for reveals where our passions are and whether they are obsessive or harmonious. Hope is attached to eager expectation. It's this expectation of what we hope for that keeps us motivated and going in the right direction provided the passion is harmonious. So, live out your hope. It will help keep you motivated and pure.

Training your mind is the key to self-control. Training your mind will require a commitment to engage in the training. The training entails you taking control of your thoughts and emotions. Take time daily to sit in quiet reflection on godly things, the nature of God, and your goals. Don't talk, sit and observe your thoughts. When intrusive thoughts enter your mind, acknowledge them without interacting with them and redirect your attention back to the task of reflection. Do this for 10 minutes a day, every day.

Part of accountability is accepting criticism and making changes. You may often receive criticism from those outside of your circle which may not be meaningful because they don't have your best interest in mind. Although you will still want to analyze this, the criticism I'm referring to is that coming from your accountability system. Listen and accept this type of criticism without being defensive. This is accountability. Use commitment and hope to make the changes.

Passion is about being motivated, inspired to right action. We can create this by placing ourselves in the position to hear inspirational stories from others and being encouraged but also by being a source of encouragement to others. It all works to the same end, inspiration. If you find yourself lacking in inspiration, seek it out and give it to others. These are the only ways it will come.

Intentionally implement the following:

1. Stay motivated in your hope by living it out. Expect good things to happen and they will; just be patient.
2. Train your mind. Give yourself at least 10 minutes a day to just sit in quiet reflection on your goals and God. Say nothing.
3. Learn to accept criticism without being defensive. More often than not, there are elements of truth in criticism. Your success is dependent on your willingness to hear it and apply it.
4. Keep yourself inspired. Put yourself in places where you can receive inspiration but also make it a habit of inspiring others. This is where harmonious passion is found.

Hope

"Do not put your trust in idols or make metal images of
gods for yourselves. I am the LORD your God."
—Leviticus 9:4 NLT

Meditation and Action

To hope in something implies a level of trust. When we hope and have
an expectation for something in the future, we base current behavior
on the expectation of what we hope for. This requires a trust that what
we hope for is real and that it will eventually reveal itself to us if we
keep our trust and commitment to it. The question is what are you
placing your trust in? In this verse, God is telling Moses and the nation
of Israel to not make idols or images of god to worship because He is
God, their God, and the only God. When things don't go according to
what we have planned, we always look for something else. It's easy to
get caught up in an emotional state and make hasty decisions. Look at
Israel as they wondered through the desert. They were willing to
acknowledge God when things were going good but when faced with
times when they needed to exercise their faith, they complained and
looked to worship other gods of their own making. The Bible is full of
these types of examples yet we still do this even today. Idols can take
many forms. What we worship is revealed through our committed
behaviors. For some it's money and material possessions, for others

it's attempts to obtain the acceptance of others, etc. What do your behaviors reveal about what you worship? As you consider today's devotion, take an inventory of this. Set your goals on things above. You won't find peace in chasing obsessive passions. To become others focused, become God focused. Spending time with Him as you work through and apply these strategies is the right place to start.

Commitment

Then Caleb silenced the people before Moses and said, "We should go up and take possession of the land, for we can certainly do it."

—Numbers 13:30 NIV

Meditation and Action

Caleb and Joshua were true warriors for God. Read through Numbers 13 to get a grasp of their attitude. They were committed to fulfilling God's promise in spite of what the opposition looked like. They were determined to take God at His word and were ready to go into the land and just take it. However, we know the other 10 tribesmen became fearful at what they saw and were disheartened. They were driven by their fear instead of their faith. As a result, they spread a negative word that they would be killed if they tried to take the land. You know how the story ends. We all face these moments in our lives. God has not given us a spirit of fear but of power. Going into battle and taking what God has promised doesn't mean you won't take some hits in the conquest. All battle will result in some scars, bumps, and bruises. However, knowing the outcome gives us the confidence to commit to the task and the willingness to take the lumps along the way. It begins with a commitment to faith and engaging in goal seeking and obtaining behavior. What is the land God has promised you and what is your attitude about going in and taking possession of it? Are you cowering at what you see and spreading a bad word or are you willing to believe God? "We should go up and take possession of the land, for we can certainly do it."

Accountability

20We want to avoid any criticism of the way we administer this liberal gift. 21For we are taking pains to do what is right, not only in the eyes of the Lord but also in the eyes of men.
—2 Corinthians 8:20-21 NIV

Meditation and Action

Think about what Paul is saying here. This chapter is discussing an offering he was taking for needy believers in Judea. In the affairs of collecting and distributing this gift, he wanted to be an example and be above reproach. He was very careful to avoid criticism. Being accountable demands that we take great care in the administration of our affairs, however, it's easy to become complacent. Sometimes doing things the right way takes a little longer. We can be so focused on the outcome that in our haste, we make mistakes. These mistakes can draw criticism from others. At times the criticism may be warranted and at times it may not. However, the message here is that it can and should be avoided. Think about the times when you've fallen into this trap. Learn from those mistakes. Paul was not only holding himself accountable but he was being accountable to others in this task of handling the gift he speaks of. Be mindful of what you're doing throughout your day and know that you're being watched. You're being watched by those around you but also by God. Take the time necessary to do it the right way.

Passion

And Pharaoh's heart grew hard, and he did not heed them, as the LORD had said.
—Exodus 7:13 KJV

Meditation and Action

Obsessive passion serves to bolster a false sense of esteem, power, and pride that hardens the heart from truth. Most people are familiar with the story of Moses. In reading about these events it can be difficult to imagine that in spite of such miraculous signs and wonders, Pharaoh refused to set Israel free. He was given so many chances yet chose to ignore reality. His stubbornness ended up costing many lives including the life of his own son. God allowed Pharaoh's heart to become hardened because that was where his (Pharaoh) passions were. The same thing can happen to us today. If you're so bent in doing the wrong thing, God will allow it. When this happens and we reap the consequences, most people's response is to blame God and become angry. However, it's not God's fault, it's ours. Remember, harmonious passions flow from the inside out; obsessive passions flow from the outside in. People become obsessed with passion when they need the behavior (outside) to make them think and feel something about themselves (inside). In Pharaoh's case it was power, authority, control. Passion is a powerful thing, that's why it so important to be led by a harmonious passion. Obsessive passions will always lead to disaster. Don't let your heart be hardened. It's not too late to change course.

H-CAP Recap

Review the verses for Hope, Commitment, Accountability, and Passion. There are many things that can serve as idols and distract us from our faith. It's human nature to seek answers and for something to trust in. It's in the difficult times that people seek for other things to answer the questions as to what's happening in their life. This leads to seeking idols. This is exactly what Israel did. Keep your trust and hope in God. Don't allow circumstances to sidetrack you. God is still there. He's doesn't create the circumstance but is there with you.

Recognize what God has called you to as you look at what lies ahead. Did you really expect it to be easy? Don't be misled because it requires work and effort. Be committed to going in and taking possession of your destiny. Of course there are giants and various road blocks. God says go; so go. You will win. Do you believe it enough (hope) to see it fulfilled through your commitment?

People are always watching you. The Bible says that we need to be above reproach. In other words take care in not giving people a reason to discredit you. Being accountable is being aware of how you conduct your affairs to avoid these things.

We're all driven by passion. The question is whether the passion is harmonious or obsessive. Harmonious passion flows from the inside out; meaning the outward behaviors are not needed to make us think or feel something about ourselves. The outward behaviors are a reflection of who we are inside. Obsessive passions work in the opposite direction. Obsessive passions will harden your heart as in Pharaoh's case.

Intentionally implement the following:

1. Keep your trust and hope in God. Don't allow yourself to be side tracked and seek other answers when times get tough. Those "other things" can turn into idols. Leave it in God's hands.
2. Don't fear taking possession of the land God has brought you to. Have the mindset of Joshua and Caleb. See beyond the giants. You can do it
3. Being accountable means that you need to monitor your actions and make sure that they are right. Be above reproach in what you do. Be accountable to yourself and others.
4. If you find your passions are obsessive and your behaviors serve to feed your ego instead of your relationship with God, stop. Harmonious passions are created by being others minded, not self-serving.

Hope

But the LORD said to Moses and Aaron, "Because you did not trust in me enough to honor me as holy in the sight of the Israelites, you will not bring this community into the land I give them."

—Numbers 20:12 NIV

Meditation and Action

Our behavior has real consequences and this is a good lesson to learn. God used Moses in great ways, however, because of his disobedience; Moses and Aaron were kept from seeing God's promise fulfilled. The entry into the Promised Land was the culmination of the whole journey. It's like being the first to the finish line only to fall just before crossing. The key word in this verse is "trust." Trust implies faith and hope. Without faith, it's impossible to please God. Faith and hopefulness is what moves the hand of God. Things that don't require hope and faith can be done under your own power and authority without God. We need to live in the realm of faith and hope and let this be visible to others. God tells Moses that not only did they not trust in God but they did not honor Him as holy in the sight of Israel. It's important that we live out our faith, not just for our sake but when others see God in us, it serves as an example and reveals God's power for others to see. Living for God is not something we do in secret. As you progress through your own journey to inherit what God has laid out for you, your own promised land, your individual goals, be careful to keep your faith and hope active by living it out. Don't become distracted by the world around you and mired in circumstances. Let others see the light in you. This is what's pleasing to God.

Commitment

> 38But my righteous one will live by faith. And if he shrinks back, I will not be pleased with him. 39But we are not of those who shrink back and are destroyed, but of those who believe and are saved.
>
> —Hebrews 10:38-39 NIV

Meditation and Action

Paul gives a lesson reminiscent of Numbers 13. God has given us everything necessary to live an abundant life. It's up to us to individually commit to going in and possessing the land. Yes, the land is full of giants. God commands us to go and possess and not retreat. If you retreat and give up, this disappoints God and causes undue hardship ending with us being mad at God and blaming Him for not making the way straight and doing it our way. Think of all the great wars our nation has been through. Victory doesn't come without sacrifice and hard fought battle. We need to be committed to the same state of mind just as Peter was challenged to step out of the boat into the storm ridden sea, just as Joshua and Caleb committed to go and possess the land. What is

God calling you to? What's keeping you from living an abundant life? If you carefully ponder these questions, you'll discover that the things that are keeping you from taking hold of your destiny is you and your fear. Be committed to having the right attitude and back it up with your behavior. Fear not and go! Don't shrink back in the face of fear. Stand, face it, and move through it. This is the place where miracles happen. Make the commitment to act.

Accountability

5But I don't consider myself inferior in any way to these "super apostles" who teach such things.6I may be unskilled as a speaker, but I'm not lacking in knowledge. We have made this clear to you in every possible way.
—2 Corinthians 11:5-6 NLT

Meditation and Action

There was an appearance that Paul was an "outsider" from the rest of the apostles. After all, the other apostles actually knew Jesus in the flesh. They walked, hung around, and ate with Him. However, this doesn't in anyway diminish Paul's calling and identity. He was given equal authority. Although others may have thought this, Paul knew who he was. He was accountable to himself and to God. He didn't need the approval of others to make him feel secure. It's when we experience feelings of inferiority that cause us to seek approval from others. Our actions at this point become self-centered because we need to fill the void to make us "feel" okay. This also leads to the development of an obsessive passion. People often use the ministry to fill an obsessive passion. Accountability lends itself to thinking and being confident in our own skin and position, not to the point of pride and disregard of others but to our position. This leads to harmonious passion. Do you struggle with inferiority? Stop entertaining the narrative that runs through your head about this. Change it and reaffirm your position in Christ. It doesn't matter what's in your past, you've already lived that. It's the present moment and the future that needs to be lived. You are priceless. Think about this and accept this for yourself. You can't give to someone something you don't have. Be accountable to the image God sees in you by living it out. Your first responsibility is being accountable to God. It's His image in you that you need to live up to, not of others.

Passion

May the words of my mouth and the meditation of my heart be pleasing in your sight, O LORD, my Rock and my Redeemer.

—Psalm 19:14 NIV

Meditation and Action

Acquiring harmonious passion requires diligence. Meditation here is used to signify the importance of pondering, considering, deep thinking, and reflection. Doing this strengthens your heart (mind, soul). The purpose of this devotional is to lead you through this process. When you meditate on something, you think deeply and hold your attention to something. In doing so, you're not forcing or creating thoughts but simply noticing what's there. Doing this regularly, allows what is focused on to become an integral part of your being. You can see how focusing on scripture can be transformative. This is what is pleasing to God. However, in order for it to be transformative, this is an activity that must be cultivated and used regularly. It's not something that is used on an occasional basis. Resilience is acquired through strength and use of that strength which continues to feed back into itself. There is also much scientific evidence on the use of meditation and its effects on increasing intelligence and emotional regulation skills. Do you think this is why we're told to do these things? Although they didn't have the benefits of science in that time, they took notice of the outcomes. Take time to rejuvenate yourself every day and cultivate harmonious passions. Practice this by setting aside a time of quiet reflection. Don't talk, you'll ruin the experience. God wants to talk to you more than wanting to hear from you. Just sit in silence and consider the ways of God and what He wants to say to you and nothing more.

H-CAP Recap

Review the verses for Hope, Commitment, Accountability, and Passion. Behaviors have consequences and our behaviors reveal where our hopes and trust are. Read and digest the example in this week's meditation and action on Hope. Keep your focus on the goal and follow through. Moses allowed himself to get caught up in the emotion of the circumstance instead of trusting in God. This prevented him from entering the land.

Fear is the one thing that keeps us from fulfilling God's plan for our lives. God doesn't work by eliminating the fear. That's not faith. Resilience and strength can only come when fear is faced and walked through. This makes us battle-hardened and impervious to fear. However, you have to create this through facing your challenges. Don't shrink back.

Paul didn't allow his past to interfere with his position as an apostle. Although many doubted his conversion due to fear and his authority as an apostle; he wasn't living up to their standards and what they thought of him. Paul lived up to the image God had of him; he lived to what God called him to do. His passions and subsequent behaviors came from the inside out (harmonious) not from the outside in (obsessive). Do you live up to the image of others or of God?

Harmonious passion is created in the presence of God. It's during these times that He talks to us and imparts His wisdom and reveals His plans for us. However, it's up to you to make the time to receive it. Take 10-15 minutes every day, at least, to just sit quietly in His presence and listen. Don't talk; just listen.

Intentionally implement the following:

1. Keep your focus on the goal, what you hope for. Don't allow yourself to get so caught up in the negative emotion of the circumstance that you violate your trust and hope as Moses had done. Hope through the difficult times.

2. Facing fear is what creates resilience, not avoiding it. God wants you to be fearless. However, you need to be willing to face the training. Enter it knowing and believing that you will win, you will survive. He promises that. Believe it and live it.

3. If you want to be accountable to God, live up to His image of you, not of the false one you may have developed as a result of negative life experiences. There are no worthless people in God's eyes. All of mankind is fearfully made in His image and have value. Live up to it.

4. Harmonious passion creates peace in the midst of chaos. This is what everyone is striving for. This is the big secret to life. Create a habit of sitting in God's presence without talking. God knows what

you have need of. He wants to do the talking. Allow Him to impart His vision for you into your heart and mind.

Hope

The desire of the righteous [is] only good: [but] the
expectation of the wicked [is] wrath.

—Proverbs 11:23 KJV

Meditation and Action

Our passions point to where our hope lies. The word "desire" in this verse points to that. What is desired is actually hoped for. Understand that the wrath this verse speaks of is not what is desired but the consequence of a negative desire, an obsessive passion. Passions can be either harmonious or obsessive. The expectation (obsessive passions) of the wicked bring only wrath. Harmonious passion breeds a hopefulness that leads to good. What are the goals you hope for? If these goals are obsessive, meaning that the pursuit of the goal is what makes you feel good, important, or worthwhile, this leads to burnout and selfish ambition. These kinds of goals will ultimately lead to self-destruction. This is how the world lives. When your goals are set and pursued because they line up with who you are, meaning that the goal and its pursuit are not needed to fill some unmet need you have, it can carry you through difficult times in a peaceful resilient state of mind. This is how God intends for us to live. This is experiencing life abundantly. Which category do you fall under? It will be one or the other; there is no middle ground. Consider your goals wisely. If you need to make a life course change, do so. The only thing that stops people from really pursuing their harmonious goals is fear. They lack the hope that it can be done because fear takes over. Remember, growth (resilience) never comes without conflict. Allow your hope, commitment, and accountability to get you there. It's not up to God to make it happen; He's already given you what you need. You need to put it into operation.

Commitment

51"Speak to the Israelites and say to them: 'When you cross the Jordan into Canaan, 52drive out all the inhabitants of the land before you. Destroy all their carved images and their cast idols, and demolish all their high places. 53Take possession of the land and settle in it, for I have given you the land to possess.
—Numbers 33:51-53 NIV

Meditation and Action

We somehow think just because God has called us to something that the way should be easy and without obstacles. We falsely view opposition as a mistaken direction as we're looking for the easy way, after all God has called us to it? This is a mistake in thinking. God told the Israelites to go into battle not only drive out and kill its inhabitants but destroy their possessions and places of worship. Why? Because if not they would eventually be a stumbling block and serve to take their focus from God. If you want God's best for your life, you have to be all in and be willing to go all the way. Anything less will cause problems in the future. Sadly, Israel didn't do this. They made exceptions and provision for these stumbling blocks and rationalized their behavior. God has called us to do the same with the world. What compromises are you making? What has God called you to do? What is your passion? Commit to go in and possess it but remember to drive out and destroy anything that gets in the way meaning things that will compete for your attention and distract you from serving God. What things in your life take away and compete for your attention to God? Recognize what these things are and readjust your priorities. This takes commitment, be either in or out! This is where the rubber meets the road and you need to ask yourself if you're willing to do what it takes to live the abundant life.

Accountability

But if the watchman sees the enemy coming and doesn't sound the alarm to warn the people, he is responsible for their captivity. They will die in their sins, but I will hold the watchman responsible for their deaths.

—Ezekiel 33:6 NLT

Meditation and Action

With accountability comes responsibility and with responsibility comes accountability. Good leaders hold themselves accountable for their actions. The responsibility falls on their shoulders. People who shirk responsibility blame and offer excuses when they fail or make a mistake. God holds us responsible. The enemy can come in many forms. We need to be vigilant and on guard always scanning our lives to not give a foothold to the enemy. We do this not only in our own lives but in the affairs we manage. Do you see the enemy approaching on the horizon in your life or perhaps in the lives or circumstances of the people or things you are entrusted to manage? What are you going to do about it? Will you passively sit and ignore it or will you take action and sound the alarm? Sometimes, the only thing we can do is to sound the alarm; warn them. Taking action may be up to someone else. The minimal action on your part is to at least sound the alarm unless it's within your power to also take action against the threat. Think about your past when you've been confronted with these situations.

Did you do the responsible thing or did you let the enemy enter unchallenged? Propose today to stand guard and be vigilant in your affairs; this is the foundation of accountability and responsibility.

Passion

Be of good courage, and he shall strengthen your heart, all ye that hope in the Lord.

—Psalm 31:21 KJV

Meditation and Action

The strength of our heart (mind, soul) is linked to our courage (passion). Notice the direction of this verse; it says to be of good courage. It's putting the responsibility for us to obtain it; it's not something that's given to us by another. This would place it out of our control and we would not be able to do as the verse says. We are to first be of good courage and then the heart is strengthened. So, the first task in building resilience is to build courage. You're actually doing this as you engage in these devotions. Your courage is built on your ability to remain hopeful. What do you see in your future? Courage also comes from your ability to engage in committed behaviors that keep your hope alive. Courage is also created through accountable relationships that feed into our hope and keep our committed behaviors on track. By doing these things, our passion (courage) begins to grow.

The strengthening of your heart that God refers to here is resilience. Notice also how the verse ends; all you who hope in the Lord. It begins with hope. You need to develop the habit of encouraging yourself. You do this by taking your eyes off of your current circumstances and looking ahead into the future and being hopeful for what you see. If you don't see hope there, you're not looking in the right direction. Look to where you want to go, what you're working for. This is where you'll find your hope. Remember, you have to create it.

H-CAP Recap

Review the verses for Hope, Commitment, Accountability, and Passion. Does your hope align with what is righteous and good or will it lead to wrath? It's the hope in our goals that gives us staying power to endure when times get tough. This is what hope does; it motivates us (passion) to continue moving forward. Keep your goals in sight, think of them often, and keep them harmonious and not obsessive.

God's looking for warriors to go in and possess. In order to live out His purpose and live abundantly, you need to become battle hardened. You can't make provision for things He's commanding you to destroy. Don't give the enemy a foothold. Tear down every stronghold that stands between you and God.

Stand guard over your heart and mind. You have a responsibility to not only guard yourself but also your family and friends. When you see the enemy approaching in the form of someone you love giving place to destruction, you have a responsibility to sound the alarm. You need to warn them of the pending destruction. If it's in your power to help, do so. Be accountable.

Courage builds hope and hope builds courage which leads to passion; the motivation for doing what we do. You can't get to where you're going if you're looking in the past. Keep your mind's eye focused on what you're aiming for, particularly in the midst of difficult circumstances. As you make it through, your courage will build which creates resilience. Keep your eyes on the hope.

Intentionally implement the following:

1. Stay motivated by keeping hope alive. Encourage yourself along the way. The more you can encourage yourself, the easier it will become. Hope gives us the motivation (passion) to endure.

2. Don't give place to worldly things that will end up competing with God's place in your heart. This takes vigilance. Violently destroy such strongholds, do not give them place in your life. God's looking to make an obedient warrior out of you. Be committed.

3. As you apply step #3, take responsibility to sound the alarm when you see the enemy approaching, not just in your own life but in those around you. We have a responsibility to the body to be accountable to each other. Speak up and stand up against ungodliness.

4. Notice that to apply these strategies it takes courage and passion. Remain encouraged in your journey. This keeps hope alive. Encourage yourself.

Hope

"But LORD!" Moses objected. "My own people won't listen to me anymore. How can I expect Pharaoh to listen? I'm such a clumsy speaker!"

—Exodus 6:12 NIV

Meditation and Action

When faced with a difficult task, it can be hard to find hope. Without hope, we fall into excuse making just as Moses did here. Without hope/faith, it's impossible to please God. It's impossible to do anything in life without hope. Being hopeful is the first step to achieving your goal. However, without God we cannot but without us God will not. It was God's plan for Israel to be set free. However, without Moses acting and doing his part, God would not. God moves and causes things to happen in our lives when we act and step out in faith. Building resilience will require you to meet the challenge. Resilience comes only after working through and surviving the conflict. The problem is that we always think the conflict will do us in somehow or because we just don't want to experience the discomfort. This leads to excuses. God's looking for warriors to engage in battle. He's not seeking water boys. What has God called you to do, what are your passions that you'd like to pursue in life but haven't because of fear and excuse making? It doesn't matter how big the dream is. It will never be realized unless you believe it can be done. God is calling you. Will you make excuses or will you rise to the occasion?

Commitment

By faith he left Egypt, not fearing the king's anger; he persevered because he saw him who is invisible.
—Hebrews 11:27 NIV

Meditation and Action

Moses, a Hebrew, had been adopted by the Pharaoh's family. He was so loved that he was considered a son of Pharaoh. He could have had anything his heart desired. However, what his heart desired was truth. He willingly gave up his position and chose to align himself with God and His people, his real family. What a step of faith this must have been. It took great commitment and courage to leave the life he knew and believe in an unseen God. However, Moses persevered. He saw the invisible God through His signs and wonders. Moses was so convinced that the Hebrew God was the God of the universe that he committed his life to His service. This commitment and hope allowed him to stand up to the evils of his adopted father without fear. Moses' obedience gave him resilience to withstand persecution which served only to make his faith stronger. Is God calling you to something? Don't give in to fear. You'll only achieve what God has for you as you commit to following through. It will be unfamiliar territory. Have hope. Commit to following Him even if that means leaving the only thing you know. Commitment to faith will never let you down. As you step out and persist, you'll be creating perseverance.

Accountability

Yet we hear that some of you are living idle lives, refusing to work and meddling in other people's business.
—2 Thessalonians 3:11 NLT

Meditation and Action

Living an unaccountable life leads to meddling in the affairs of others. We can't effectively live our own lives while enmeshing in the lives of others. It's not that we shouldn't have concern for the welfare of others; however, this goes beyond that. People try to control the lives of others because they are idle. They don't have enough to do and or refuse to confront the matters in their own life so they direct their attention and energy to living through others. People who do this claim to have all the answers but can't seem to apply them to their own lives. It's a smoke and mirror trick but the trick is on them. Do you find that you get too involved in the affairs of other people? If so, get involved in living your own life. You'll find that it's a fulltime job just managing your own affairs. The problem is that you may not want to confront those issues which are why you turn to managing and direct the affairs of others. If you want to grow in the area of accountability, take control of your life today and stop meddling in other people's business. This will take an intentional decision. Hold yourself accountable in this area and allow others to hold you accountable. When checked on this, listen without being defensive, and make corrections. Accountability is to serve to keep us on track. It's a good thing.

Passion

25Do not lust in your heart after her beauty or let her captivate you with her eyes, 26 for the prostitute reduces you to a loaf of bread, and the adulteress preys upon your very life.
—Proverbs 6:25-26 NIV

Meditation and Action

The book of proverbs is about acquiring wisdom. Chapter 6 deals with warnings against adultery. This can refer to not only infidelity between spouses but also infidelity with God. The part that's under examination for today is the terms "do not" and "let." These warnings are repeatedly given throughout the Bible because they need to be. It's our nature to satisfy the "flesh." Unless we're vigilant, we will be subject to the outcomes of this verse. The impulse to satisfy the desires of the flesh is the definition of obsessive passion. This is the part of us that needs redeemed and transformed. This is the part that requires no training; we are automatically driven by these negative impulses. The change process is what requires attention, action, and vigilance. Note how the verse begins with "Do not let." This means it's our responsibility. We decide what to influence us or not. It's not up to God. People often blame God for their obsessive passion which serves only to derail them by shifting responsibility from the one who is ultimately responsible, you. Blaming is an age old reaction, recall the Garden of Eden. Developing a harmonious passion will require you to take responsibility. Look to where you want to go and resist temptations of the flesh. Rely on your accountability system and be encouraged. This will create the courage (passion) you need to be hopeful and strengthen your spirit.

H-CAP Recap

Review the verses for Hope, Commitment, Accountability, and Passion. You'll never achieve anything in life by making excuses. There will always be a reason not to do something that you find challenging. Resist the temptation to find excuses as Moses did. God will give you what you need. You have to believe it can be done in order for it to get done. God has chosen you; believe it and do it.

Some commitments are harder than others. Review Moses' experience. Sometimes making a commitment and doing the right thing requires us to step out of our comfort zone. Remember that growth never comes without some level of conflict. Commit to the vision God has given you and pursue it with whatever it takes. Commitment makes hope realized.

Accountability serves to keep us on track. It may be difficult to hear at times but it is vital to our well-being. Don't waste time living your life through others, controlling, others. Live your own life. If you stay busy enough living out what God has for you, you won't have time to "meddle" in the affairs of others.

Don't be misled by obsessive passions. If you're in the habit of blaming and not taking responsibility, this is a sign of a lack of accountability but also that your passions may be obsessive. Obsession lends itself to blame, denial, and justification; sure signs of passion run amuck. Creating harmonious passion gives you strength to resist temptations of the flesh.

Intentionally implement the following:

1. Believe what God has called you to do. Of course it will be challenging. If it wasn't, you wouldn't need God. He'll give you what you need to accomplish the task, just believe.

2. Your growth will not come without being stretched, challenged. Don't be surprised at this. Commit to right action regardless of the obstacle. Be willing to step out of your comfort zone. This is how winning is done.

3. Living an abundant life doesn't leave time to meddle in the affairs of others. Of course this is not speaking to helping and serving others. As this week's verse indicates, it's the wasting time involving yourself in the lives of others and trying to direct their life when you can't even live your own. Walk and live the path God has directed you to and hold yourself accountable to it.

4. Resist the temptations of the flesh. Don't allow yourself to be led by obsessive passions. If you remain busy serving others and being accountable, you won't have time to indulge in obsessions.

Hope

For I fully expect and hope that I will never be ashamed, but that I will continue to be bold for Christ, as I have been in the past. And I trust that my life will bring honor to Christ, whether I live or die.

—Philippians 1:20 NLT

Meditation and Action

Paul provides a great example of hope and faith being lived out. He's the ultimate survivor and a model of how life is to be lived. Things didn't always go as planned for Paul. He suffered many hardships just like we do. However, it was his response to these hardships that made him resilient. Paul is an example of the fact that just being a Christian doesn't mean that our lives will be easy. His resilience is attributed to his state of mind. He was determined no matter what he faced that Christ would bring him through alive. Even if it brought death, his thoughts were of being with Christ. This hope allowed him to be content with whatever or wherever he found himself. This verse gives us a picture of this state of mind. He says, "I fully expect"; "I trust that my life." These words exemplify his hopefulness that God would be there for him and accomplish His purpose through him. Because Paul believed it to such depth, it influenced his behavior (commitment). If you're struggling to believe, to hope, it's what you're telling yourself that's hindering you. You need to use effective language that directs you to hope, not excuse making. That type of language leads to doubt, complacency, and ineffective behavior. What do you tell yourself, "I expect....., I trust......" or are you prone to excuses? Change your dialogue.

Commitment

> Do not let this Book of the Law depart from your mouth; meditate on it day and night, so that you may be careful to do everything written in it. Then you will be prosperous and successful.
>
> —Joshua 1:8 NIV

Meditation and Action

The key to success is to have the right mind set. Sometimes, where you want to go and where you end up are two different places. What your mind is focused on is where you'll end up. You may be trying to go one way, but if your mind's eye is focused on something else, that's where you'll ultimately end up. Just as Joshua and Caleb did back in Numbers 13 about possessing the land, they took God at His word in spite of what they saw with their natural eye. They chose to see the possibilities with their mind's eye. How did they cultivate this steady and immovable state of mind? By meditating on the word of God and being careful to doing what it says. In other words, they were committed to meditation and action. You face the same decision. Are you willing to make the commitment and dedicate yourself to being careful to serve God and keep His word in your heart? By reading this devotional and meditating on its principles and committing to following through on its actions, you're committing to becoming prosperous and successful in your spiritual life. Commit to making it a part of your daily life. It'll make you strong.

Accountability

If you listen to constructive criticism, you will be at home among the wise.
                                        —Proverbs 15:31 NLT

Meditation and Action

One thing all successful people have in common is the willingness and ability to listen and heed constructive criticism. This is the mark of a wise person. Sure, it's difficult to listen to negative things about our plans, ideas, actions, etc. We often perceive this as an attack which causes us to react defensively even in the face of truth. This is because we don't want to accept fault. This attitude leads to failure. Success isn't about being right all the time; it's about producing, creating, and living. Accept the fact that you don't have all the answers. Such thinking will lead to obsessive passions. Don't fear being wrong. Accepting responsibility for wrong decisions and taking corrective action is the mark of a true leader and demonstrates accountability. Think about the times in your life when you reacted poorly to constructive criticism. It's not too late to heed that advice and take corrective action. Go to that person and credit them for helping you to see the error in your thinking or behavior. This last step is most important and is what builds accountability. The choice is yours. Will you be wise or a fool?

Passion

> All of us used to live that way, following the passionate desires and inclinations of our sinful nature. By our very nature we were subject to God's anger, just like everyone else.
> —Ephesians 2:3 NLT

Meditation and Action

You can tell where a person's passions lay based on their commitment (behaviors). Paul describes two different lifestyles here. The first of these is serving the desires of the flesh which is part of our sinful nature. This type of living is subject to God's anger. The second lifestyle is indicated at the beginning of the verse, "All of us USED to live that way." Paul is talking to believers so the expectation is that they no longer serve the desires of the flesh but seek to please God. This is a result of salvation and mind renewal. The connotation Paul leaves is the change from the former life that is left behind and the new one that has taken its place. Those who follow the sinful nature are a slave to that nature and this is where their passion (obsessive) is. This is the priority even though you're not recognizing it as such. Because this is what comes natural, it will take diligent effort to redirect these obsessive passions into harmonious passions. To do this, your priorities need to reflect this effort which only comes with committed action and accountability. This is the transformation that Paul speaks of. To build and keep harmonious passion alive, keep your priorities God centered. Intentionally engage in efforts of serving others, doing at least one kind thing for someone each day. It will make your day to make another's day and will keep your mind centered on godly things. The more you busy yourself in service to others, the less time you have serving the flesh.

H-CAP Recap

Review the verses for Hope, Commitment, Accountability, and Passion. Hope is living in expectation regardless of what the circumstance may be. As you review this week's verse on Hope, pay attention to Paul's language that reveals his state of mind. Outward circumstances just didn't matter. He lived for what he hoped for regardless of what took place in the past or present. This was a decision he chose to live by.

The commitment mentioned in this week's meditation is clear, keep God's word in your heart, and meditate on it night and day. Your mind will always be thinking about something and process information from a particular lens. If not of godly things, then it will be something else. This is the level it takes to keep your mind focused. God should always be on your heart and mind. Keeping these strategies in mind as you go throughout your day is the way to fulfill this task.

Accountability means that you need to leave yourself open to the instruction of others and not be so closed minded that you think that your way is the only way. People who don't take direction well fear failure and are prideful. This will ultimately lead to a downfall. The mark of a wise person humbly takes direction and is accountable to others.

All behavior is purposeful and driven by passion. The question is what type of passion is driving your behavior. Paul describes two kinds of living, the former lifestyle before Christ and the lifestyle after. Before Christ, our passions are self-serving and obsessive which leads to God's judgment. The second is transformative. By allowing Christ to become our passion, our behavior needs to reflect service to others. As we give, we get.

Intentionally implement the following:

1. Don't allow circumstances to determine your hope. Hope should remain in spite of circumstance. Notice that Paul makes this decision to look in this direction regardless of what his circumstances were. Decide to be bold for Christ whether you live or die.

2. Your mind will always be occupied by something. You can let the world fill your mind and influence you or you can intentionally choose to fill your mind and heart with the biblical principles outlined here. Keep God's word in your heart and mind 24/7.

3. Great leaders are accountable to others; they listen and take direction. This is the application of wisdom. Don't fear being wrong. You're only wrong when you don't listen and implement the wrong decision. Listening to others before you decide is the time to avoid making wrong decisions.

4. Because all behavior is purposeful, what type of passion do yours point to, obsessive and self-serving or harmonious, serving others?

Hope

Love never gives up, never loses faith, is always hopeful,
and endures through every circumstance.

—I Corinthians 13:7 NLT

Meditation and Action

Hope and passion coexist in a way that without the other, neither can survive. Hope gives purpose to our passion and passion gives the reward for our hope. True passion (love) and hope never give up. Paul uses these terms because within this context means that it will be challenged. The world stands ready to throw up various road blocks to your goals, particularly your spiritual goals. The most important thing to remember during these moments is that hope and love never give up. It's during these times that hope and passion grow. You just need to sit and wait during the process. It works through "every circumstance" not some. However, it's up to you to keep it going. When you find that your hope and passion is under fire, you need to keep your vision focused in the future, keep looking at the goal. Refuse to dwell on thoughts of the current circumstances bringing an end to what you've been hoping for. This leads only to discouragement. Keeping hope and passion alive is your task and is part of the growth process. It needs to be nurtured. This is what will create resilience. Resilience will never come if you give up. It's not supposed to be easy and we're never promised that it will be easy. If you're struggling right now, stop and reflect. Like quicksand, the more you struggle and waste energy, the faster you sink. Keep your eye on the prize; take some deep breaths, lean on your accountability system, and watch God move.

Commitment

Diligent hands will rule, but laziness ends in slave labor.
—Proverbs 12:24 NIV

Meditation and Action

Keeping busy, particularly with the right things brings prosperity. Laziness ends in bondage and breeds only more laziness which leads to hopelessness and helplessness. Look around the people you know and associate with. Do you know anyone who sits around and complains all the time about everything but never does anything about their circumstances? They always talk about how hard and unfair life is. Many times this can also be accompanied with being a busybody in other people's business. A spirit of laziness brings bondage to being lazy. It sucks the life out of you and if you've noticed, when you're around people like this, they tend to suck the life out of you too. Maybe this is you and you're seeking a change. If so, change is right in front of you waiting. Begin by committing to the right type of behaviors to occupy your life. Such behaviors include serving others. Meditate on God's word, let it sink into your mind and allow it to change your direction. Receive God's plan for your life; allow Him to place a passion for a new direction in your life. Commit to doing the action steps outlined in this devotional and add to it each day. It will be challenging but don't quit. When the going gets tough, you're on the brink of creating perseverance and resilience. Be diligent; keep moving forward, that's how winning is done!

Accountability

Whoever stubbornly refuses to accept criticism will suddenly be destroyed beyond recovery.
—Proverbs 29:1 NLT

Meditation and Action

By now you should be noticing some recurring themes. This is done intentionally to reinforce the principles. The Bible also presents them in this fashion because exposure and repetition is how learning takes place. The ability to accept constructive criticism is the mark of someone who is accountable and responsible. While it's true that criticism can hurt, growth never comes without conflict. If you look back at the criticism you've received in your life, you'll find that there are elements that may be more true than not. Here's the test, if it hurts, there's probably an element of truth in it. This is why it hurts. We don't want to face that truth which is the natural reaction. We see this from the beginning of time in the Garden of Eden. However, we need to learn to resist this natural reaction to defend ourselves. The only way to grow is to accept responsibility. To do otherwise leads to destruction which ends up being more painful than the criticism itself? The accountable person learns to train themselves to look beyond the criticism and see that the end will be worse than acceptance and taking action. How do you normally react to criticism? Is your first reaction to defend or do you recognize that acceptance of the criticism is less painful than ignoring it? Train yourself to respond and not react to criticism. If it hurts, look for the truth in it and take appropriate action to remediate it. This is accountability and is a mark of a true leader and servant.

Passion

For where your treasure is, there will your heart be also.
—Matthew 6:21 KJV

Meditation and Action

Seriously think about this verse and its implications for you. By examining your behaviors, what do they say about your priorities, your passions? Avoid looking at this through what your intentions are but stick to what your behaviors are. For instance, if a stranger looked at your checkbook, what would that reflect about your priorities? If a stranger looked at the way you conducted yourself, the words you use, your actions toward others, would it be obvious that you're a believer? Regardless of intention, we act out of what's in our heart. If you don't like what you see, change it. The type of treasure that fuels our behavior can be obsessive or harmonious. Which one dominates your heart? Remember, as a believer, God has already given you everything you need to be successful in your spiritual journey. He's already given you the keys of resilience, Hope, Commitment, Accountability, and Passion. However, you have to put them into motion. This is not God's deal, it's yours. You can transform your mind and heart (passion) by engaging in right behaviors. By making them a habit, you'll be making them your treasure and the benefits will be great. Look to the future with hope. Commit to right behaviors. Create and rely on accountable relationships.

Store up treasure in heaven for yourself through serving and encouraging others. This will create harmonious passion in your life.

H-CAP Recap

Review the verses for Hope, Commitment, Accountability, and Passion. Love (passion) and hope work together. Love never fails because it's hopeful and hope will never end when it's rooted in love. However, these need to be nurtured. Love and hope will be challenged much like the challenges that all relationships face. However, true love endures. True love is harmonious, not obsessive. Nurture love and hope.

You're either moving forward or backwards. There's no such thing as remaining static because while you're standing still, the world is passing you by which leaves you falling behind. Remaining busy in the right things is the key to growth. What's your attitude about working in such tasks? Don't fear the commitment to working out your faith. Be diligent in the application of your new found skills.

Don't shirk criticism. While no one enjoys being criticized, there are important lessons that need to be learned. While it can be true that some criticize for the purpose of being hurtful and offer no instructive purposes, the type of criticism the Bible speaks of is "constructive" criticism coming from those in our accountability system. While this type can be just as hurtful, you need to reexamine the lens from which you're receiving it. This is what feeds the hurt you experience. Learn to see what truth may be in the criticism and make the appropriate changes if necessary.

What do your behaviors, how you live your life, reveal about what you treasure? Are your passions self-serving (obsessive) or others-serving (harmonious)? Obsessive and self-serving passion will lead to many forms of poverty to include monetary, emotional burnout, and spiritual depravity. Make sure your treasure, what motivates you, are harmonious passions. Avoid being motivated by obsessions.

Intentionally implement the following:

1. True love endures all. True love is rooted in hope. Keep nurturing your hope and it will grow into a harmonious passion when the behaviors serve to edify God and not yourself.
2. Keep busy through the application of these strategies. Stopping, taking breaks will cause you to fall behind. There's no such thing as taking a break from life. If the behaviors are right (harmonious) it will energize you. Stay busy.
3. When on the receiving end of criticism from others, hold yourself accountable to listen. Seek the truth in what they say and take action to fix it. Avoiding and reacting negatively is a prideful defense mechanism which will keep you from moving forward.

4. Make regular deposits into your heavenly savings account. Become an investor in mankind. Such deposits include giving and serving others.

Hope

14For we have become partakers of Christ if we hold the beginning of our confidence steadfast to the end, 15while it is said: "Today, if you will hear His voice, do not harden your hearts as in the rebellion."

—Hebrews 3:14-15 NKJV

Meditation and Action

Keeping hope alive can be harder at times than others. Remember, hope is not something that we get a single dose of and it's just there. It must be cultivated to grow stronger. Paul says that we're only partakers of Christ if we hold onto hope to the end. Hope gives us a confidence that what we hope for will eventually materialize but we need to hold onto it with a tight grip and not allow it to be ripped from us by circumstances. During difficult times, it can be hard to engage in committed behaviors and hear words of promise because we allow the gravity of the circumstance to overcome us. This is what Paul refers to when he tells us not to harden our hearts. This is our choice. We can't blame God for anything. We're responsible for our own actions and how we respond to life. Everyone is susceptible to life. What's your typical response when things get tough? Do you blame God, become angry, and withdraw or do you run to your accountability system and correct your mental vision. Remember, hope requires you to see the world through your mind's eye, your spiritual lens, not necessarily your natural eye. Difficult times cause us to shift focus from what we see in our spirit to the circumstance. Retreat is the last thing you want to do. Allow yourself to be encouraged by others during these times and get into the habit of encouraging yourself.

Commitment

> King Jotham became powerful because he was careful to live in obedience to the LORD his God.
>
> —2 Chronicles 27:6 NLT

Meditation and Action

Jotham was the son of Uzziah who was also a king. Many people like Uzziah start out right but become corrupt and disgraced in the end. As a result, they're not remembered for the good they did but how they crashed and burned. Uzziah was a godly king; however, in his rise to power and fame, he became prideful which led to his downfall. Give the short chapters of 26 and 27 a read through. Jotham served God during his short reign but he was also committed to avoiding the sins of his father. This was the reason for his success. Jotham became a powerful king because he was committed to being obedient to God. Although the people he ruled were corrupt and Jotham's reign was rather short, it's not about how long he lived but what he did while he was alive and the legacy he left. What will your legacy be? Will you go down like Uzziah who became a leper or Jotham? Your decision is made by what you commit to. Remember, commitment is an obligation to act regardless of what you feel. It's a choice. Commit to following God which includes what you occupy your mind with and how you behave. Let your legacy speak well of you.

Accountability

No one serving as a soldier gets involved in civilian affairs--
he wants to please his commanding officer.
                                        —2 Timothy 2:4 NIV

Meditation and Action

Accountability is about minding and doing your own business and not involving yourself in the affairs of others. It's about doing what YOU need to do. You are accountable for your behavior. As Paul mentions in this verse, a good soldier seeks to please his commanding officer. He or she wants their commanding officer to know that they can be trusted to get the job done with as little supervision as possible. It's easy to get sidetracked in life with so many things that can compete for our attention. However, the accountable person is mindful of what they need to do and doesn't involve themselves in things that will get them off track. Do you find that you're easily distracted by what's going on around you? Do you find yourself getting too involved in the affairs of other people around you? Do you find yourself getting involved in worldly things that compete for your attention to spiritual things? Maybe you've even been told this before. Stop involving yourself in directing the lives of others and focus on what's expected of you. Your action step for the day is to take an inventory of your affairs and make sure you are on task and to distance yourself from meddling in the affairs of others. Make it a habit to monitor your behavior and seek to please your commanding officer, Jesus, and you will be well on your way to mastering this trait.

Passion

> Now may the God who gives perseverance and encouragement grant you to be of the same mind with one another according to Christ Jesus.
> —Romans 15:5 NASB

Meditation and Action

God is the source of perseverance and encouragement. These terms define who He is. However, like all things of God, they can be used for good or evil. They can be used to enhance life and to live it abundantly or they can be used to cause destruction. This is the difference between harmonious and obsessive passion. As the preceding verse indicates, the Scriptures were given for our benefit so that we may learn from them, learn from the examples of others. We call this vicarious learning. These examples serve to give us hope which can lead to harmonious passion when heeded. This is achieved by being "like minded" with others. The key is being like-minded with the right individuals. Serving an obsessive passion leads to hanging around those who feed into this negative passion. If spiritual growth and resilience is the objective, you need to actively and intentionally surround yourself with like-minded people. This will create a passion in the right direction. Again, you can see how all the traits within the H-CAP model are used to create itself. The direction you apply them will determine the outcome. If you have obsessive passions, eliminate those relationships that serve to keep them alive and create and maintain relationships that are God serving. As you do this, harmonious passions will develop. This is where peace of mind is found.

H-CAP Recap

Review the verses for Hope, Commitment, Accountability, and Passion. Holding on to hope is hard in the midst of difficult times. However this is the test and the only thing that can bring us through. Why then is it the first thing we discard when things get tough? Hold on to your hope, lean on your support system, and get encouraged.

Commitment is a decision to engage in certain behaviors. Behaviors can lead to obsessive and self-serving passions which lead to destruction or harmonious which lead to strength and peace of mind. What will be your legacy? Commit to the right behaviors.

A good soldier's mindset is on pleasing their commanding officer by demonstrating that they can be trusted by remaining diligent and on task. There are many things in the world that can compete for our attention. If not mindful, one can be easily led away. Don't allow yourself to be distracted by worldly things. Remain focused by continuing to apply these strategies. Hold yourself accountable.

God is the source of perseverance and encouragement because they are the essence of His being. He also imparts them to us. When aligned with other like-minded people, the church becomes a powerful force that can change the world. However, in order for the body to be strong, the individuals that make up the body must be strong and like-minded.

Intentionally implement the following:

1. Hold onto hope. Hope is tried, refined, and strengthened in difficult times. Hold on to it. Find encouragement.

2. You have a choice to commit to the right or wrong behaviors. God will not force you to make right decisions. Do you want to be remembered as a fool who wasted their life or someone who invested in the lives of others? Commit to serving, encouraging, and teaching others.

3. As Christians, we are soldiers involved in a spiritual war. The enemy is crafty and the untrained mind can find it easy to become distracted by the trappings of the world. Don't be misled. Seek to serve and please God. Diligently apply these strategies every day to guard your heart and mind.

4. God is the source of encouragement and perseverance which create harmonious passion. However, as this week's verse implies, it requires us to be aligned with other like-minded people. Create and sustain relationships that feed this.

Hope

This truth gives them confidence that they have eternal life, which God--who does not lie--promised them before the world began.

—Titus 1:2 NLT

Meditation and Action

The general theme of the book of Titus is that the gift of God, salvation, should not only transform our character but also how we relate to others. Titus provides a manual for how we should conduct ourselves. Paul says that it is this truth, the belief in this truth, which gives us confidence that we have eternal life. If this state of mind truly dominates our thinking, it will be revealed in our committed behaviors, it will reflect in our accountability system, and our passions. We will always live out whatever state of mind we're in. With this understanding, you need to take responsibility for creating the proper state of mind that creates hope and confidence in God. This is where transformation begins. These things are created through hope. Look to the promises that God has given through His word but also the promises God has spoken to you for your personal life. What are your passions? How has He called you to fulfill your passions? Allow these passions and the hope of their fulfillment keep you motivated and moving forward. Take time every day and reflect on these promises and allow them to fuel your passion for them. This is true transformation in action. This is where miracles happen!

Commitment

If you are willing and obedient, you will eat the best from the land;

—Isaiah 1:19 NIV

Meditation and Action

Isaiah was a prophet in Judah during a time of great tension between Egypt, Syria, Israel, Babylon, and Assyria. However, the problem was that Judah was more interested in playing politics to keep the other nations at bay instead of trusting in God. The nation also had the appearance of being religious but was far from being spiritual. It was a time of political and spiritual decay. Very similar to what we are facing in America and around the world today. We turn away from our roots which are founded on biblical principles and seek to solve our problems with the corruption of politics. This can take place at a national level but also an individual level in your own relationships. God is always willing to forgive and return His blessing; however, it is up to us to cleanse ourselves. We must first repent and commit to right action. Only then will we eat the best from the land. What do you trust in? Has your life turned into an outward appearance of being religious without a real spiritual relationship with God? If so, you're only fooling yourself. While it may be a hard thing to accept, you need to put your trust in God and not politics. Commit to being obedient to God and make change in your own life in spite of what's going on around you. You are responsible for your own behavior and salvation.

Accountability

Do not seek revenge or bear a grudge against one of your people, but love your neighbor as yourself. I am the LORD.
—Leviticus 19:18 NIV

Meditation and Action

Accountability involves being accountable to self, others, and most of all, God. Holding grudges and an attitude of getting even keeps us from being accountable and keeps us out of the will of God for our lives. The law described in this verse is plain and simple. We need to learn to love our neighbor as our self. Why do we need to have a love for self, isn't this pride? It can be if the love is turned toward self-satisfaction without God. Loving self and having a healthy view of self is important because we can't give to others something we don't have; in this case love and accountability. How we love and hold ourselves accountable to the ones we love is a direct reflection of what we think of ourselves. The difference is that people who don't have a healthy view and love of themselves have two types of relationships. The first is characterized as moving away from others and isolating yourself. The other is characterized as being a doormat. This type of person gives the appearance of being loving but the reasons for these behaviors is that they do for others because it makes them feel wanted and needed. In other words, accountability and love for others doesn't flow naturally because of who they are but because they need it to feel that they measure up. Where are you on the continuum? Do you love and do for others because of what it does for you or because that's who you are? If the former, begin today by being honest with yourself. Recognize who you are in Christ and the price that was paid for you. You are priceless!

Passion

Don't use foul or abusive language. Let everything you say be good and helpful, so that your words will be an encouragement to those who hear them.

—Ephesians 4:29 NLT

Meditation and Action

It's a running theme that your behavior points to where your passions are. The ways to influence harmonious passions are to commit to the behaviors stated in this verse. Notice its focus is on outward observable behavior. Also notice that the verse begins with what not to do and ends with what to do. The words we use have a significant impact on the lives of others. Words can be used to tear people down or build them up. Look at your own life. I'll bet that you can recall some hurtful things that were said to you long ago. Even though it may have happened many years ago, the pain can still feel new. The same goes with positive and uplifting words. Calling yourself a Christian and using foul and abusive language serves as a poor example and is one of the reasons why people are turned off by the church. By focusing our words and behaviors on what is good and helpful serves to encourage others. Research indicates a ratio of about 3:1 for positive and negative communications. Meaning, for every negative contact that tears people down, it takes 3 positive interactions to counter that one negative one. As you commit to right behaviors, include giving encouragement and stay away from foul and abusive language. As you commit to these, your harmonious passions will flourish.

H-CAP Recap

R eview the verses for Hope, Commitment, Accountability, and Passion. You can trust God's promises for salvation and your personal life. You just have to believe in them. Believing requires you to look in the direction of your hope and live as if. Remember, just because He's called you to something, doesn't mean it will be easy. Allow your hope to motivate you.

It's God's will that everyone live an abundant life. However, it's up to you to live it. Many people want the abundant life but are not willing to commit to the right behaviors to make it happen. Be obedient and committed to right behaviors, only then will God give you the desires of your heart.

Part of accountability is treating others as we want to be treated. The Bible relates that the right state of mind is to love others as ourselves. It's necessary to have a healthy view and love of self. Our ability to love others is a reflection of how we view ourselves. You are priceless in the sight of God and are made in His image. Live and love like it.

People will judge you by the words (language) you use.We're to speak words of encouragement to others. You can also leave a wrong impression by using foul language in the form of swearing, condemning, tearing others down, etc… Such language makes people look foolish and is not edifying. Seek out people to uplift.

Intentionally implement the following:

1. Hope always requires action on your part to make it work. You must act on it. The difficulty of the circumstances has nothing to do with it. Choose to believe.

2. God can and will only bless as you act. Be committed to following Him regardless of what circumstances you may find yourself in. Be willing and follow it up with action.

3. If you love yourself, pour that onto others by offering generous words of encouragement. Don't be selfish and stingy in giving to others. This ultimately reflects your own worth.

4. Create a habit of encouraging others. You'll find this fulfilling which will reinforce harmonious passions for godly things.

Hope

11And we desire that each one of you show the same diligence to the full assurance of hope until the end, 12 that you do not become sluggish, but imitate those who through faith and patience inherit the promises.

—Hebrews 6:11-12 NKJV

Meditation and Action

There's a lot of meat on this bone. This verse provides an excellent example of growing hope. Creating and maintaining hope requires diligence and action. It's a state of mind that leads to transformation. Every human being is capable of this as expressed in Paul's statement. It was his desire for each one to show the same diligence to hope and that we hold onto this hope until the end. Because he challenges us to hold onto it until the end implies that it can be lost. How can we fumble and give up the ball? This happens when we allow circumstances to take our eyes from where we're trying to go. When we focus on the circumstance we become sluggish, we begin to see cracks in our hope and suddenly come to think that maybe I won't make it after all. These are the challenges of life that everyone faces. However, Paul also gives us the strategy to maintain hope during these times. Simply, imitate those who through faith and patience overcome. Note, that in order to imitate, you have to have accountability. You not only have to have someone to imitate but you need to be in contact with that person to receive encouragement. It's through this process that builds strength and resilience which keeps hope alive during difficult times. This is your responsibility and requires committed behavior to act. Keep your hope alive.

Commitment

Watch your life and doctrine closely. Persevere in them, because if you do, you will save both yourself and your hearers.

—I Timothy 4:16 NIV

Meditation and Action

As we've been discussing, living a life committed to spiritual resilience requires being vigilant. Paul tells Timothy to persevere in watching your life and doctrine, the code you live by and making sure the two line up closely. Paul further mentions that it's by being diligent and monitoring these things that results in our salvation and how effective our lives are. We can't leave things to chance and simply live our lives without any forethought. We must live purposefully. This is something most people don't do. Reflect on your own life while considering this passage. How often do you go through your day just addressing things as they surface as if being on auto pilot? When was the last time you truly reflected on your actions in light of your faith to make sure the two align with each other? We need to get in the habit of thinking about this every day. Your challenge for today and throughout is to create the habit of watching your life with consistency to make sure you're being the example you need to be. When you make mistakes, and you surely will, fix them. Doing so strengthens your personal walk with God but also leaves an example to help others do the same.

Accountability

12Listen to me, you stubborn people who are so far from doing right. 13For I am ready to set things right, not in the distant future, but right now! I am ready to save Jerusalem and show my glory to Israel.
—Isaiah 46:12-13 NLT

Meditation and Action

This chapter outlines what the prophet Isaiah was telling the Babylonians about their false gods compared to the one true God. Because of their stubbornness, they refused to give up their false gods and idols. They failed to see the hand of God and recognize that they had placed their hopes in things that were not real. Stubbornness will keep us from seeing the obvious. We can get so fixated on what we think is reality that we become blind to the truth because we want things to work out our way, we want control. Being a prophet, Isaiah's role was to hold Israel accountable for their actions by warning them. When they did not heed the warnings, they suffered God's wrath being the natural consequence of their actions. When they heeded the warning and turned from their wicked ways, they experienced God's blessing. The mark of accountability is being able to admit when we're wrong and take corrective action. It's not so much the wrong doing, although important, but the willingness to accept responsibility, admit the wrong doing, and making it right. If your tendency is to be stubborn because you want things your way, your task is to be honest with yourself, admit it, and take corrective action. Do this starting today and make it a habit. Doing so will build accountability into your life and bring prosperity.

Passion

Holdfast the form of sound words, which thou hast heard of me, in faith and love which is in Christ Jesus.
—2 Timothy 1:13 KJV

Meditation and Action

The book of 2 Timothy is Paul's goodbye to Timothy. The books of Timothy provide information regarding spiritual warfare along with encouragement to be diligent, courageous, and to make the most of opportunity. In this verse we get a glimpse of how diligence, courage, and opportunity making are obtained. Paul tells Timothy to hold fast the form of sound words. In other words, he's telling Timothy to remember the things he has heard Paul say regarding faith and Christ. It's the act of remembering, bringing previously heard and learned information into the forefront of our mind that brings encouragement. When we're exposed to important information, we just don't listen to it and forget about it. That serves no purpose. We need to process that information through application for it to become meaningful and useful. However, due to life circumstances, it's easy to get caught up in autopilot mode which serves only to being reactive to life instead of being responsive. Reaction is kneejerk, hasty, and automatic. Responding requires thought. Reaction feeds into being caught up in the emotion. Responding requires listening and remembering, followed by action. Encourage harmonious passions by remembering what you've heard about the faithfulness of God and what He's done in your life up to this point. Look into the future with hope about what He's yet to do. Allow this to encourage your spirit and give you strength for what you're facing. This is the act of how it's done which is why Paul is telling Timothy this. Learn to apply this to your daily routine.

H-CAP Recap

Review the verses for Hope, Commitment, Accountability, and Passion. As you see from this week's verse, maintaining hope requires diligence. You must hold onto it until the end. To do this, we need accountability. We need the right people around us to imitate and to be encouraged. These things keep us focused and keep hope alive.

Watch your life closely. Monitor and scrutinize your motives and actions to make sure they're appropriate. Paul says that we need to persevere in this meaning that we need to make a commitment to it on a regular basis. This action is what keeps us on track and in so doing provides an example for others. Do you see how commitment is linked to accountability?

Making a decision to do the right thing will require accountability. As in this week's verse, Isaiah was accountable to God to follow through with what He told him to do. If he failed, Israel would have no example, no direction, and continue to be lost. Israel also needed to be accountable by heeding Isaiah's direction. Don't allow a stubborn attitude keep you from seeing and doing what's right.

See how this week's verse on passion weaves into itself the traits of hope, accountability, and commitment. Paul was giving explicit instruction to Timothy to help him keep his passion alive and moving in the right direction. This would require Timothy to commit and do what Paul was telling him. Paul was a mentor to Timothy which also means there was accountability. Apply this verse as if Paul is writing it to you. Allow it to feed your passion.

Intentionally implement the following:

1. Hold on to your hope. Don't give it up and don't allow yourself to be sidetracked due to circumstances. Receive encouragement from others to help keep you grounded.
2. Diligently monitor your life to keep it going in the right direction. As a navigator checks their charts to make sure they're on course, so we must monitor our actions.
3. As you do the above steps, you should notice if you've been hindered by a stubborn attitude. This is a sign of wanting to take control. Give it up.
4. Hold fast to the things you're learning as you apply these traits. Doing so will create a harmonious passion for your goals.

Hope

Then Caleb silenced the people before Moses and said, "We should go up and take possession of the land, for we can certainly do it."

—Numbers 13:30 NIV

Meditation and Action

Israel stood on the threshold of receiving what God had promised to them after leaving Egypt. God was ready to give it to them and wanted to bless them. Caleb tried to encourage the people that they could do it. However, we know how the story ends. Israel refused to believe the word of God and chose to believe in what their fear was telling them. Again, we see this recurring example between seeing with the natural eye and the mind's eye. Circumstances are not always as they appear. Yet we become slaves to our emotions that are tied to the natural. Seeing with just the natural eye leaves us blind to faith and hope. You can't see hope with the natural eye. So why do you keep trying to base spiritual decisions based on what you see? Hope comes from what is not seen. This is the mistake Israel made and they paid dearly for it. It cost them 40 years of wandering in the desert. The problem is that we read this story and reflect on what a mistake this was yet do the same thing. God has something special for your life; a promised land. Do you have the hope to go in and take it or do you just see the giants? It takes intentional action to see and maintain your focus on hope. Allow yourself to be encouraged in your pursuit as Caleb did. This is a process I call mental optometry. We all need a mind's eye correction from time to time. Focus on the promise, not the circumstance. Keep moving forward; that's how winning is done!

Commitment

> But I tell you this--though he won't do it for friendship's sake, if you keep knocking long enough, he will get up and give you whatever you need because of your shameless persistence.
>
> —Luke 11:8 NLT

Meditation and Action

Successful people don't take "no" for an answer. That's part of the reason why they're successful, because they're persistent. This applies to the spiritual as well as the natural. Luke gives us the formula in this verse. Simply being committed to not giving up will get you where you want to go. We need to pursue our goals shamelessly and relentlessly. That means without fear. It's the fear that we won't make it, the loss of hope, which causes us to give up. Of course, our goals need to line up with God's or we'll end up going in the wrong direction which will cause a great deal of heartache. God will allow us to go there. This state of mind comes from a stubborn obsessive passion by being committed to the wrong thing. Notice that we can be persistent for the right or wrong things. God will not override your will to choose. Application of this trait needs to be done in light of the other traits you learn and apply as you go through this devotional. Staying vigilant, watching your life, making sure you're on the right track (I Timothy 4:16) will serve to make sure the goals you pursue with shameless persistence are a harmonious passion and not obsessive. Don't give up. Remember, commitment is an obligation to act on your goals regardless of emotion.

Accountability

> Without wise leadership, a nation falls; there is safety in having many advisers.
> —Proverbs 11:14 NLT

Meditation and Action

The act of accountability requires a relationship with someone or something. Effective leadership is inextricably linked to the nature of the relationship a leader has with their advisers, the people they choose to surround themselves with. The people you choose to associate with and have in your inner circle speak to your character and will also guide your future. A wise person seeks out people who will give them sound advice and direction and accept direction even if it's not what they want to hear. Wise and effective people weigh this input carefully before a decision is made. This is the safety that the author of this Proverb talks about. It's also important as you receive advice from others that you don't become defensive. Such an attitude will hinder you from hearing what they have to say. Who's in your accountability circle? Do you surround yourself with people who just tell you what you want to hear or are they free to be honest? Do you look out for their best interest and do they look out for yours, or are these relationships one sided? To build accountability, take an inventory of your circle. Do you need to make changes? If so, commit to right action and listen to sound advice. This is wisdom in action.

Passion

The righteous care about justice for the poor, but the wicked have no such concern.

—Proverbs 29:7 NIV

Meditation and Action

This verse compares and contrasts harmonious and obsessive passions. Those who operate out of an obsessive passion are all about them, a what's in it for them attitude. They're so busy and consumed with their own affairs that they don't notice the needs around them. Sure, they may have times where they think about others and even do some good deeds. However, more often than not, they don't operate out of this principle. Remember, you can tell what a person's passions are by their behaviors. People driven by harmonious passion, care for the well-being of others. They demonstrate this by doing for others. However, their doing is not done to fill a void within themselves and to make them "feel better." They do for others because it's who they are. You can create this within yourself simply by making it a habit to give of yourself to others, not for your benefit but for the benefit of another. It's not about you, it's about others. You can give of yourself in many ways and this doesn't have to include money, although it can if you have it to give. You can give of yourself in time and words. Do you know people around you that can benefit from you helping them? You can also give the gift of words in the form of encouragement. A simple kind word can make someone's day. Don't be stingy with caring. Get in the habit of meeting a need for someone daily simply because they need it.

H-CAP Recap

Review the verses for Hope, Commitment, Accountability, and Passion. You may have recognized this week's verse from an earlier meditation on commitment. However, it's equally effective in cultivating hope. Hope comes not from what is seen with the natural eye by with your mind's eye. What God says to you and what the world is showing you can be two different things. Which one will you choose to look at?

This week's verse is a good example of persistence paying off. Don't give up. This is what commitment is all about. It will happen, how bad do you want it and are you willing to do what it takes to see it through?

Effective accountability means that you surround yourself with people you trust to tell you what you need to hear and not necessarily what you want to hear. Listen to sound advice without being defensive. This is where wisdom begins.

Creating harmonious passion requires a commitment to serve others. As you give to others, this creates a sense of gratitude that you can't get anywhere else. It motivates us to do more of it. This is the experience of harmonious passion. It creates an awareness of the needs of others which allows us to care. Follow through with the doing part of this to keep the passion alive.

Intentionally implement the following:

1. Hope comes from what is not seen, not what you see in the present. Choose to look beyond your natural vision and allow yourself to see what God has for you.

2. Commitment is all about persistence which is necessary to build resilience. Never give up. You may get knocked down, just get back up. Be encouraged through the application of the remaining traits.

3. Do you have effective and quality relationships in your inner circle? If not get them and listen to them. Get rid of a stubborn attitude.

4. Meeting needs of other people is what harmonious passion is all about. It's about others, not self. Self becomes obsessive.

Hope

Why are you downcast, O my soul? Why so disturbed within me? Put your hope in God, for I will yet praise him, my Savior and my God.

—Psalm 42:11 NIV

Meditation and Action

You go where you're looking. This means that to whatever you direct your vision to; you will eventually orientate your body and movement in that direction. This is not only a physical and neurological principle; it's also true with our state of mind. You may say and or desire to go in one direction but if your mind's eye is focused in another direction, that's where you'll end up. Once you arrive, it usually ends with blaming God or others and feeling discouraged. Does this sound familiar? Here's the prescription for correcting your mental vision; put your hope in God. This requires you to redirect the object of your vision (mind's eye). Allowing yourself to be encouraged by the word of God and through others in your accountability system brings hope into focus. Notice how David says to "put your hope in God." This means that we have to do something in the midst of our discouragement. It's not up to circumstance or people, you need to take action. Putting your hope in God means that you will commit to engaging in behaviors that will make your hope realized. Worshiping God in the midst of discouragement is a great way to lift your spirit.

It's an act that's contrary to the emotion at the time, but don't focus on the feeling. Commit to the behavior because it's the right thing to do. It will also restore your hope and get you back on track. Can you make yourself do it?

Commitment

I have refused to walk on any evil path, so that I may remain obedient to your word.

—Psalm 119:101 NIV

Meditation and Action

The psalmist, most likely Solomon, cuts right to the chase for obtaining and maintaining spiritual resilience. It's a commitment to not giving in to the temptation of the "evil path." It's what I call the law of resistance and submission. To resist a force, requires submission to another. In this case, it's the resistance of evil, temptation, and submission to God. They work hand in hand. The act of submission will give power to resist and the act of resistance gives power to submission. This process can work in either direction, good or evil. You need to decide what you will submit to and what you will resist. If a resilient spirit is your goal, submission to the word of God in your life is the only way for you to resist the world. It's a drop dead commitment. It's not a matter of convenience or feeling but a decision to act. This act is not about simple willpower. Willpower is just about the resistance part. In addition to resisting, you need to add the submission part. You're substituting one for the other. This is what makes this process work. Reflect on your own life, to what do you need strength in resisting? Your power to do this lies in what you submit to. Submit to God by diligently applying these strategies and the thing you resist will become weaker. Try it.

Accountability

Lead me in the right path, O LORD, or my enemies will conquer me. Make your way plain for me to follow.
—Psalm 5:8 NLT

Meditation and Action

Accountable people know when to ask for help. Many people don't like to ask for help because they think it a sign of weakness. They want to be viewed as having all the answers. They like to take credit when things work out right but blame and point fingers when things go wrong. This statement can hurt if this is you. However, don't let the hurt of the truth lead you to blame as you read this. Let it sink in. In doing so, you're being accountable. Just keep reading. Asking for help and direction whether it be from God or other trusted advisors is not a sign of weakness but the sign of a wise and prudent person. The natural consequence of not doing this is clear as mentioned in this verse, *or my enemies will conquer me.* Of course, if it's your nature to not seek advice, when you are conquered your normal reaction will be to blame and point fingers. The point of this devotional is to help you see this before it happens. Your task in building accountability is to recognize this and take corrective action. Don't be prideful and don't wait until you get into trouble before you ask for help. Seeking direction from trusted sources along the way can spare a lot of heartache. It's an easier path to follow once you get past the emotion of asking for help.

Passion

11For I long to see you, that I may impart to you some spiritual gift to strengthen you, 12that is, that we may be mutually encouraged by each other's faith, both yours and mine.
—Romans 1:11-12 RSV

Meditation and Action

Paul had an incredible faith. We look to him as a spiritual giant. He had such wisdom and strength and seemed almost invincible in faith. He was able to endure any hardship without fear. This is what we're striving for in our own lives, resilience. In this verse, we see the nature of imparting spiritual gifts mentioned by Paul. He talks about being mutually encouraged by each other's faith. To be encouraged by another gives hope. Look back in your own life and consider the last time you were encouraged by something. What did it do for you? Did it lift you up; help you to see things in a new way? This is all hope. However, in addition to creating hope, it also spurs us on to keep moving forward. Hope inspires action (commitment) but also passion (motivation). These are the gifts that Paul is referring to. It's the ability to endure and pass the gifts onto others through mutual encouragement. Notice that Paul says that he longed to see them. Longing for something indicates a passion, a drive for something. For him, he was looking forward to not only sharing with others but also receiving from others. These acts require accountability as indicated by the word, *mutually*. Your spiritual resilience depends on your ability to be accountable and commitment to encouraging others as well as allowing yourself to be encouraged. Take advantage of these opportunities and create them.

H-CAP Recap

Review the verses for Hope, Commitment, Accountability, and Passion. Everyone has times when they feel hopeless. This doesn't mean you're weak or something's wrong. It's just human nature. If David and Jesus can experience these times, why should it be a surprise when we experience it? The question is what to do when we experience it? The answer, redirect your attention, your mind's eye, from what the actual circumstance is back to God.

Refuse to walk on any evil path. The temptation is there for everyone. This is what the world does. Learn the process of resistance and submission. Submission (commitment) to applying these skills will give you the ability to resist temptation when it hits. Don't be alarmed if you have to engage in this process countless times. The more you devote yourself to the submission part, the easier resisting is.

Everyone needs help to get where they want to go in life. The church is no different. This is why the Bible speaks of the need for fellowship. Don't wait until you're drowning to ask for help. Seeking direction from trusted sources along the way will spare you from last minute panic.

Being encouraged in our efforts as we are pursuing our faith is the source of passion. Passion is the motivation for doing what we do. It needs to be fed just like the other traits. The best way to feed it is giving and receiving encouragement. Mutually encourage each other.

Intentionally implement the following:

1. If you're getting tired and find it hard to see hope, allow yourself to be encouraged from God's word and from others. This will reboot your hope.
2. Remember, the law of resistance and submission. There is a direct correlation to the degree of your submission to your ability to resist. Submit to applying these traits, think about them, and bind them around your neck. The more this is on your mind, the easier it will be to resist.
3. Don't fear asking for help. It's not a sign of weakness but of strength. Let your accountability system work for you.
4. Allow yourself to be mutually encouraged in the faith by trusted others and in the progress your making in applying these traits. This will build your passion.

Hope

For I know the plans I have for you," declares the LORD, "plans to prosper you and not to harm you, plans to give you hope and a future.

—Jeremiah 29:11 NIV

Meditation and Action

Although these words were written thousands of years ago, it's a promise that is true for us today. God was speaking these words through Jeremiah to His people and we are His people. What was true then is still true today. God has a plan for your life. Have you discovered what that is? What is your passion? How do you want to be used by God? What are you willing to do? Knowing that God's plan for our lives is to prosper us and not harm us is something to look forward to. However, it's easy to misunderstand the "harm" part. Some can interpret this to mean that we should not experience any harm as if we should go through life unscathed. What this means is that God does not cause the harm. It does not originate from Him. He does allow us to suffer the consequences of our own behavior and what naturally occurs in the world. However, these things are not sent by God. It's just life. God's plans are for us to grow in the knowledge of His word and to live life abundantly. This is the hope we are to live in. The message is that we can live in this hope even while experiencing life. It's only through hope that abundant living can be experienced. Keep this promise alive and active by reminding yourself of it. It can only transform you to the degree you're willing to believe it.

Commitment

When a man makes a vow to the LORD or takes an oath to obligate himself by a pledge, he must not break his word but must do everything he said.

—Numbers 30:2 NIV

Meditation and Action

The definition of commitment is rooted in the word, obligation. It's an obligation to act regardless of how we feel. The reason that word is used is because it's normal to not "feel" like doing something we know we should at times. However, to be obligated means you override the feeling and do it anyway. Have you ever wanted to sleep in and not go to work or school? Why did you get up and go, because of an obligation? The following through of a commitment is also trustworthy. Others know that you can be counted on. These things are equally true in our commitment to God. Although we are not saved by works but through faith, our faith is demonstrated by our works. It's our works or committed behaviors that train our mind and spirit that bring resilience just as an athlete must be committed to training their body to perform. You can't run a successful race without putting time into training. Consider your commitment to God. Have you let things slide because you just weren't "feeling it?" As Christians, we have an obligation to run the race and finish well. Spiritual resilience will not come in any other way. What have you been obligated to; can you be trusted to make good on your obligation?

Accountability

6But let him ask in faith, with no doubting, for the one who doubts is like a wave of the sea that is driven and tossed by the wind.7for that person must not suppose that he will receive anything from the Lord; 8he is a double-minded man, unstable in all his ways.

—James 1:6-8 ESV

Meditation and Action

Being accountable is a process of obtaining information, seeking wise counsel, and taking decisive action. There is no doubting. This is also linked to being hopeful. We anticipate X happening, that is our hope based on our passion and commitment to make it happen. The point being is the commit to action based on our faith and our willingness to be held accountable. A state of indecision is being double-minded. Part of living an abundant life is about taking some risk and living in faith based on our commit to excellence. This is all of the H-CAP traits working together. We can often doubt a direction within ourselves and it may be necessary to seek advice from people who know. You must seek them out though. Don't wallow in your indecision, seek out the answers, make a decision, and believe. At times, it may not work out. Ok, back up and regroup and go at it another way. Don't give up! If you know what you're worth go out and get it but you have to be willing to take the hits. Are you struggling with indecision? Seek out direction, and make a committed decision to act. God won't move unless you're willing to step out of your comfort zone and put your faith to the test. Make your hope and faith a stable force in your life.

Passion

12Since we have such a hope, we are very bold, 13not like Moses, who would put a veil over his face so that the Israelites might not gaze at the outcome of what was being brought to an end.
—2 Corinthians 3:12-13 ESV

Meditation and Action

Passion gives us boldness. In reading Paul's letters of the New Testament, his boldness and lack of fear stands out loud and clear. Next to Christ, he was arguably the most resilient and fearless of believers. However, this is just not to be admired, it's to be recreated. It's available to all willing to grow to this level. The boldness mentioned in this verse comes from harmonious passion. Passion creates boldness and fearlessness. Here, Paul compares and contrasts this passion from the old covenant law to the love and grace of the new covenant. Moses needed to hide the glory of God that shown upon his face. The radiance Moses experienced came from being in the presence of God. It was a reflection of God's passion for man and Mosses' passion to serve. Being in the presence of God changes us from the inside out. We are to let this shine for others to see, not hide it. Have you ever noticed how and why people are drawn to passionate people? It's the passion they exude that stands out, it's like a light in darkness. We're to live out our passions. As we live them out, others will be attracted by our passion because true passion is contagious. Note that passion stems from hope. Your ability to be hopeful about the future creates the passion for moving forward. This passion directs our commitment and accountability. This is the example that Paul lived by which is reflected through his actions. Let your passion for God give you boldness.

H-CAP Recap

Review the verses for Hope, Commitment, Accountability, and Passion. God's plan is to prosper you. You have an assurance that He has a plan for your life. If you allow yourself to see and believe this, it can get you through the toughest of times. Remember, God doesn't promise anyone an easy life; just that we can have hope, a reason for hope, in the midst of trouble.

Take this week's verse on Commitment into consideration for your life. This reflects the true meaning of the word. This level of commitment brings results. Think how different your life would be if you held yourself to this standard. Don't allow your behaviors to be dictated by what you feel. Take control of yourself. Be committed to right action for the sake of it being right, not feeling.

States of indecision can be a difficult place. When faced with these times, seek out wise counsel from trusted others and ask God to give you guidance. This is your due diligence of holding yourself accountable. Go with the decision that brings you the most peace. God will honor that.

Passion gives confidence to overcome. It gives boldness to the one who holds such confidence. This confidence is a result of many factors to include hope, committed behaviors, and the level of our accountability. Allow this confidence in your faith to shine, put on display for others to see. Don't hide it.

Intentionally implement the following:

1. Do you truly believe that God has a plan for you and that this plan includes living an abundant life? Living it out with confidence (assurance) is dependent on your willingness and level to which you believe it. Let the thoughts of this always be on your mind so it sinks in.

2. As you engage in #1, commit to right action. Remember that being committed is an obligation as outlined in this week's verse. A commitment to living a spiritual and resilient life requires an obligation. It's not about what you feel.

3. As you live out your hope filled life and commitment to right behaviors, it's normal to experience indecision. Holding yourself accountable and seeking sound counsel during these times is important. Make the best decision and act decisively. Step out in your faith.

4. Allow the growth you've been making in the application of these strategies to give you confidence and boldness. Allow this new found confidence to show in your life for others to see. People will want what you have. Note, that what they see is Christ in you, not you.

Hope

21Yet this I call to mind and therefore I have hope: 22Because of the LORD's great love we are not consumed, for his compassions never fail.

—Lamentations 3:21-22 NIV

Meditation and Action

The book of Lamentations is about the mourning over the destruction of Jerusalem. The message it conveys is that even when current circumstances appear disastrous, the faithfulness of God will always give us a reason to hope. As chapter 3 unfolds, the author, Jeremiah, takes a turn from looking at the destruction and hopelessness to hope. He does this by remembering the grace and love of God and His restorative power. God's love for us never fails no matter how wrong things go to include our bad decisions. We can choose to lament and beat ourselves up over our losses or we can focus on turning our life around and making it right. Knowing that God's love for us is endless and never fails, can give us the hope we need to look beyond our circumstances and start rebuilding for the future. Note that this does not happen automatically. Jeremiah says that "I will call to mind." You have to intentionally direct your attention (mind's eye) in this direction in order to get your body to follow. It's about readjusting your focus to things that produce hope. There is nothing more hopeful than unconditional love that is never ending. God is always there waiting to help you pick up the pieces. It doesn't mean that it'll be easy, but it will certainly be easier with Him than without Him. Make it a habit to remember the unending love God has for you. This means that you can always make it right. It's never too late.

Commitment

12But be sure to fear the LORD and serve him faithfully with all your heart; consider what great things he has done for you. 25Yet if you persist in doing evil, both you and your king will be swept away."

—I Samuel 12:24-25 NIV

Meditation and Action

Samuel was the last of the judges. It was a transition time from being ruled by God, a theocratic system, to being ruled by a king, a monarchy. Recall that the people wanted to have a king on a throne and be ruled by man as opposed to being governed by God. Samuel warns the people and gives them directives to keep them on track spiritually. He begins with service. Serve God faithfully. In other words, he reminds them of their commitment, their obligation to serve if they wanted God's blessing. Their service must be done faithfully and with all their heart, meaning being consistent. To help them in this task, they were to reflect and remember all the things God has done for them in the past. This was to serve as a reminder for them and keeps

God in the forefront of their minds. You'll find this to be a consistent formula for success, determined action and reflection (going where you're looking), in whatever you do. The key is keeping your mind's eye focused on the right thing. If you don't stay focused, you'll easily be led astray. Be proactive and keep God in your heart and mind and let this be your compass. Commit to serving God through your service to others. Persist in these things. If not, you will do the opposite by default which is persisting in doing evil.

Accountability

18For John had been saying to Herod, "It is not lawful for you to have your brother's wife." 19So Herodias nursed a grudge against John and wanted to kill him. But she was not able to.

—Mark 6: 18-19 NIV

Meditation and Action

More often than not, grudges are created because we don't want to admit to a wrong that we've been called on. Sometimes the truth hurts and that hurt can produce anger. In this passage, Herod had taken his brother's wife, Herodias, for himself. John called him on it and from then on she wanted John dead. Although Herod feared John because he knew that he was a righteous man, Herodias' anger grew. The foolishness of Herod and his failure to take a stand and do what's right, caved to her request which eventually resulted in John's beheading. This is a case of accountability gone awry which resulted in the murder of an innocent man. When caught in a situation, there's always a window of opportunity to make it right. During these times, it's important to have others around you who have your best interest in mind to seek advice. John told Herod and tried to hold him accountable but he refused to listen. Herod was blind to this because his alliance with Herodias was lustful which made his mind and heart weak. He chose his sin over sparing the life of an innocent man. He refused to be accountable to the truth. If you allow a grudge to grow as a defense mechanism, it will eventually lead to your destruction. Are you currently nursing a grudge? If so, hold yourself accountable. Do you find yourself so caught up in your sin and lacking accountability that you're not making good choices? Reconcile the matter and let it go. Seek wise counsel. Doing so will free you from bondage. This act takes a commitment strategy and will create accountability in your life.

Passion

1As a prisoner for the Lord, then, I urge you to live a life worthy of the calling you have received.2Be completely humble and gentle; be patient, bearing with one another in love.

—Ephesians 4:1-2 NIV

Meditation and Action

The calling we have received is living out our salvation for others to see. This can be done in whatever circumstances God has called you. Paul uses the word "urge" he urges us to live a life worthy of our calling. The fact that we need to be urged to do something means that we can also choose not to do something. In other words, we can have a calling and experience salvation but not live it out. It's the difference between wearing the Christian label and living it. Paul gives us the answer to living a life worthy of our calling. It's being humble, gentle, patient, and bearing with each other. As we've been examining, it's about being others focused. Christ is the example, He's the standard we need to live up to and strive for. Recall the slogan, "What would Jesus do." When we have as a goal to put others first, meeting needs of others, the natural consequence of this is harmonious passion which leads to humility and patience. Paul knows that this does not come natural to us and this is why he urges them. Urge yourself in the same manner. Don't wait for motivation to strike you. Action needs to come first. It's the action that creates the harmonious passion, not the other way around. Urge yourself to take right action and be determined to carry it out. Right feelings follow right behavior.

H-CAP Recap

Review the verses for Hope, Commitment, Accountability, and Passion. Remember that you will always go where you're looking. When times are tough and things appear to be hopeless, it's easy to look at how bad things are. Learn from Jeremiah's experience. Be encouraged by looking to hope. This is simply done by reflecting on God's grace and mercy. His love never fails no matter how bad things get. You can count on that. Allow your reflection to lift your spirit.

God demands faithful service. This means commitment. Take time to reflect on what God has already done for you and allow this to feed your hope and passion. To serve God means serving other people. If you don't make a commitment in this direction, you're committing to do evil. It's one direction or the other. There is no in between.

The obsessive passion of sin has a way of altering our good judgment. It's during these times is when we need accountability. Listen to the warnings that others may tell you. God always provides a way out if you're willing to hold yourself accountable

Right feelings follow right behavior. Because we have such a great salvation, we are urged to live it out. Living it out for others to see comes from the passion within. If you truly hold to the belief that God so loves you and that He wants you to share the glories of heaven with you, allow this to transform your life. Allow the change that takes place on the inside to reflect change on the outside.

Intentionally implement the following:

1. Always take time to reflect on what God has done in your life and the mercy He's shown and how He's spared you. Allow these memories to give you encouragement and grow your hope. Look in this direction and go in this direction.

2. If you want to receive God's blessing and live an abundant life, you need to make a commitment to living out your faith. Living it not just when times are good but in all times. We live and serve God through serving others. Commit to passing it on.

3. Everyone has times when they struggle with temptation. The object is to resist it and not give in. When we're feeding the sin, the last thing we want to hear is to "stop." Allow this internal conflict to be the alarm. This is the window of opportunity God is giving you to get out. Hold yourself accountable and listen while there is still time.

4. We do have a great calling and Paul challenges us to live up to it. This means living out your passion. Allow the internal changes of God's grace given to you reflect through your outward behavior. Live it through service to others. This feeds the passion.

Hope

4And endurance develops strength of character, and character strengthens our confident hope of salvation. 5And this hope will not lead to disappointment. For we know how dearly God loves us, because he has given us the Holy Spirit to fill our hearts with his love.

—Romans 5:4-5 NLT

Meditation and Action

Resilience creates character. Good and strong character is forged in the fire; in the crucible of life of which no one is immune. Many Christians have the false belief that if God really loved them, life would be easier and that life should be easier for the Christian, we shouldn't have to struggle as much. Nowhere in the Bible is this mentioned. If anything, Christians are under greater scrutiny because our beliefs and actions run counter to the world. Jesus Christ and all the martyrs that followed are a testament to this. The difference is that we can endure in spite of the world. However, it's the reason why we can endure. That reason is hope. We have a confidence that the world does not have; the assurance of salvation and eternity with Christ. We have the never ending and unfailing love of God. In other words, we have what the rest of the world is seeking yet fails to see. It's the hope in these things that enables the Christian to stand the trails of life. When we stand together, bear each other's burdens, and provide support to each other, this brings peace to chaos. It moves the hand of God which increases our hope and confidence. This creates resilience. This is exactly why you're reading this book. Allow this verse to sink in and stir up your hope and confidence that all things are possible. Don't allow circumstances to dictate your future. Look to your hope.

Commitment

11Obey what I command you today. I will drive out before you the Amorites, Canaanites, Hittites, Perizzites, Hivites and Jebusites.12Be careful not to make a treaty with those who live in the land where you are going, or they will be a snare among you.

—Exodus 34:11-12 NIV

Meditation and Action

There's a saying, without God we cannot but without us, God will not. God will make a way for us. However, this does not mean we are left without responsibility. God commands faithfulness. This is our part. It's a commitment to serve God with all our heart and mind. Sometimes we falsely think that just because we serve God that He will make the path easy. Sometimes He does and sometimes He doesn't. Sometimes, it's necessary to go into battle. Even when we're promised the victory, this doesn't mean that we won't take some hits, bumps, and bruises during the fight. This is how perseverance is created. The ONLY part we need to concern ourselves with is doing what is expected of us which is living the way our faith commands. The rest is up to God. This includes not forming alliances with those who live in the land (the world). Don't be willing to compromise your faith. As the verse says, this will be a snare and cause you to stumble. We need to learn to give up the things beyond our control and just do our part. Commit to serving God and then He will drive out the enemy. We need to act first. Are you facing a battle and struggling by trying to control things that are beyond you? Are you giving place to the world? Commit to giving it up and just focus on being obedient. He'll fight the battle, just let Him.

Accountability

Don't lord it over the people assigned to your care, but lead them by your own good example.

—1 Peter 5:3 NLT

Meditation and Action

In this chapter, Peter is giving direction to elders and young men of the church for effective leadership. He tells them to be shepherds and not to lord leadership over people. In other words, don't smother and micromanage people to the point that it frustrates them. Simply lead by example. People who are experienced leaders and who are accountable know how to make an impression and get the most from people. People who lord their position over others do so out of insecurity and they throw their weight around as a mean to bolster their own low self-image. People who do such things lack appropriate accountability. To learn this effectively, it's important to align yourself with people who are effective leaders. Watch them. Notice how they lead by their own actions and words. Allow them to impact your life in this manner. The people you have influence over will respond and adopt your style of interaction, good or bad so it's important to go about it the right way. Effective leaders serve, it's a model called servant leadership. Christ is the best example of this type of leadership. What kind of example are you leaving for your family, friends, and co-workers? Your task from here on is to be mindful of the example you're projecting. Make sure it's the right one. Treat others as you expect to be treated and lift people up through encouragement.

Passion

For since the creation of the world God's invisible qualities--
his eternal power and divine nature--have been clearly seen,
being understood from what has been made, so that men are
without excuse.

—Romans 1:20 NIV

Meditation and Action

Look around and take notice of creation, the trees, grass, the sky, atmosphere, all manner of life. Each form of life has its own cycle and is held in balance by our planet. These things are too intricate to be formed by accident. The nature of the design points to a creator who is God. This is why we are without excuse. The ability to reflect on the beauty of creation works to increase our passion for spiritual things. It serves to keep us grounded. Notice in reading the verses that surround this passage. It talks of how man suppresses the truth due to inherent wickedness. Because we fail to recognize and acknowledge what is clearly in front of us, God gives people over to the wickedness of their own hearts. It's not that God intentionally blinds people to His truth, He simply allows us to follow the desires of our own heart. The question for you is which desires are you going to follow? Godly desires (harmonious passions) need to be cultivated. Obsessive passions are innate and won't require any work. They're already there waiting to be unleashed. Consider how God reveals Himself though nature and begin to recognize the workings of God on a daily basis. Remember, this is an intentional act of commitment and works to create and maintain harmonious passion. As you do this, you don't have to speak anything to God. Just sit and admire. Allow Him to speak to you. This is what real prayer is and is where God will fill your heart with passion.

H-CAP Recap

Review the verses for Hope, Commitment, Accountability, and Passion. Growth doesn't come without conflict. It's only through the trying of our faith that hope is strengthened and good character formed. It's the hope we have from the word of God that gives us the assurance that no matter what we're facing, God will be with us. Hold on to this thought.

God demands obedience. It's only as we are obedient that He will drive out the enemy. The Bible warns us of not making a treaty with the world. Letting our guard down and making exceptions will lead to your fall. If you're too busy being obedient to God, you won't have time to be deceived by the world.

Be mindful of the example you leave for those around you. Effective leaders don't assume the position because they desire power and control. The most effective leaders are those who aren't afraid to get dirty; they lead by example. Effective leaders serve. Christ is the ultimate example of this. Model it.

Creation reveals the nature of God. To examine the intricacies of all creation can produce a sense of amazement. The details can only point to a designer and creator. It's far too complex to be an accident. Allow yourself to be amazed at the beauty of creation and the grace of God and allow it to fill your heart with a passion for spiritual things. You are part of that creation.

Intentionally implement the following:

1. Hope is what we hold onto for strength. It's the reason we get up every day. However, hope and character don't grow unless they're put to the test. Hold on to your hope, commit to doing right, and lean on your supports. You'll make it.

2. God demands obedience before He'll drive out the enemy and give us the land. Complacency will lead you to making compromises with the enemy. Busy yourself with being obedient and you won't have time to entertain compromises.

3. Lead by example by following Christ's example of leadership. Serve.

4. Keep your passion alive by taking time to reflect on creation itself. This includes you.

Hope

For whatever things were written before were written for our learning, that we through the patience and comfort of the Scriptures might have hope.

—Romans 15:4 NKJV

Meditation and Action

The Bible is full of examples of successes and failures. By examining these examples, it gives us the benefit of hindsight. The right course of action is always easier to see from this position. It's just like Monday morning quarterbacking. In the heat of the moment, it can be easy to get caught up in the emotion of misguided obsessive passions which can make it easier to make wrong decisions. This will be even more difficult when we're not surrounded by the right people (accountability). However, if we study these examples long enough they will become embedded in our memory. This will serve to increase the likelihood of us making the right decision under fire. As we meditate on these examples, we need to find personal meaning for them. This is exactly why they are recorded in the Bible. These are not just written for the sake of being good literature. They were recorded with the intention of learning from the examples of others which leads to hope; hope that we don't have to make the same mistakes. Remember, there's nothing new under the sun. The troubles you face are not new to you or anyone else. We all face the same difficulties at various times and at varying degrees. Take comfort in the fact that others have been there and that difficult times don't last forever. Look to what you hope for and stay committed to behaviors that will make it happen and surround yourself with likeminded people. You create your own success. God's already mapped it out, just follow the right examples.

Commitment

Now reform your ways and your actions and obey the LORD your God. Then the LORD will relent and not bring the disaster he has pronounced against you.
—Jeremiah 26:13 NIV

Meditation and Action

Jeremiah was a priest called to be a prophet in Judah. His message to the nation is exactly as it is for us today, reform your ways and actions, obey. We fail to realize that our own actions cause most of the emotional turmoil and circumstances we find ourselves in. We then have the audacity to blame others and God. This is not being accountable. Our only mission in life is to live for God. God should be at the center of our thoughts and actions. When we accept and commit to this, God blesses us. Again, this does not mean that we live a life without trouble, that's not reality. We are promised peace of mind and resilience. However, these traits must be cultivated through the creation of hope, commitment, accountability, and passion. We will always make mistakes along the way. However, it's not the mistakes that God keeps track of but our ability to reform, make right, and redirect our attention to Him. This is the process. What exists in your life that has not yet been turned over to God? Take some time and consider this. Commit to being accountable to God, others, and yourself. Commit to reforming your actions that reflect this commitment whatever they may be. Only then will God fulfill His side of the deal.

Accountability

For God did not give us a spirit of timidity but a spirit of power and love and self-control.

—2 Timothy 1:7 RSV

Meditation and Action

The achievement of self-control begins with accountability. Self-control is not something that is attained timidly. It demands immediate and decisive action on our part. We see from this verse that we all have the ability to tap into this spirit of power; the question is, are you? When we have examples in our lives that demonstrate and model power, love, and self-control, it's easier to put on these traits and model them to others. The key ingredient here is finding these people and allowing them to influence you. Think about the most significant relationships in your life good or bad. What traits have you taken from these relationships, good or bad? We all take things from these relationships. This is why it's so important to have quality relationships so the impact is positive. Although we don't have control over this as we're growing up, as adults, we certainly do. Examine the nature of your relationships that are having a negative influence in your life. Be accountable and take action to change those relationships and create relationships that demonstrate love and self-control and model their behavior. This is the first step in creating power in your life.

Passion

6Likewise urge the younger men to control themselves. 7Show yourself in all respects a model of good deeds, and in your teaching show integrity, gravity, 8and sound speech that cannot be censured, so that an opponent may be put to shame, having nothing evil to say of us.

—Titus 2:6-8 RSV

Meditation and Action

Harmonious passion is achieved through the motivation we get from being encouraged and giving encouragement. This is what the word "urge" means here. Along with encouraging others to do the right thing, show yourself as a model. In other words, be a role model of how a dynamic Christian life is to be lived. We are to model this in our committed behaviors through our deeds and speech. Reflect on your own behavior and manner of talk. Can it be said of you that you act and speak differently from non-believers? If not, you're being a model of the world which will lead to confusion. What you say and what you do are incongruent and this is why people mock the church. Your deeds and the manner in which you carry yourself speak for itself. When your behaviors speak to a harmonious passion for the things of God, although you may be the object of ridicule for your belief, it is your accusers who are put to shame because their accusations are not based on truth leaving them to look stupid. Carrying out this verse will require commitment and accountability because you not only need to act on it but you need to encourage others in their faith. You will also receive encouragement from this. Intentionally engaging in these behaviors keeps passion for God alive and will increase your desire to pursue Godly things. Don't fear in living passionately for God. You're the light in a world of darkness.

H-CAP Recap

Review the verses for Hope, Commitment, Accountability, and Passion. The Bible was written as a guide to teach us how to live. We can read about the successes and failures of others and learn from these examples. Although it can feel like it, you're not the only one who goes through tough times. Use the Bible as encouragement by seeing how God always comes through. He will for you too. Hope on that.

If you want God's blessing, reform your ways, meaning change your behavior. You can't expect God to bless until you make the commitment first. It's okay if you make mistakes, just take responsibility for them and keep seeking God. It's only then will He pour out His blessing on your life.

God has given us everything we need for love, power, and self-control. The problem is we don't use it. As the saying goes, if you don't use it, you lose it. Self-control needs to be exercised by training the mind. To strengthen this ability, you need effective models. Surround yourself with like-minded people who do exercise sound judgment and self-control. Allow them to influence you in these areas.

Be passionate in living for God. Be a role model, an example, of the Christian life. Yes, the world may mock you. However, let your good deeds, service to others, your passion, speak for itself. Live out your passion.

Intentionally implement the following:

1. Use the Bible as a source of encouragement. Learn from the actions of others, good and bad and apply what you learn. Human behavior is always the same which is why these stories are still relevant. Learn from them and have hope that God will never let you down.

2. If you want to live an abundant life, you must make the first move to commit to reform.

3. Gain self-control by going to your spiritual gym. Train your mind by applying these strategies but also through relationships with like-minded people. They will keep you on track.

4. The best model of behavior you can be is to live out your passion for God. You may be made fun of, so what. Your accusers will be condemned by their own behavior. Just let your passion shine.

Hope

So keep up your courage, men, for I have faith in God that it
will happen just as he told me.

—Acts 27:25 NIV

Meditation and Action

Paul is on a prison ship, a prisoner on his way to Rome when the ship
is hit with a terrible storm. As would be expected, this creates a state
of panic among the crew and passengers. Paul provides encouragement
to everyone on the ship but also tells them that everyone must remain.
Some of the sailors, fearing death, tried to escape with the lifeboats
leaving the rest stranded. The crew also considered killing all the
prisoners to keep them from escaping. Paul assured them that everyone
would survive regardless of what their circumstances were telling
them. They just needed to stick together. The ship would be lost;
however, if they listened to him and followed his instructions,
everyone would survive. What gave Paul this hope and what kept him
from just saving himself? He believed what God told him. Because he
believed it, he was able to convince the rest of the crew and
passengers. It was confidence in his hope that God would fulfill what
he had promised. This made the rest of the people believe that he knew
what he was talking about. This confidence enabled him to remain
calm and provide decisive direction which was enough to convince the

experienced crew and others to trust him. Paul started this journey being a prisoner but ended up taking charge of the ship and saving everyone on board. What position do you assume when confronted by the storms of life that lead you into the rocks? Do you remain a prisoner to your circumstances and panic or do you rise up in your hope and take action? Others are waiting and need an example.

Commitment

"Every commandment which I command you today you must be careful to observe, that you may live and multiply, and go in and possess the land of which the LORD swore to your fathers."

—Deuteronomy 8:1 NKJV

Meditation and Action

The instructions for living a blessed life are simple and few. Moses gives God's commands to Israel; be careful to observe to obey God's commands. When we do this, we are able to reap God's blessing to live, multiply, and possess. When Moses talks about being careful to observe, this means being mindful and vigilant to ensure you're living as you ought. Serving God and living a Christian life is not a mindless activity which we go through each day on auto pilot. However, this is exactly how most people live, on auto pilot. They just go through the day doing what they know with little accountability and complain about the outcome of their life pointing fingers and blaming others as to why they aren't where they want to be. This is not active observation of living for God. This is active observation about you. Commitment requires an obligation to someone or something. In the case of spiritual resilience, it's a commitment to living and being a godly example. To do this requires being aware of our actions and the impressions they leave. Living on auto pilot means you're not in control, circumstances are. Are you living on auto pilot? Obtaining your goal of spiritual resilience requires you to take control. Decide to commit today to accept Jesus Christ into your life and follow Him!

Accountability

Good planning and hard work lead to prosperity, but hasty shortcuts lead to poverty.
—Proverbs 21:5 NLT

Meditation and Action

The mark of accountability is planning and hard work which incorporates the connection to commitment. It can be very tempting to take shortcuts but doing so will result in coming up short. Having accountable relationships is crucial in keeping us from giving into the temptation of taking shortcuts. These relationships are also important in effective planning and hard work. This is what successful people do and is one of the reasons why they are successful. They don't take short cuts and they surround themselves with like-minded people. Examine your circle of relationships. Do they promote planning and hard work or for taking the easy way out? If you find you really don't have people in your life that can be that example to you, your first order of business is to seek out and create these relationships. Tell people your goals and ask them to hold you accountable in reaching them. This in and of itself is accountability. Do you have a plan of where you want to be 3, 5 years from now? Let a trusted person, who is where you want to be 3 or 5 years from now, know and ask them to help you plan and hold you accountable to the plan. Doing so will ensure your success of making it reality.

Passion

Care for the flock that God has entrusted to you. Watch over it willingly, not grudgingly--not for what you will get out of it, but because you are eager to serve God.
—I Peter 5:2 NLT

Meditation and Action

Serving is not about us but others. The key is to serve God willingly, not grudgingly. The difference between harmonious passion and obsessive passion is the willingness part. People whose behavior flows from willingness means that their behaviors come from the inside out, it's who they are. Obsessive passion comes from the outside in. Harmonious passions are under your control, obsessive passion controls you. God has called us all to serve in some capacity. You can develop a passion for caring and serving others simply though your accountable relationships. Get involved in your church, commit to serving in some way. As you see the results of your work, passion will develop. Another way would be to set aside one day a month that you devote to giving your time to a local charitable organization in your area. It could be serving food at a soup kitchen, helping at a food bank, etc.. The act of doing good deeds will serve as an encouragement for hope which will foster a passion for others. However, the key is to be consistent with this behavior. It's not a one time or an occasional thing. If you're ready to go to the next level, start making a plan of where you can serve and keep it consistent. Once you know how your efforts benefit others, the natural result will be compassion. It happens automatically.

H-CAP Recap

Review the verses for Hope, Commitment, Accountability, and Passion. The degree of hope you have will reflect your level of confidence. When we believe in something and expect it, we can act with confidence. What an example this week's verse provides. Will you allow your hope to give you confidence to take action when trouble hits or will you give up?

The blessing of God is given under one circumstance, that being obedience. Living for God, requires a commitment to serve Him through serving others, not yourself. The world says me first; God says, others first. Who is your master, the world or God?

You're not going to get to where you want to go on your own. You'll need accountable relationships with others to give you support and guidance along the way. Your success will depend on the quality of these relationships. Seek them out.

Harmonious passion is evident through a simple willingness to do something. It's not coerced. Harmonious passion is about doing because you love to not because you have to. This can be created by serving others. Doing things for other people has a way of changing the brain and mind. It causes us to care which leads to action. This is love.

Intentionally implement the following:

1. If you lack confidence, you also lack hope. Allow your hope to grow to the point where you can stand and confront fear in the face because hope says you can win.

2. People often want the blessing of God but don't want to live the life it takes to obtain it. God requires commitment; a commitment to following His example through service to mankind and worshipping Him. Put your money where your mouth is.

3. Don't underestimate the strength of accountable relationships. You won't make it alone. We need other people. Just as iron sharpens iron, so we need accountable relationships.

4. Don't serve God begrudgingly. That's meaningless. Serve God with passion. Meeting needs of hurting people can create that passion.

Hope

Now may the God of hope fill you with all joy and peace in believing, so that you will abound in hope by the power of the Holy Spirit.

—Romans 15:13 NASB

Meditation and Action

Paul describes God as being hope. He's the definition of it. It's only through hope that we can experience joy and peace. It is absolutely impossible to have joy and peace without hope. We can be hopeful for many things. No one is completely hopeless. The object of hope can differ and can certainly lead to feelings of hopelessness when hope is misdirected or when we lack the commitment to engage in the behaviors necessary to make our hope realized. This kind of hope is called a pipe dream. This form of hope comes from being driven by obsessive passions. It's a motivation to certain behaviors for the purpose of filling a hole in your ego. It's self-serving. So, you can see that even misdirected hope is hope; it's the object that we need to consider. Hope is the belief for something; Paul links believing to joy and peace. Hope is reciprocal and feeds into itself as we engage in committed behaviors that put feet to our hope. This means that hope is more than a cognitive assentation; it requires action to give it life. This action requires accountability and passion. All of these feed back into hope which creates the end state of resilience. Make mankind your passion. This is where abundant living begins. Hope that brings joy and peace stems from passion that's harmonious. Hope that results in frustration and anxiety is linked to obsession. Focus on the right thing.

Commitment

Therefore, since we are surrounded by such a great cloud of witnesses, let us throw off everything that hinders and the sin that so easily entangles, and let us run with perseverance the race marked out for us.

—Hebrews 12:1 NIV

Meditation and Action

Have you ever noticed that when a runner runs a race, they try to minimize the weight they carry? Today, there are a variety of shoes on the market that weigh mere ounces. The less weight on the runner's body, the less drag they have and can run faster. Likewise, the weight we carry in the form of emotional baggage can hinder us from running (living) our life. Paul tells us to throw off this weight that hinders us and run with perseverance. It's very easy to get emotionally caught up in the external things of life. It takes a commitment to training yourself to run (live) without being distracted by "things." Perseverance doesn't kick in until you've reached your limits though. This is where your faith and hope come in and are strengthened. Something is only strengthened as it goes through the process of stress and recovery.

Until that time, it isn't perseverance. Are you running your race effectively or are you allowing yourself to be hindered by the weight you carry from unfinished business from the past? Commit yourself to perseverance. Shed the excess baggage, resolve to punch through the wall by creating and using your accountability system, focus on your end goal, and perseverance will begin to grow. It'll be like catching your second wind.

Accountability

He will die for lack of self-control; he will be lost because of his great foolishness.

—Proverbs 5:23 NLT

Meditation and Action

A lack of self-control is a result of a lack of accountability. When you are accountable to either the wrong people or to no one, you seek to serve your own pleasures. Those with this state of mind find it difficult to do for others and struggle with selfishness. Those who do such things do not take criticism well nor seek direction from others. Destruction is the only path this state of mind will find. When the natural consequences come as a result of this behavior, blame and defensiveness follow. Although we all at times tend to go in this direction, this is a matter of degree. For those who catch themselves and gain control, this internal struggle may not even be noticed by others. Self-control then begins with accountability. You need to have a standard of expectation for yourself and others need to have the same for you. Do you have a tendency to struggle in a particular area of your life? Does this struggle lead you to lose control? You create your own success. Take control! Begin by creating an environment and fill it with individuals who can hold you accountable. Do this and you will take your control back.

Passion

7If your gift is serving others, serve them well. If you are a teacher, teach well. 8If your gift is to encourage others, be encouraging. If it is giving, give generously. If God has given you leadership ability, take the responsibility seriously. And if you have a gift for showing kindness to others, do it gladly. 9Don't just pretend to love others. Really love them. Hate what is wrong. Hold tightly to what is good.
—Romans 12:7-9 NLT

Meditation and Action

God has given everyone gifts to serve. Creating and maintaining a harmonious passion requires you to do as this verse demands. It's in the doing that creates the passion. Don't wait for the motivation to strike you before you act. Remember, commitment is an obligation to act regardless of emotion (whether you feel like it or not). As you engage in serving others with your gifts, motivation will come. You can build passion through implementing the other traits of Hope, Commitment, and Accountability. We all have the capacity to give whether its time, money, or both. What can you give to others? We can all offer an encouraging word. Take the time to notice what others are doing and tell them how much you appreciate the work they do. Everyone can be kind to others either through giving an encouraging word or through doing something nice for someone. Doing these things generates a love for others. Take a moment and reflect on the people you come across on a daily basis. What can you do to make their day better? Decide on a course of action and hold yourself accountable in getting it done. If you do this, you will create a hate for what is wrong and your passion and desire for what is good will increase.

H-CAP Recap

Review the verses for Hope, Commitment, Accountability, and Passion. Hope that comes from God brings peace and joy. These traits are linked with passions that are harmonious as opposed to hope that leads to frustration and anxiousness. It's the object of your hope that matters. Have the right goals.

Emotional baggage left over from past experiences has a way of accumulating and weighing us down. Don't get into the habit of emotionally stuffing things such as hurt and fear. These things build up over time and will negatively influence your relationships, sense of self, and overall outlook. It's time to shed that baggage. Focus on your hope, commit to resolving those issues, and lean on your accountability system. This will give you perseverance.

The Bible emphasizes the need for self-control for obvious reasons. This requires living up to a standard which also requires accountability. Everyone is accountable to someone including being accountable to yourself. What is the standard you hold for yourself? Successful people surround themselves with individuals they can trust to give them good advice even if the advice is not something they want to hear. Hearing this and acting rightly on such direction is accountability.

Everyone has gifts that can be used to serve others. This is what God has called us to do. It's find your niche and using it (giving it) to others. This generates a passion for the right things. As you engage in these behaviors, it also reinforces your hope and commitment to goal seeking and obtaining behavior.

Intentionally implement the following:

1. Make sure what you hope for is in line with what God has for you. It will make a difference between following an obsession, which stems from selfish ambition, and a passion that's harmonious.

2. Commit to dumping the emotional baggage that slows you down from living your life. It's keeping you from obtaining what God has for you, living.

3. Self-control begins and ends with accountability. Don't underestimate this. You need to have trusted counsel to keep you on the right track. Listen to them and seriously consider the truth in what they say.

4. Harmonious passion is lived out when you use your gifts to serve others who need them. It's life changing for you the giver and also the recipient.

Hope

"Give, and it will be given to you. A good measure, pressed down, shaken together, and running over will be poured into your lap. For with the measure you use, it will be measured to you."

—Luke 6:38 NIV

Meditation and Action

Hope is created and feeds into harmonious passion when we give to others. Giving to others generates this type of passion. When people struggle with hope and self-centered states of mind, this causes people to be emotionally unavailable to others. This prevents them from having meaningful relationships with significant others because they find emotional intimacy difficult. A sure cure and correction to this mind set is to engage in committed behaviors that require the meeting of needs of other people. Meeting needs can take many forms and not all require the giving of money. Time and attention is the main ingredient that people are looking for. They just want assurance that other people care about them. This can be done through simple random acts of kindness to others. The rule is that you get by giving. This is contrary to the world's way of thinking which says to get as much as you can and do unto others before they do unto you. What's your measuring stick for success? If your focus is on storing up treasure for yourself, you're missing the mark and being driven by obsessive passions. Your hope is in the wrong thing. Let mankind be your business. You'll find yourself and your true passions in giving and doing for others. As you do this, hope, believe that God will bless you.

Commitment

"These things I command you, that you love one another.
—John 15:17 NKJV

Meditation and Action

To live an effective life, particularly a Christian life, requires that we love others. This demands a commitment because this can be a difficult task. It's easy to love those who love us back. However, the kind of love the Bible talks about here is about loving all people. Consider the love of God toward us. He didn't love us because it was reciprocal. He loved us first. He loves those who do not love Him or even acknowledge His existence. This is what draws us to him in the first place, His love. This act does not come natural to us, therefore it must be cultivated. It's part of our spiritual development and will require a commitment on our part. Remember, commitment is an obligation to act rightly regardless of what we feel like. Your training will consist of doing for others. Begin by asking God to reveal opportunities to show love and helping others. However, you'll need to be mindful of these opportunities and be looking for them because this is a prayer He'll answer right away. The problem is that you can get caught up with distractions and miss it. These distractions may not be pleasant or convenient but an opportunity in disguise. Commit to setting a goal for yourself to do one kind thing for someone every day and add to this every day thereafter.

Accountability

1Here is a trustworthy saying: If anyone sets his heart on being an overseer, he desires a noble task. 2 Now the overseer must be above reproach, the husband of but one wife, temperate, self-controlled, respectable, hospitable, able to teach, 3 not given to drunkenness, not violent but gentle, not quarrelsome, not a lover of money. 4He must manage his own family well and see that his children obey him with proper respect. 5(If anyone does not know how to manage his own family, how can he take care of God's church?)

—I Timothy 3:1-5 NIV

Meditation and Action

In this chapter, Paul outlines the qualifications for church leadership. Leadership is the goal. However, it's the qualifications that outline the goal that give the direction to get there. The directions contain all of the elements we've been discussing, self-control, hospitable, teachable which means being able to accept criticism and learning from it, not given to argue which means not being defensive. These qualities will enable one to manage well. The traits outlined here are the standard and in order for a standard to be developed requires accountability. Note, that these traits are qualifications for everyone and not just for leaders of a church or a fortune 500 company. If you have a family, you're a leader. If you're a low or mid-level manager, you're a leader. Everyone has some responsibility for something. So these traits apply to everyone. Do you lack any of these qualities? If so, create a plan to grow them. Your plan must include aligning yourself with trusted people who you can count on to hold you accountable. By taking this step, you'll be creating an environment that's conducive to your success. Think about whom these people can be for you and begin the process of creating those relationships today.

Passion

12And we are instructed to turn from godless living and sinful pleasures. We should live in this evil world with wisdom, righteousness, and devotion to God, 13while we look forward with hope to that wonderful day when the glory of our great God and Savior, Jesus Christ, will be revealed.
—Titus 2:12-13 NLT

Meditation and Action

Developing passion requires action on our part. We have to create it through right behaviors. Righteous living demands us to turn from a godless way of living. Many people wear the Christian label, yet live ineffectual lives. This is because they have one foot in the world and another in the church. However, this doesn't work. This is an identity crisis for the church and is the major reason why the world mocks the church. Although we live in the world we are not to be of it. This requires wisdom, righteousness, and devotion. To accomplish this, you'll need to tap into and activate the other traits you're implementing from Hope, Commitment, and Accountability. With devotion to God and right living comes wisdom and passion. It's the passion we exude that attracts other people to us. It's through our passion that others see that we're different. It's through passion that leaves others wanting what we have, in this case, Christ. However, we need to make sure that the direction of our passion is right. Note, the verse uses the term "sinful pleasures." Sin is pleasurable which can lead to obsessive passion and destruction. What message are you leaving? What do people see when they look at your life? If you don't like what you see, change it. Devote yourself (commit yourself) to serving God and others. Don't give place to obsessive passions. The good news is that if you're reading and applying the strategies in this devotion, you're doing what it takes; just keep going. It's a lifestyle, a way of being, not something we do and then quit.

H-CAP Recap

Review the verses for Hope, Commitment, Accountability, and Passion. Living an abundant life is not a race to see how much you can accumulate before you die. Your quality of life in the sense of having peace of mind, loving what you do, and joy is found in doing for others. In giving, God says we will receive. We can believe this to be true. Have hope in this goal.

Showing love to others is a command. At times, this can be more challenging. However, the lesson here is that love is an intentional act. It's not based on feeling. Love is a commitment. You can show love through simple acts of kindness. Commit to making this a habit. It will transform your life.

Everyone is a leader in some capacity in that they have responsibilities that they are expected to carry out. That being the case, you need to cultivate the traits outlined in this week's verse on Accountability. Hold yourself accountable to this standard and seek relationships with those who have them.

This week's verse on Passion uses all of the traits in the H-CAP model. Our hope and committed behaviors need to come from a harmonious passion. This comes through being wise and learning from experience and avoiding getting caught up in sinful pleasures that come from our proclivity to obsessive passion. Devote yourself to serving others and seeking a relationship with God. This will keep obsessive passions at bay.

Intentionally implement the following:

1. God assures us that when we give to others, it will be given back to us. Don't worry about the time line. Just hope and believe that it's coming in one form or another.
2. Love is a command, not a request. Commit to loving others by helping, doing for others, encouraging others. In other words, serve.
3. Everyone is a leader in some capacity. That being the case cultivate, temperance, self-control, respect, hospitality, teach, don't be given to drunkenness, not violent but gentleness, not being quarrelsome, not a lover of money, and manage your family well. How do you do this? By following the H-CAP model.
4. Make it a habit to avoid obsessive passions (sinful desires) and seek to strengthen your relationship with God. Allow God to be revealed in you.

Hope

13Brothers, I do not consider myself yet to have taken hold of it. But one thing I do: Forgetting what is behind and straining toward what is ahead, 14I press on toward the goal to win the prize for which God has called me heavenward in Christ Jesus.

—Philippians 3:13-14 NIV

Meditation and Action

When we read Paul's letters to the church that make up many of the books of the New Testament you can quickly see that he was a man with extreme faith. His hope and faith were unshakable. This is what you're striving for. It is possible to reach this level of faith and living. However, it's a journey, not a place you arrive at and once there kick up your feet and enjoy the surroundings. Notice Paul's state of mind. He says he doesn't consider himself as arriving (taking hold of it). Although we may think, yes, he has indeed achieved the goal. No, to think that you've arrived, taken hold, means that there's nowhere else to go from there. Paul was always seeking greater things, not for himself, but though his faith and hope in Christ. He did this by not looking back and reliving past experiences but he looked to what was ahead. Hope is in what's ahead of you, not in the past. People spend too much time looking in the rear view mirror of their life with regret and guilt which serve only to erode our hope for the future. The only way to keep moving forward to your goal is to live in the here and now and look to what's ahead with hope. In your attempts to move forward, do you find yourself focusing on the rearview mirror of your life? Remember, you go where you're looking. You can't reach your goals and make them a reality unless you're looking in that direction. Hope lies in what's ahead, not what's already been lived. Press on toward the prize. Pressing on means striving, working. Your hope is fulfilled to the degree you're willing to commit.

Commitment

19"Go therefore and make disciples of all the nations, baptizing them in the name of the Father and of the Son and of the Holy Spirit, 20"teaching them to observe all things that I have commanded you; and lo, I am with you always, [even] to the end of the age."
—Matthew 28:19-20 NKJV

Meditation and Action

This is the Great Commission. It's a command given to all believers as to how we need to live our lives. It's a commitment that also employs accountability, hope, and passion. Human beings are created for relationships and we're called to disciple others in the faith. This requires a commitment to act and cultivate relationships with others and encourage each other in the hope of our faith. We are to teach others as we are taught. This is how the gospel is spread throughout the world. What you've received needs to be passed on to others. It's not a gift that is to be kept by you alone and locked up and not shared. Your faith grows and builds resilience as you put it in operation. What can you do to fulfill the command in this verse? You need to get off the sidelines and into the game in order to grow. Make a commitment to align yourself with other like-minded believers. Be a disciple and disciple others. This takes committed action on your part. Following this command will also develop right passions that bring peace and contentment.

Accountability

A person without self-control is like a city with broken-down walls.

—Proverbs 25:8 NLT

Meditation and Action

The walls of a city serve to protect it from outside influence or invasion. The same process occurs for our mind (spirit). In this case, our self-control serves as the wall of protection and defense. Without it, the city (our mind/spirit) is left unprotected and able to be breached by any sort of negative influence. When builders set out to build a structure, there are checks and balances put into place to ensure that the plans are being followed correctly. You have the workers that do the building and you have supervisors who manage the building process to make sure the builders do it correctly. Likewise, you have inspectors that check the work of the builders to ensure the supervisor is doing their job and make sure the codes are being adhered to. The point is that the process has accountability built in which results in a safe, strong, finished product. Self-control begins and ends with you. You are the one held responsible. A wise person will surround themselves with people who can tell them the truth even when they may not like it. Do you have such people in your life? If not create them, if so, listen to them. Doing these things is like building your wall of protection against negative influences. You are the builder of your future. Don't pass this responsibility to someone else.

Passion

Never let loyalty and kindness leave you! Tie them around your neck as a reminder. Write them deep within your heart.
—Proverbs 3:3 NLT

Meditation and Action

Loyalty is an indicator of what we are passionate about. Think about your life and what you're loyal to. What does your loyalty say about your passion? Sometimes we need reminders of our commitments (loyalties). Things can crop up and desires can flow and take us in another direction. Think about how adultery starts. Most people who have affairs will say that they never intended it to happen. That's because they allowed themselves to get caught in a series of circumstances where desires surface and overwhelm the senses which eventually overrides the brain. The next thing you know, sin is conceived which brings forth death. They've broken the bond of loyalty and trust with their spouse. This is why the psalmist says to tie them around your neck as a reminder. Loyalty isn't something we make a one time commitment to; it's an ongoing state of mind. It's an obligation that needs to be checked as it's tested through life experiences. A good way to keep your loyalty to Christ going in the right direction is to feed your harmonious passion. The verse also tells us to never let kindness leave you. This is the key. Keep acts of kindness going. Make them part of your daily routine. This will act as a reminder and will keep your passion flowing in the right direction. What is something you can do for someone else today?

H-CAP Recap

Review the verses for Hope, Commitment, Accountability, and Passion. Hope lies in what's ahead, not what has already been lived. Allow your current thoughts and behaviors to be influenced by your hope, not the past. Your future remains unwritten; you haven't lived it. You be the one to determine your destiny by your hope, not your past.

The great commission is a command for all believers. It's not a request. It will take a committed effort on your part to make this happen. You do this simply through right living. By applying these strategies to your life, the passion that is created will drive this behavior. It begins with your commitment to making it happen.

Accountability is important for self-control. Self-control and your accountability system act as the walls around the fortress. You need to protect your mind from negative outside influences and even your own bad decisions at times. It's our accountability system that serves as the checks and balances. Ensure that this part of your life is stable.

Your loyalties will reveal your passions. This needs careful monitoring and you need to feed the passion. Just make sure your feeding the right passion. Feeding harmonious passion is done by making God the center of your intention, serving others. Feeding an obsessive passion makes you the center; it's what the behavior does for you.

Intentionally implement the following:

1. You can't move forward looking in the rear view mirror of your past. Hope lies in the future. Make this the focus of your mind's eye.

2. Making disciples requires a commitment. Keep applying these strategies and pass them on to others through the difference they make in your life. In doing that, you'll be meeting this requirement. Keep moving forward.

3. Accountability and self-control go hand in hand. Build the walls of your fortress and guard it with people you can trust and go to for wise counsel.

4. Feed the right passion. It's easy to make the distinctions. Harmonious passions flow from the inside out and obsessive passion flow from the outside in. What's your motivation?

Hope

Our hope for you is unshaken, for we know that as you share
in our sufferings, you will also share in our comfort.
—II Corinthians 1:7 ESV

Meditation and Action

Paul's letters to the Corinthian church are very personal. Paul had to be
harsh and firm with them because many would not accept his authority
as an apostle and he was being challenged by others who were trying to
Judaize the church. Paul experienced a lot of suffering in his attempt to
share the gospel and establish the church among them to the point that
he felt like giving up. Contrary to what many Christians believe, God
doesn't shelter believers from suffering. What good would this serve? If
we're sheltered and protected from suffering, we'd never learn how to
live through it. The object is how we go through suffering is what
makes the difference. People without hope are crushed by suffering.
This leads to states of hopelessness. People of hope, live through their
suffering and become stronger as a result. This is what suffering can
teach us and this was Paul's message. Suffering is universal; no one is
immune. You're going to experience it. You can confront it with hope
or you can allow yourself to be overwhelmed. We can be comforted by
one another which will keep hope alive. This is how hope and
accountability work together. If your expectation (hope) is going to be

effective and bring results, it must be steadfast. With this state of mind, you too can be unshakable. If you're going through a tough time, accept the circumstance for what it is, do what is within your power, and leave the rest to God. Look toward your hope, be patient, and lean on your supports for comfort and encouragement.

Commitment

Be careful to obey all these regulations I am giving you, so that it may always go well with you and your children after you, because you will be doing what is good and right in the eyes of the LORD your God.

—Deuteronomy 12:28 NIV

Meditation and Action

The commitments you make and live by will impact the generations that follow you. The legacy you leave can be good or bad. It all depends on what you're committed to. In this verse, Moses gives a warning that the land that they were to possess could be a place of entanglement or enjoyment. It all depended on them obeying God. This verse applies equally to us all these years later. The land that we're called to possess when we accept God's gift of salvation (the quality of life we will live and the effectiveness of our lives) depends on our obedience to God. Because there were many stumbling blocks in the land, they were told to eradicate them when they went in to possess it. They failed to do this. We face a similar task in today's world. The world around us has many stumbling blocks that compete for our attention. We must be careful to commit to the right things because what our children see us do will influence the decisions they make and so on. Take a moment and consider the implications this verse has for your life. What do your behaviors say about where your commitments lie? What kind of legacy are you leaving? Do you need to make some changes? Acknowledge what you need to change, be accountable to write it down as an objective and be committed to taking action and monitor the changes you make. The future is made by the decisions you make today!

Accountability

Do not let sin control the way you live; do not give in to sinful desires.

—Romans 6:12 NLT

Meditation and Action

The Bible speaks endlessly about the importance of self-control for a reason. It's easy to give control over to others. We do this when we blame people and circumstances for our thoughts, emotions, and actions. The truth though is that no person or thing can make you think or feel something you don't want. Take a moment and think about the last time you had a negative thought or feeling that stemmed from what someone did or said. Were they the real cause of your thoughts and feelings or could it be your own thoughts (interpretations) about what they did and the meaning you attributed to it? I would say the latter. How about when we act negatively to life's circumstances? Do we blame bad luck for the reasons we do things we shouldn't? This is giving control to others. We need to learn to be accountable for ourselves and take responsibility for our own behavior. We can no more blame others for our thoughts and feelings than to blame our sinful desires and sinful behaviors on others. To take your control back, decide to accept responsibility and take action to make it right. The verse says to not give in to such sinful desires. This means that this is under our control. Don't be fooled with the world's reasoning that says "it's not your fault, assigning blame is just hurtful." You do have control. Responsibility begins and ends with you.

Passion

11Now finish the work, so that your eager willingness to do it may be matched by your completion of it, according to your means. 12For if the willingness is there, the gift is acceptable according to what one has, not according to what he does not have.

—2 Corinthians 8:11-12 NIV

Meditation and Action

Our willingness and passion to do something can be seen not only in how we go about what we do but also in the final product. Willingness means intention. Passion brings intention and purpose to the things we do. Have you ever received something from someone or asked someone to do something for you and they didn't really want to do it? Did that attitude reflect in the result? How did it feel to be on the receiving end of that? Perhaps, you were the unwilling person. God deserves nothing but our best. As Christians, we should be in the habit of striving for perfection, however, not in an obsessive manner. It's not that we will ever attain or reach excellence but it's the striving for excellence that makes us excellent. As this verse tells us, if the willingness is there, our work is acceptable. Don't give God or others, second best. There's no reward in that. Even if things don't work out as planned, there's assurance and peace knowing that you did your best and nothing more could have been done. These steps create and feed into keeping a harmonious passion alive and growing even in the midst of mistakes or failures. Do you need an attitude check? Serve God and others willingly. Strive for perfection in your service. These actions will yield beneficial results and others will take notice of your faithfulness. Passion is contagious.

H-CAP Recap

Review the verses for Hope, Commitment, Accountability, and Passion. No one is immune to difficult times. It would be impossible for hope to grow if it weren't challenged. When facing hardship, keep your eyes on the prize, lean on your accountability system for encouragement, and wait. Just as it takes time for a seed to germinate and grow to produce fruit, so it is with hope.

Even though we're surrounded by many distractions and temptations, God promises that if we just obey, commit to living by His standards, we can have strength to resist these temptations. If we commit to living out our faith, God will bless us. It's only as we live out our faith can we pass it down to our children. What example are you leaving?

Take control and be responsible for your behavior. Don't blame others for your sin. You choose the behavior, you choose the consequences. It is a choice. You can't change it unless you first take ownership of it.

Passion is contagious. In everything you do, seek to do it with excellence. Be the best at what you do. This is what God desires for you and will honor your efforts. The passion we put into it will be visible in the final product. Serve with intention.

Intentionally implement the following:

1. Difficult times will come and go. They don't last forever. Hope is easy when things are going good. You need it the most when times are tough, however; this is when people drop it. Keep looking toward your hope.

2. This strategy reinforces what was also covered with Accountability. Even though we're surrounded by many distractions, keep your mind's eye focused on the goal and remain committed to right behaviors. God demands obedience and loyalty. Your ability to resist temptation lies in your willingness to be obedient.

3. Accountability is taking responsibility. If God says to resist, this means it is within your power. Don't allow yourself to be overcome by the emotion of wrong doing. This leads to blaming. Be accountable.

4. Let your passion be contagious. Allow your passion to show through your behaviors and interactions with others. Strive for excellence.

Hope

23Let us hold fast the confession of our hope without wavering, for he who promised is faithful. 24And let us consider how to stir up one another to love and good works.
—Hebrews 10:23-24 ESV

Meditation and Action

Hope is used here with the connotation of expectation. This is noted through the words "hold fast" and "without wavering." The confession Paul speaks of is your faith, what you believe in. This is what we need to hold on to with a tight grip. Paul uses this language to reinforce the message that hope is dynamic. It's a living thing that must be cultivated and protected. Protected against what? We need to protect it against the world and its self-indulgent influence. Without vigilantly guarding your hope, the world's influence can slowly creep in and influence (change) the lens in which you view the world. A good way to protect yourself is through having a good accountability system in place. Paul says to stir one another to love and good works. This means that we need to provide encouragement to each other. Iron sharpens iron. We can't make it alone; we need each other to pick each other up. This is what keeps hope alive. When we experience times of weakness, we can count on others to lift us up and walk with us. This is how Hope and Accountability work together. As we grow through that experience, we in turn do the same for others. This back and forth comforting and encouraging strengthens individual hope and creates resilience. You can see through this verse how hope is created on the individual commitment to hold on to it but also maintained through our willingness to hold ourselves accountable.

Commitment

> They rejected his decrees and the covenant he had made with their ancestors, and they despised all his warnings. They worshiped worthless idols, so they became worthless themselves. They followed the example of the nations around them, disobeying the LORD's command not to imitate them.
>
> —2 Kings 17:15 NLT

Meditation and Action

In this chapter God's longsuffering for the nation of Israel had run out. As a result of their disobedience, He allowed Israel to be taken captive by Assyria. This verse has implications for us today in that as Israel, when we forget God's mercy, when we imitate the ungodly, turn a deaf ear to hearing the word of God, allow false gods into our lives, God will allow us to be taken captive by the world. God does this for our good with the hope of it waking us up to our sin and returning to Him. However, we can also become bitter, blame, and succumb to our surroundings. The choice is yours. Sadly, many Christians find themselves in this situation. Being in the world yet to be not of it, can be difficult to navigate which is why it requires a commitment to vigilance. If you're not being vigilant in monitoring your faith, you can end up just like Israel did. They slowly assimilated and made accommodations for ungodly things in their lives until God had enough. Learn from this lesson. Allow it to serve as a wakeup call. Commit to following God's example and living for Him. Reject the world's way of justifying wrong behavior. Don't be normal, commit to standing out in the crowd through your acts of service and dedication to God. What do you need to change in your life, what do you need to give up to get back on track? Recommit to getting out of the world and into God.

Accountability

When you enter the land the LORD your God is giving you, do not learn to imitate the detestable ways of the nations there.

—Deuteronomy 18:9 NIV

Meditation and Action

We're constantly surrounded by negative influences. God's warning to Israel going into the land was to not mingle with the people and take part in their customs. In fact, He wanted them to destroy everyone and everything in the land. Why, to avoid this problem in the first place? In the same way, we need to eradicate sin from our lives. To do this, we need to be accountable to God, self, and others. It can be easy to fall into temptation. However, if you create a system of accountability and are open to allowing these people to check you without being defensive, you can spare yourself a lot of heartache. Strength comes when you have a multitude of advisors whom you can count on. However, you have to be willing to heed their direction. The Bible says that although we are in the world, we are not to be of the world. Destroy the influence and the footholds of the world that you've given place to. The moral of story is to keep people around you who hunger and seek after the things of God and allow their state of mind to positively influence you. Separate yourself from people, places, and things that serve to distract you. This is what accountable people do.

Passion

Never be lazy, but work hard and serve the Lord enthusiastically.

—Romans 12:11 NLT

Meditation and Action

It's human nature to want to take the path of least resistance. We always want maximum profit with the least investment. However, in the end, you will always get out of life what you put into it. The enthusiasm Paul talks about here is passion. Over 90% of the world's population lives their lives on autopilot and this includes the church. They find little enjoyment in what they do and just tolerate others or their jobs. They find little satisfaction in their jobs because most people fall into careers out of necessity instead of choice. In other words, the job or career chose them instead of the other way around. Life sets in and before you know it, you're just doing what you need to do to survive. This is not how God intends for you to live. We can live with passion (enthusiasm). However, change can only come with intentional action. We cannot be complacent. Are you part of the 90%? Passion is created by doing the right behaviors that feed into it. Turn off the autopilot and begin to live intentionally. Take control and set a course of behaviors of doing for others, meet needs of people you come into contact with. Remember, meeting needs can be as little as the giving of a kind word. Knowing that you added to someone's day and made it special for them in some small way will create passion and meaning in your life. Don't be lazy, do it!

H-CAP Recap

R eview the verses for Hope, Commitment, Accountability, and Passion. Hope and Accountability work together. Paul tells us to hold on to hope without wavering. This means hope can waver. Hope can waver when experiencing difficult times. It's during these times that Paul urges us to stick together and be a source of encouragement. This keeps hope alive.

Commitment to serving God requires you to disavow the ways of the world. Refuse to allow yourself to be negatively influenced by the world's way. In today's times more than ever, what was considered as wrong behavior is now considered right and what was right behavior is now wrong. Commit to excellence.

Living for God in the midst of a falling world will be the most difficult task you'll face. The onslaught of negative influence is unrelenting. Having stable relationships around you that can help keep you on track in your commitments is vital. Be accountable. Imitate godly people, not worldly people.

Your level of passion is revealed in your behaviors. God demands excellence. Laziness has no place in the kingdom of God. Resist the temptation to take the path of least resistance. Live intentionally and join the 10% club.

Intentionally implement the following:

1. Keep hope alive and keep it from wavering. Cling to your support system and renew your hope. You don't have to go it alone.

2. Serving God will require you to destroy the strongholds presented by the world. Refuse to allow yourself (your mind) to be taken captive. Commit yourself to right living.

3. As you apply step #2, don't forget to feed your accountability system. This will be your source of strength and encouragement.

4. As you apply the above steps, your passion for godly things will increase. As changes occur on the inside, it will reflect on the outside.

Hope

Be patient, therefore, brothers, until the coming of the Lord. See how the farmer waits for the precious fruit of the earth, being patient about it, until it receives the early and the late rains.

—James 5:7 ESV

Meditation and Action

Just because a seed is planted doesn't mean it will grow. There are other factors that dictate the potential for germination and the quality of growth once a seed sprouts. The farmer plants in the hopes of a good return. They never plant not expecting their crops to grow; they also never plant without tending to what they've planted through watering, fertilizing, and taking steps to ensure the minimization of insect damage. In doing all these things, the farmer waits until harvest time. Our faith/hope operates in the same manner. Being made in the image of God, we're all given a measure of hope from God at creation. However, it must be cultivated in order for it to grow. It requires feeding which comes in the form of encouragement through exposing yourself to the right environment. This is where accountability comes in. It's up to you as the farmer of your hope to create an environment conducive to growth. You then have to wait. Growth occurs over time. It must take its natural course. While you're waiting, live your life with expectation. Keep yourself surrounded with likeminded others on the same journey. As you go through life, your hope will be challenged not unlike a bad storm can threaten a farmer's crop. However, as you make use of your accountability system and survive, your hope will grow stronger. The process continues to repeat itself and as you grow, you become more resilient, enabling you to withstand the storms of life. This is abundant living at its best, knowing we win. Have hope.

Commitment

If your sons will keep My covenant And My testimony which I shall teach them, Their sons also shall sit upon your throne forevermore."
—Psalm 132:12 NKJV

Meditation and Action

God promised David that his blood line will forever sit on the throne. At the time this psalm was written, Israel would be without a king until the birth of Jesus who is from the lineage of David. However, note the contingency of this promise, your sons must keep My covenant and My testimony. God's promises fall into two categories, His general grace and blessing that applies to all mankind whether they believe in Him or not and the promise of eternal life which is offered only to believers. It's possible for non-believers to enjoy God's blessing when they act on biblical principles even though they don't acknowledge it as such. He causes the sun to shine on the just and unjust alike. However, salvation, spending eternity with God, is offered only to those who believe and live out their lives for Him. We are to become living sacrifices. This is the deal. Salvation is not about saying a prayer of forgiveness and accepting God and then going back to living as you once did. You're fooling yourself. It's not that we won't make mistakes; however, it's our response to our sins and our continuous pursuit for holiness that shapes and builds our faith. Anything short of this and we run the risk of God saying, "You had a form of godliness but denied its true power, I never knew you." Commit yourself to keeping God's witness alive in your life by living it. You can do this by applying all the steps you're learning in this devotional. Do one of them today and every day.

Accountability

Students are not greater than their teacher. But the student who is fully trained will become like the teacher.
—Luke 6:40 NLT

Meditation and Action

The reason we're to follow the example of Christ is because we are to strive to become more like Him. This is the growth process through learning. Through this verse we see the developmental process of growth between the student and the teacher. From a spiritual perspective, the teacher is Christ and we are the students. Any good student seeks to become like the teacher in deed and knowledge. Over time, the student begins to think and act like the teacher. Through the exposure of the relationship and learning, you mature and learn how to apply knowledge under different circumstances. As this happens, they become fully trained and are now like the teacher and are able to teach others. This is how knowledge and skills are passed down. Two things must happen in order for this process to work, 1. The student needs to align themselves with the teacher and allow themselves to influenced. 2. The student must have a heart for learning. This is accountability. In order for one to become proficient at something, they need to be taught. The first step is to seek out someone who knows and is willing to teach you. You then need to submit to their authority to learn. If your goal is to develop spiritually, seek out someone willing to teach you and be a spiritual mentor. Submit yourself to their authority and let the learning begin.

Passion

Their loyalty is divided between God and the world, and
they are unstable in everything they do.

—James 1:8 NLT

Meditation and Action

Loyalty is linked to passion and behavior (commitment). You can
see where one's loyalties lie based on their passions and behaviors
to fulfill them. To achieve success in anything, you cannot have
divided loyalties. You cannot serve two masters. By nature, this is
an unstable relationship and is the source of confusion. With regard
to spiritual resilience, there are distinct differences between being
of the world and being in it. We certainly can't change our location
of being on earth, in the world itself. However, we can choose
whether we'll adopt the culture. The world as we know it has a
pervasive culture of instant gratification, lust, selfishness,
intolerance where morality is now relative. We've come to accept
immoral behavior and the breakup of traditional family values as
the new normal while those who espouse right living and moral
awareness are considered racist, intolerant, and bigots. Sadly, many
Christians have fallen into this trap of wearing the Christian label
yet live the new normal lifestyle. It's hard for people to want to be
different, we want to fit it. However, as James tells us, you must

choose. Are you in the habit of wearing the Christian label and have you found yourself to look more like the world as opposed to being different. To what have you been loyal to, the obsessive passions of the world or harmonious passions of the Spirit? If the former, seek to separate yourself from the worlds ways of living and begin serving God with purpose. This purposeful behavior will result in a harmonious passion of goal directed behavior.

H-CAP Recap

Review the verses for Hope, Commitment, Accountability, and Passion. Hope is a growth process as described in this week's verse. For it to grow, it needs your attention to supplying it with the necessary care. Feed it with encouragement from yourself and others. Doing so will enable your hope to weather the most difficult of times.

God promises to bless us not only with the gift of living an abundant life on earth but with eternal salvation. Although He freely gives this, we must be obedient in serving Him through the denial of self and service to others. It's you giving God permission to live through you. You can only get the benefit of His promise as you commit to this. It's not really a trade off or cost of doing business. It's a win, win situation for us. How could you not commit when what you get far outweighs what you give?

Our goal in developing spiritual resilience is to become more like Jesus. Just as Paul told his disciples, "follow me as I follow Christ." We need a model and a teacher to show us how to apply the model. We also need a heart (passion) for learning. Find someone to teach you and allow their way of life, state of mind, to influence you to be more Christ like.

Allow your passion to serve Christ reveal your loyalty to Him. Don't seek to be "normal." Stand out from the world. Be different. Pursue excellence in what you do particularly in your service to Christ which is shown in your service to others. Allow your passion to be contagious.

Intentionally implement the following:

1. Feed your hope. In order for it to be there when you need it, you need to be in the habit of feeding it so it can grow. Because it's a growth process, this takes time. Don't expect instant gratification. Feed it with plenty of encouragement and as you face obstacles and feed it during this process, it will grow. It's an ever growing trait.

2. God's blessing is determined by your willingness to commit to Him. Do you want all of God's blessing or just a small blessing? The sacrifice on your part is really no sacrifice at all once you consider what you get in return. The only thing that would hold you back is fear. Commit.

3. You will only be as strong and or as smart as the source of your teaching. Seek out people who are more knowledgeable than you in the faith. Learn from them. Allow them to influence your way of thinking. Just make sure you choose the right models.

4. Allow your passion to influence others around you. Don't seek or settle for being average. Seek God's best for you and be the best.

Hope

When doubts filled my mind, your comfort gave me renewed
hope and cheer.

—Psalm 94:19 NLT

Meditation and Action

Doubt is the growing point of hope. We all have times where we begin
to doubt whether the things we hope for will materialize. We need to
recognize that this is a normal process and not condemn ourselves
simply because we doubt. The Bible is full of stories of spiritual giants
who've doubted including Jesus. The reason these stories are recorded
is for the purpose of giving us hope. Growth never comes without
conflict. In other words, hope can't grow unless it's being challenged.
We see this back in the very beginning with Adam and Eve. God told
them not to eat of the tree of knowledge. It was a challenge to their
hope. Their downfall was that they put their hope in the wrong thing.
So, doubt in and of itself is not the enemy per say but what you do
with it. It takes a challenge for hope to grow. The key to overcoming
doubt is to not allow it to overcome you. You can do this by
comforting yourself. The term comfort here implies encouragement
and support which is comforting to the mind. When we're encouraged,
our hope is renewed which dispels doubt and we grow. The cycle
keeps repeating itself as long as we live. The world will always

challenge your hope. It's your ability to face the challenge in spite of doubt, encouraging yourself, and allowing yourself to be encouraged by others that gives you strength to overcome. This is the process of resilience. Are you being challenged? Find someone to encourage, encourage yourself, and seek out and receive encouragement from others. Do these things, and you're guaranteed to make it.

Commitment

"But as soon as they had rest, they did evil again before You; Therefore You abandoned them to the hand of their enemies, so that they ruled over them. When they cried again to You, You heard from heaven, and many times You rescued them according to Your compassion.
—Nehemiah 9:28 NASB

Meditation and Action

We can always depend on God to take us back into right relationship with him when we do wrong. It's His unconditional love. However, it's up to us to come before Him, acknowledge our sin, and accept His forgiveness. The theme of the book of Nehemiah is to trust in God and living for Him no matter what obstacles are encountered along the way. It's easy to become complacent when we let our guard down. This makes us vulnerable to negative influence and most people don't give this much thought. It's like boiling a frog. By gradually turning up the heat, the frog adjusts and never knows it being cooked. Sin can work in the same insidious way. You can make allowances when your guard is down and before you know it, your whole life can be turned upside down and you're left wondering what happened. Remaining vigilant is an ongoing process. Regardless of the obstacles and or roadblocks you face in life, like Nehemiah, they continued to build the walls and fight at the same time; you need to commit to continue your vigilance even in the midst of opposition. Refuse to give into complacency. Make excellence your standard and demand nothing less from yourself. Don't fall into the trap of receiving God's blessing and then getting comfortable and forgetting. Remain committed.

Accountability

10If anyone comes to your meeting and does not teach the truth about Christ, don't invite that person into your home or give any kind of encouragement.11Anyone who encourages such people becomes a partner in their evil work.

—2 John 1:10-11 NLT

Meditation and Action

This verse is a caution to wrong relationships. Earlier we discussed the instructions God gave Moses when entering into the land. Israel was not to allow themselves to be negatively influenced by the customs of the people there. When we become entangled in relationships that influence us in a negative way, we are aligning ourselves with them and become partners in their evil work. Note how the word "encouragement" is used here. Encouragement creates hope and passion. We can hope in the wrong things and passions can be obsessive as in this case. Don't align yourself (building accountability) with these people. Complete separation is the only remedy. This is not saying we shut off ourselves from the world. However, we don't have the same type of relationships with people who do not share in our love for Christ. The reason is because God is a jealous God. There is no room for any other. Do you have relationships that influence you in a negative way? Identify them and separate yourself and take steps to grow relationships that build on your relationship with Christ. Doing so will enable you to love and reach out to the lost without being sucked back into the world.

Passion

11You will be enriched in every way for great generosity, which through us will produce thanksgiving to God; 12for the rendering of this service not only supplies the wants of the saints but also overflows in many thanksgivings to God.
—2 Corinthians 9:11-12 RSV

Meditation and Action

Generosity breeds thanksgiving to both the giver and receiver. There is no better way to create harmonious passion than through acts of generosity. It's through meeting the needs of others that ignites the spark which produces the flame. Once the flame is created, it's up to you to keep it burning by feeding it. If you've been applying the tasks of this devotional daily, you're already experiencing the development of passion. Keep your acts of giving going. If you've been slow to get started, all it takes is for you to give something away every day. It can be as little as a kind word, a word of encouragement, a gift of money, or time. If you see a need and it's within your ability to meet it, simply do so. We get as a result of our giving. Our giving is not a loss of something. This is the world's state of mind, "if I give, I'm now without." This attitude blocks our willingness to give and serve others and is fueled by a poverty mentality. If you want to "get" you have to "give." I'm asking you to have hope and believe the word of God. This goes against the world's way of thinking. Commit yourself to action, regardless of what your emotions are telling you. Jumping into this principle is like pouring gasoline on fire. In the same manner, you'll begin to experience a passion for the things of God while the things of earth grow strangely dim. Are you up for this?

H-CAP Recap

Review the verses for Hope, Commitment, Accountability, and Passion. If you're not being challenged, hope can't grow. Don't think it some strange thing when confronted with obstacles to your goals. Keep hope alive by seeking comfort (encouragement). Doubt in and of itself is not the enemy. It's common to all of us. It's what you do with it. Think of it as an opportunity for growth, not destruction.

Stay committed to living your faith. Don't become complacent as Israel was in the habit of doing. Learn this lesson. Yes, God will take you back, but think of the heartache and loss to yourself and family you can spare yourself from if you just remain on task. Hold yourself accountable and stay committed.

Make sure you take steps to align yourself with the right people who can build your hope and feed your passion in the right direction. Don't give place and encouragement to people who do not hold themselves to the same standard. Doing so is contributing to their behavior.

The flame of passion is ignited by your decision to act. Give and serve others. As you are enabled to meet the need of another, even just giving a kind word of encouragement can serve to set ablaze your passion for continued service. Don't let fear keep you from right behavior. Give to get.

Intentionally implement the following:

1. Doubt is an opportunity for growth. It's normal. Seek to be encouraged when hit by doubt and it will enable you to see those opportunities. Remember; see with your mind's eye, not your natural eye.

2. Remain faithful in your commitment to live out your faith. Learn from others. The Bible is full of examples of the destruction suffered as a result of turning away from God. You don't have to go down that road. Commit to staying the course.

3. Your ability to apply #1 and #2 will be contingent on your success with this step. Seek out relationships with people stronger than you. Model their behavior and thought processes.

4. Add to your behaviors the intentional act of giving, serving others. There is no better thing you can do that will feed your motivation than to give to others and knowing that you made a difference in their life.

Hope

19 If in this life only we have hope in Christ, we are of all men the most pitiable. 20 But now Christ is risen from the dead, [and] has become the first fruits of those who have fallen asleep.

—I Corinthians 15:19-20 NKJV

Meditation and Action

The believer is promised peace, joy, and abundant life. In the midst of life's most difficult challenges, we have the assurance that we can still experience peace. However, these promises aren't just for this side of life. To view God's blessing in this narrowly defined manner is short sighted. We live out our faith, what we hope for, not just for the benefits for this side of life but also for eternity. The ultimate goal is living in eternity with Christ. The culmination of our hope will be fulfilled after death, after this life is over. Our hope is in the belief that death is not the end but really the beginning. Because Jesus was raised from the dead, death has no hold on the believer. Because of this act, we're promised eternal life with Christ and we can live without fear. We're promised everlasting peace, joy, and an end to all suffering. We're promised that everything we experience in life can't compare to the riches we'll one day receive. It's this hope that serves as the foundation for everything we hope for. This is the source of all hope. Don't get caught up living just for the now. Allow your current behavior to be influenced by the ultimate goal of reigning with Christ.

This is hope fulfilled. Keeping this mindset and allowing this to be the lens in which you view the world can change your life. However, you have to look in that direction in order to go in that direction. Remember, you always go where you're looking not where you say you want to go.

Commitment

The laborer's appetite works for him; his hunger drives him on.
—Proverbs 16:26 NIV

Meditation and Action

Appetites can direct good or bad behavior. You can always tell what a person's passions are by their behavior (the things they are committed to). The key is to be hungry for the right things. A prepared heart is one that commits and submits to God. What comes out of our mouth is a reflection of what's in our heart. A heart that's committed to the things of God will direct helpful and encouraging speech, and sometimes admonishment when it's not delivered from spite. A proud heart leads to speech that reflects self-interest and defensiveness. A purposeful heart is one that is committed to growing in the knowledge of God's word and applying it. A perverse heart is stubborn, obstinate, and pertinacious. What do your behaviors reveal about what drives your passions? If you find that your appetites are misdirected, commit to seeking and obtaining goals that bring honor and praise to God. You can do this by setting your mind on heavenly things as opposed to earthly things and by serving others. Making a daily habit of this will build a resilient and faithful spirit within. Committing to the right behaviors will feed a harmonious passion (appetite). It's this passion that will feed into itself and keep the motivation alive for more committed behaviors. It will work for you.

Accountability

Run from anything that stimulates youthful lusts. Instead, pursue righteous living, faithfulness, love, and peace. Enjoy the companionship of those who call on the Lord with pure hearts.

—2 Timothy 2:22 NLT

Meditation and Action

The heart of accountability lies in the taking of responsibility. Paul is clear in giving instruction to young Timothy in the pursuit of godly living. Youthful lusts are misguided and full of emotion. The power of emotion is that when entertained, they lead to action which results in sin (death). The mark of an adult should be wisdom. They have the mind to recognize these lusts and instead of being directed by emotion, turn to righteous living instead. This is reinforced through the type of companionship we keep. Do your relationships reinforce youthful misguided decisions or the wisdom reflected though righteous living? If the former, you can make a wise decision today to eliminate those relationships and create ones that will reinforce the mind set of spiritual success. Paul emphasizes this to Timothy by using the word "run." You need to run from the influence of youthful lusts and immature thinking. You need to take it that serious. It's the equivalent to running from danger. Take a moment and reflect on what relationships you need to eliminate and which ones you need to create or reinforce. The quality of your spiritual life depends on it.

Passion

He who seeks good finds goodwill, but evil comes to him who searches for it.
                                        —Proverbs 11:27 NIV

Meditation and Action

Harmonious passion can always be found if you search for it, likewise will obsessive passion. Remember, it's the nature of mankind to go with obsessive passion. This will feel more natural because it's serving the flesh. This takes no effort on our part and will not be hard to find. However, goodness and goodwill take effort. These are things we need to develop and anything that needs to develop, by the nature of the word implies a growth process. Remember, the traits of Hope, Commitment, Accountability, and Passion is innate to all of mankind. This is God's image in which man is made. However, life has a way of eroding these traits. Although they can erode, they are not destroyed. They need to be cultivated and worked in order for them to be the new normal. It's the same process of anything you'd seek to achieve whether it is getting in physical shape, education, career, etc. You need to commit to a new set of behaviors and lifestyle to make it happen. Create a habit of seeking right living and commit to acts of goodwill. Following this rule will create and keep a harmonious passion which will feed into itself. However, you must always be vigilant to keep it alive. A fire that is not fed will eventually die out. The same goes with passion. It must be fed. Seek good and do good.

H-CAP Recap

Review the verses for Hope, Commitment, Accountability, and Passion. The ultimate fulfillment of our hope comes after death of the physical body. Hope applied during our lives in our physical body allows us to live effective and abundant lives. However, it's not just for these blessings do we seek hope. Our goal, the prize, is heaven. Allow this goal to be an encouragement to you.

We are driven by our appetites (passions). A commitment to the right behaviors will give the motivation for right passions. These behaviors include service to others, monitoring your life to make sure you're holding yourself accountable, feeding your hope with encouragement, and the worshiping of God.

Get in the habit of exercising mature decision making. Run from situations, places, people, that would otherwise tempt youthful and immature decisions that feed into emotion. This will always lead to destruction. Create and invest in relationships that will reinforce mature thinking and self-control. This is where wisdom is found. Apply it.

Harmonious passion must be sought after unlike obsessive passions which will always be there to tempt you. The question is which one will you feed? It will take intention to feed and develop your harmonious passions. Commit to behaviors of goodwill toward others. Seeing the impact you make on the lives of others will keep passion alive. Feed the right one.

Intentionally implement the following:

1. Eternity is the ultimate goal for the Christian. It's this hope that gives us the strength to endure. The Bible says that anything we experience in this life can't compare to what we'll receive in heaven. Allow this thought to remain firm in your mind and reflect on it regularly as a source of encouragement.

2. As long as you commit to the right behaviors, everything else will feed back into itself. It's not that you will be on autopilot. You will always need to make intentional decisions and be vigilant. Commit to keeping the H-CAP traits alive and working.

3. Your state of mind and behavior will reflect your relationships. Create a buffer against making destructive decisions based on emotion. Surround yourself with the right people.

4. You have the choice of feeding you obsessive passions or to create harmonious passions. Obsessive passions are fed by not following step #3. It's following youthful lusts. Not making mature decisions and following emotion. Commit to behaviors that influence your desire for spiritual growth.

Hope

Remember this--a farmer who plants only a few seeds will get a small crop. But the one who plants generously will get a generous crop.

—II Corinthians 9:6 NLT

Meditation and Action

A farmer can only expect a crop in proportion to the seed he sows. The same lesson applies to how we live our lives. You get what you give. It has often been said that in life there are givers and takers. Takers never have enough no matter how much they have. This comes from a poverty mentality; poverty not in money but thought, state of mind, well-being, hope. This kind of life is driven by fear and obsessive passion and leaves little room for hope, at least hope in the right things. However, the giver receives in abundance. They can expect a generous return on their investment. Note, that the return may not be material or wealth but something much more valuable. Things like peace, satisfaction, contentment, well-being, resilience, and hope. These things are priceless. It's the gift and ability to live abundantly in the midst of a broken world. The giver gives because they have hope and because they have hope, they give. Which category do you fall into? Are you a giver or a taker? Do you hoard your possessions, time, the withholding of giving yourself to others for fear of being taken advantage of or some other loss? If so, you're already poor. Creating hope begins with taking the focus off of yourself and recognizing the needs of others. Give others a reason to hope by meeting some need for them. Doing so will create a hopeful attitude in you and in so doing you will become rich.

Commitment

But someone will say, "You have faith; I have deeds." Show me your faith without deeds, and I will show you my faith by what I do.

—James 2:18 NIV

Meditation and Action

Commitment is where we give feet to what we hope for. Our behavior shows where our commitments lay and to what we hope for. You can hope for something endlessly, however, unless you're willing to put feet to your hope through committed behaviors, your hope is nothing but a pipedream or false hope. Hope and faith are displayed (backed up) through our behavior. The behaviors we commit to reveal our hope and faith. Examine your behaviors with an outsider's perspective. What do they reveal about what you place your hope in? Do your behaviors align with your hope and faith or do they go in opposite direction? Does your witness align with what you say you believe in? If not, be committed to acting out your faith so it can be seen by others. It's what others see you do that makes the difference as behaviors speak louder than words.

Accountability

24Do not associate with a man given to anger; Or go with a hot-tempered man, 25Or you will learn his ways and find a snare for yourself.

—Proverbs 22:24-25 NASB

Meditation and Action

In learning to create the trait of accountability, the meaning and influence of significant relationships is reinforced over and over again. The reason being is because the Bible makes it clear that this is the primary function that sets the course for our state of mind and what we allow to influence it. Our spiritual well-being depends on it. The author, most likely Solomon, who is noted as the wisest man who ever lived, makes this association crystal clear. Hang around ill-tempered people and you will learn and adopt their ways. It's that simple. The only counter to this is to hang around those who are not hot-tempered and prone to emotional decision making and action. This is an intentional decision and not made passively as if it will happen on its own. Choose your friends wisely. Hang around those who display self-control, restraint, contemplation. This will also rub off on you. The choice is always yours. Take a moment and examine your life and what changes you need to make and take the appropriate action. Avoid the snare!

Passion

What is desired in a man is loyalty, and a poor man is better than a liar.

—Proverbs 19:22 RSV

Meditation and Action

Loyalty is inspired by passion. However, we need to be loyal to the right things. Loyalty is defined by a commitment to something, an obligation. True loyalty is hard to find. We're often loyal until something happens that we don't like or things don't work out as planned. Instead of sticking it out, we rationalize and make excuses and jump ship. This isn't loyalty. Being committed while things go your way doesn't require any loyalty. Loyalty is tested and reveals itself by the commitment to stick it out during the rough times and making it through. Up until that point, there is no loyalty. This is how many people live their lives as Christians. They are willing to serve God and seek Him when things are going good, as things are working according to their plan. However, at the slightest bit of discomfort or when things take a turn for the worst, they bail. The attitude is that if

God allows this to happen then it's He who breaks the obligation so in turn I'm justified to walk away. We need to remember, that it's Satan who is in control of earthly things. Due to the fall, God merely allows life to take its course. All of mankind suffers at various times. This was true even with Jesus. However, perseverance and resilience can only be created through trial. It's not that God has bailed; it's an opportunity for the growth of passion. Are you truly loyal?

H-CAP Recap

Review the verses for Hope, Commitment, Accountability, and Passion. The Bible promises that if we give we'll get back in abundance. This thought runs contrary to the world of take, take, take and do unto others before they do unto you. Give generously and you can expect to get generously. The return may not be immediate but it will come. Have hope in the investment you make in others. It's investing in the Bank of Heaven which can never go bankrupt and the returns are unmatchable.

Commitment is putting your money where your mouth is. You can say that you're a believer but your behavior will prove it. We're not saved simply by what we say. Our words and behavior need to match up. Otherwise, we lie. Show your faith by living it.

You become those you hang around with. It's that simple. As you apply step #2 on Commitment, add this to your "to do" list. End relationships with ill-tempered people and invest in relationships with those who exhibit temperance and sound judgment.

Are you loyal or a fair weather Christian? God demands loyalty which is a hard trait to find in people. Loyalty is tested in the fire of life, not when all is right. Allow your hope and passion to carry you through difficult times. Remain loyal to the cause to the end.

Intentionally implement the following:

1. As you give and pour into the lives of others, have hope for a good return on your investment. The return is in the future and may not be immediate. It seldom is. Keep looking ahead.

2. Your behaviors reveal what you truly believe. Back up what you say you believe in through right behavior.

3. Continue to seek out and maintain right relationships that move you forward. If you're not moving forward, you're going backwards.

4. Stick it out. Be loyal to your faith in all circumstances, not just when things are going good.

Hope

When you go through deep waters, I will be with you. When you go through rivers of difficulty, you will not drown. When you walk through the fire of oppression, you will not be burned up; the flames will not consume you.

—Isaiah 43:2 NLT

Meditation and Action

What an increasable promise we have that God will protect us. He will always be there and walk with us through any circumstance. Because of this, we have reason to face life with boldness and without fear. How would your life be different if you really believed this? The problem for many is that they don't truly believe it. Many have a false belief that because they're a Christian, they shouldn't go through difficult times or that because they go through difficult times; God is punishing them or has left them. Understand the context of the verse. God is speaking through Isaiah to the nation of Israel; they are His people. He's reminding them of His promise to them, giving them hope. God doesn't spare anyone from experiencing life. However, He does remind us that as we go through life, when it feels like we're about to drown, when it looks like we're on a one way collision course to crash and burn, when there's seemingly no way out, He's with us. He sees, knows, and feels our pain. If you can remind yourself of this as you endure and not complain and think that He's left you, it can provide hope much like a good friend who stands by you and walks with you and holds your hand. How would your life be different, how would your attitude change as you faced life, the same life everyone faces if you believed and acted on this? Do it and discover this truth for yourself.

Commitment

3Not only so, but we also rejoice in our sufferings, because we know that suffering produces perseverance; 4perseverance, character; and character, hope. 5And hope does not disappoint us, because God has poured out his love into our hearts by the Holy Spirit, whom he has given us.
—Romans 5:3-5 NIV

Meditation and Action

The right state of mind when confronting life is important. Although trials can be painful, there is a purpose to our suffering. While we may view our hardship through the natural mind and try to make sense out of non-sensical things that happen, we need to keep in mind that God allows us to suffer through the natural progressions of life on earth. We need to remember that God always works things out for our good as we go through trials. The good that God works may not be the outcome that we have in mind such as a healing, the prevention of a death, etc. However, it will always be the strengthening of our faith to the building of perseverance (resilience) and hope. It is a true saying that what doesn't kill us makes us stronger. The rejoicing that Paul refers to is not to be happy for the trials themselves but in the knowing that God will walk with you through it for the perfecting of faith and character. It's the rejoicing that God will somehow bring peace and restoration to your life. Remember that you always go where you're looking. The key to getting the most out of negative situations is to look to this verse and others like it and to lean on your accountability system to help you through. By committing yourself to these steps as you walk through your trials, you will come out stronger. Look through the obstacle to what's on the other side.

Accountability

Learn to do right! Seek justice, encourage the oppressed. Defend the cause of the fatherless, plead the case of the widow.

—Isaiah 1:17 NIV

Meditation and Action

Selfless giving and doing for others not only serves to create hope, commitment, and passion but it also reinforces accountability. We need to learn to do right. It's not that we don't know right from wrong because we're born with a sense of this concept. However, doing right for the sake of rightness in spite of having emotions to the contrary takes learning. It takes accountability. You need to have others around you who model this behavior and who can provide encouragement for you as you do them. This type of learning is called scaffolding. It's learning that takes place as you engage in behaviors under the leadership of those who are masters of the behavior. You learn as they do and model their behavior. It's when we apply this through helping others, in this case, being an encouragement to others, defending the causes of the fatherless and widow that strengthens the core of the H-CAP traits. Doing for others takes the focus off of us and helps us to become others centered. Take this step in accountability by taking action. Seek out those in need and provide encouragement. If it's within your means to do more than that by the giving of time and money, do so.

Passion

> For we dare not class ourselves or compare ourselves with those who commend themselves. But they, measuring themselves by themselves, and comparing themselves among themselves, are not wise.
>
> —2 Corinthians 10:12 NKJV

Meditation and Action

The world lives in competition. Our value is based on conditions and acceptance of others and how we measure up compared to others. This mindset is the root of obsessive passion. The Bible tells us that we're to run our own race. Christianity is not a competition or a sprint to the finish; it's a journey, a marathon. It's how we run our race that counts not whether we get there ahead of someone else. You can't run your best while you're focused on what others are doing. The reason Paul says that this is not wise is because it slows us down and takes us off course. Focusing on the "competition" of it promotes self-pride. Once we start comparing ourselves to others, obsessive passion kicks in. We then find ourselves engaging in behaviors for the purpose of making us feel good. This is the opposite of what God wants for your life. Note, however, that we should strive to be the best and give our best in whatever we do. However, this striving comes from the inside out and not the outside in. It's the striving for excellence that makes us excellent. It's Christ and His goals for our lives that become our race.

Examine your own life through the measure of living out what God has intended for you. Whose race are you really running? If you find yourself in the "rat race" you're running the wrong race. Stop, get your priorities in order and run toward what God is calling you to do.

H-CAP Recap

Review the verses for Hope, Commitment, Accountability, and Passion. We have the assurance that as we go through life, God will not leave us. Although difficult times may seem unbearable, He is with us. Just because we experience hardship is in no way an indicator of punishment or God turning His back on us. Hope in the fact that as this week's verse indicates, He is with you.

God allows us to experience all that life has to offer, the good and the bad to build character and perseverance. Don't be surprised by these things but be committed to the process. Commit to learning these lessons and let it build character.

Learning to do right does not always come intuitively. Sometimes, as the verse indicates, you need to learn it. From whom you learn it is the one you will need to be accountable to. Learn from the right people.

Obsessive passion will lead you to focus on the competition of life. The only competition is with you. Are you meeting your goals, are you following the passion God has put on your heart or are you too busy worrying about what others have and what you don't? Run your own race.

Intentionally implement the following:

1. Be assured, God will never leave you. Don't use the circumstance as a measure of this. Have hope in what He has told you. He is there. Lean on him through the forms of encouragement you can give yourself and from others.

2. People aren't born with good character, it's created. It's created through trial and learning to live rightly through difficult times. Commit to making the right decisions to build good character.

3. As indicated in step #2, the learning process requires a teacher. Who you align yourself and model your behavior after is about accountability. Learn from those who know and have a proven track record.

4. Don't allow obsessive passion to take your focus from running your own race. Living out your faith is a one man race. Just do your own part and let God take care of the rest.

Hope

And we know that God causes everything to work together for the good of those who love God and are called according to his purpose for them.

—Romans 8:28 NLT

Meditation and Action

As we experience life, God assures us that He will always work things out for our good. This is a promise that we can hang our hope on. We need to be mindful that we don't always see the bigger picture. When things don't go as planned and we get frustrated, angry, and act out, we're only seeing things from our narrow perspective. We have to have hope/faith that regardless of what we see, God is doing things we cannot see. The payoff may not come at that moment because He may have other people He has to work through. With hope, comes trust. As we hope, we must trust that God will do as He said. If we truly believe this, it will produce a peace in the midst of chaos. We can give up the worry because God has it under control. Even if it doesn't work out as we wanted it to, God still has a plan. We need to conform ourselves to God's plan, not the other way around. Believing that God must work according to our wishes is what leads to anxiety, frustration, and blaming. How would your life be different, if no matter what happened in your life, you believed this verse to be true? Imagine living a life of being anxious for nothing. It is possible and it gives you something to hope for but to make this hope realized requires action on your part. Trust, believe it to be true and live it out. This builds resilience and will make you different from the rest of the world, even most believers.

Commitment

Those who live according to the sinful nature have their minds set on what that nature desires; but those who live accordance with the Spirit have their minds set on what the Spirit desires.

—Romans 8:5 NIV

Meditation and Action

Paul experienced the same struggles as we do. Our human nature is flawed due to the fall. All of mankind battles against the temptation of doing wrong. Although we have the desire to do what is right (this is our conscience) our flesh (desires) wants the opposite. We're in a constant battle between what we know we should do and what our flesh desires. However, there is a way to win this battle against the flesh. Remember, we will always have fleshly desires. The goal is to not eradicate them and not have them in first place; this is impossible as long as we have earthly bodies. The goal is to change the outcome of the desires. This is controlled by what your mind is focused on. Remember, you go where you're looking. When sinful desires creep in, and they will, if you give it attention, it will gain a foothold and become stronger. You can acknowledge a sinful desire without engaging the desire. By engaging I mean to dialogue with it in your mind. This is giving it power. The more you interact with the desire in your mind, the stronger it gets, good or bad. Intentionally look in another direction; shift your mind's eye to godly things. If you commit to setting your mind on the things of the Spirit and actively engage with those thoughts, you will strengthen the spiritual nature. Two things cannot occupy the same space at the same time. It's a law of physics. If your mind is focused on godly things, it can't be occupied by sinful desires at the same time and vice versa. However, you must act and intentionally look in the direction you want to go in.

Accountability

23When Abigail saw David, she quickly got off her donkey and bowed low before him. 24She fell at his feet and said, "I accept all blame in this matter, my lord. Please listen to what I have to say.

—I Samuel 25: 23-24 NLT

Meditation and Action

David was seeking revenge against Nabal for how he treated him and his men. Revenge is a natural emotion but left unchecked can lead to destruction. Here, Abigail confronted David and reminded him of

Nabal's foolish nature and his own which was to do and fulfill the work of God. Abigail held herself accountable by humbling herself and taking responsibility. However, David also was accountable in that he listened to what she had to say and decided against killing Nabal. Who was she that David the warrior listened to her? It was because David had a spirit of accountability and knew that what she was saying was right. To kill Nabal in his anger would have amounted to murder leaving a scar jeopardizing his ability to be used by God. Because David listened to this counsel, he withdrew. How do you react to direction particularly from those who may be subordinate to you? If your mind set is one of being above others, you will likely not take direction well. However, if you acknowledge that you don't always have the right answers and are open to direction from others, this is a mark of a wise person. Take action by listening to others, be slow to anger.

Passion

16So I say, live by the Spirit, and you will not gratify the desires of the sinful nature. 17For the sinful nature desires what is contrary to the Spirit, and the Spirit what is contrary to the sinful nature. They are in conflict with each other, so that you do not do what you want.

—Galatians 5:16-17 NIV

Meditation and Action

To live by the Spirit or to live by the sinful nature is living out a harmonious versus an obsessive passion. They work in opposite directions. Harmonious passion works from the inside out and obsessive passion works from the outside in. You can ask yourself this question, "Do I need the behavior to fulfill some desire in me?" If the answer is "yes" it's obsessive. Behavior that edifies our spiritual nature comes from within. They promote oneness with God and willingness for service. The two natures will always be in conflict with each other but you need to be aware of the battle within. This awareness requires an intentional act and must be closely monitored. If you create and live out a harmonious passion, you won't gratify desires of the flesh. However, if you're living out your obsessions, you can't be living for the Spirit. Two things can't occupy the same space at the same time. Without being vigilant and guarding your passion, you will automatically lean toward an obsessive passion as this is the nature of man. It's what's natural. If you remain consistent in living out your faith, your spirit will become stronger and resilient. Note that the inner conflict is the red flag waving for you to take notice that something isn't right. Don't simply dismiss it. Take notice and follow the right passion.

H-CAP Recap

Review the verses for Hope, Commitment, Accountability, and Passion. Be encouraged with the fact that God will work things out for your good. Don't focus on the circumstances but on what the promise is. Receive encouragement from others to lift your spirits. Look to what's coming, not what you have.

Commit to setting your mind on things of the spirit. When hit by lustful thoughts or desires, don't give them place. Commit to a simple observation and refocus on the task at hand. If the desires get too strong, you may have to stop what you're doing and engage in an incompatible activity until the desire goes away. These are committed strategies that work if you commit to using them consistently.

Accountability is taking responsibility for your behavior. Sometimes you may need to heed direction from people you don't expect to hear from. This doesn't mean that you should discount what they have to say. Good advice can come from unlikely places as in the case of this week's verse. Listen and take responsible action.

If you live by the Spirit and live out your harmonious passions, you'll be resistant to living out obsessive passions. It's the law of resistance and submission. Both passions may be at work within you, just choose the right one.

Intentionally implement the following:

1. When hit with difficult circumstances, get into the habit of reminding yourself that God will work it out. Tell yourself this over and over. Receive encouragement from others and let God work.

2. Commit to not giving place to lustful thoughts that will turn into desires. Simply refuse to give them place. You can't stop the thoughts and chase them away; that gives them more power. Redirect your focus to something else and let it pass.

3. Sound advice can come from unlikely places. If you're being accountable, you'll listen and give consideration before acting. This is what accountable people do.

4. If you live by the Spirit, you won't have time to entertain desires of the flesh. If you resist one thing, you have to submit to something else. In this case, it's resisting obsessive passions and submitting to your harmonious passions. They will both be present, you must choose which one you will follow.

Hope

16 Therefore we do not lose heart. Though outwardly we are wasting away, yet inwardly we are being renewed day by day. 17 For our light and momentary troubles are achieving for us an eternal glory that far outweighs them all. 18 So we fix our eyes not on what is seen, but on what is unseen. For what is seen is temporary, but what is unseen is eternal.
—II Corinthians 4:16-18 NIV

Meditation and Action

This verse provides an excellent example of hope in action when faced with difficult times. Our outward bodies are subject to the aging process of wear and tear. As we age we lose strength and stamina. You begin to feel the aches and pains and recovery comes slower than it used to as in young adulthood. However, inwardly, our hope continues to get stronger. This is one thing that gets stronger as we age. We should get better in its application through experience. Life can be harder at times than others. This verse tells us that no matter what we face here on earth as far as difficulties, these troubles can't compare to the joy and glory we'll experience in heaven. This is to bring us hope. This is what we're to be looking at when we go through tough times: 1. It won't last forever. 2. Knowing that in the end, we do win; we will achieve and receive something greater. This is like having money in the bank. You don't have to worry about that check not clearing because you have plenty in reserves. Jesus experienced this in the Garden of Gethsemane. He pleaded with God to let what was to take place, pass. However, the Bible says that for the glory that was set before Him, He endured the cross. It's the same for us. Fix your eyes on what's ahead. This is where your hope is. You won't find it in your current circumstance. Hope is what is not seen. Look to where you're going, and allow yourself to be encouraged. This is where you'll find hope.

Commitment

> Then you will have success if you are careful to observe the decrees and laws that the LORD gave Moses for Israel. Be strong and courageous. Do not be afraid or discouraged.
> —I Chronicles 22:13 NIV

Meditation and Action

The key to success is clear, be careful to observe God's ways, be strong, courageous, and fearless. How is it that we can be strong, courageous, and fearless and not succumb to discouragement? This is accomplished by observing the things of God. The word, observe, means to not only take notice of but to put into practice. By the act of doing, we set our mind's eye on a goal, a target. By keeping the goal in sight through our actions, this takes our focus off of the circumstances that will serve to make us fear and doubt. Fear and doubt are normal when faced with circumstances that are unfamiliar to us. However, when we focus on that aspect, the fear and discouragement will grow and push out any courage we had. If we choose to focus on observing God and finding comfort and support through our accountability system, we can be encouraged which creates hope and strength. The commitment on your end lies in the observing to do part. Are you facing difficult and challenging times and feel discouraged? Don't isolate yourself. Commit to observing things of the Spirit and behave accordingly which includes tapping into your accountability system. This will provide encouragement and strength.

Accountability

Walk with the wise and become wise; associate with fools and get in trouble.
—Proverbs 13:20 NLT

Meditation and Action

The wise Solomon says it all in this verse. If you want to be wise, associate with those who display wisdom. To do this takes intentional action. You get the other side of this verse simply by default. The message being that you become like those you associate with. There will always be more people and opportunity to associate with fools than wise individuals simply because there are more of them. Therefore, to choose correctly will require an intentional act of seeking out and aligning yourself with right minded people. Examine your relationships. Do you associate with more fools that serve to negatively influence a Christian style of life? This can be a hard task for some because you may not want to recognize this. However, accountability demands action (commitment). It won't happen on its own or by default. If your goal is to develop accountability in your life, it begins with right relationships. No individual trait in the H-CAP model operates separately. In order for each trait to be fully developed, you need to use all of them. Accountability is no exception. Surround yourself with people who are wiser then you. Find them and befriend them.

Passion

The humble will be filled with fresh joy from the LORD.
The poor will rejoice in the Holy One of Israel.
         —Isaiah 29:18 NLT

Meditation and Action

A common trait of living out harmonious passion is humility. The opposite of humility is pride and to feed into pride leads to obsessive passion. Pride and obsessive passion work from the outside in. Pride is a false sense of security which makes you the source, the center of attention. Humility is like being behind the scenes and allowing God to be seen through our behaviors. It's not about us but God. It's God who needs to be the object of how we live, not us and how strong and good we are. Do your actions reflect your faith in God or do they reflect you? Create a harmonious passion by serving others. Do things for other people and make meeting needs of others your focus. If you're following this devotional, you've already set into motion the practice of serving and giving to others. Remember, serving can come in a variety of forms. Just do something nice for other people. These acts of kindness will change your heart by creating a passion for helping and caring for others. This is the joy that this verse speaks of. It also creates humility. This needs to be cultivated and fed regularly to maintain it. However, once you get started it will feed into itself to keep the momentum going. The toughest part is starting. What can you do today for someone else that has no strings attached? The very act of thinking about doing one thing for someone each day will keep you in the right mindset.

H-CAP Recap

Review the verses for Hope, Commitment, Accountability, and Passion. Hope is found in the future, not in what's taking place in the moment. If you want to get through your current circumstance, you need to look to your hope, what is presently not seen, the ultimate outcome. This serves to motivate us to stick it out. It provides encouragement. Make hope work for you. Don't fix your eyes on the present; fix them on what's ahead.

The Bible tells us to be strong and courageous. That means we have to choose to be these things. The time to choose is when you're gripped by fear. Think about it. There's no real need for courage and strength in action when things are good. It's when you're being challenged that these traits need to be brought out. Commit to observing God's ways and activate your hope by looking to what's ahead. This is how hope and commitment work together. Together, they provide courage and strength.

This week's verse on Accountability cannot be more clear and simple. Just as the saying goes with food, "you are what you eat" so it is with relationships. You become who you choose to associate with. Choose wisely.

Harmonious passions are not prideful as in obsessive passions. The goal is to create and maintain a humble attitude. Allow Christ to be seen through your life, not you. You can do this by making your service to others your priority. Do something each day to make someone else's day. As you do this, a passion for service will develop and increase as you put it into operation.

Intentionally implement the following:

1. You will always go in the direction you're looking. In order to receive strength and encouragement from your hope, you need to fix your eyes on it. Hope is in the future, it's where you're going, not the present. Allow your hope to work for you. Look ahead.

2. Hope and commitment work together. In order to receive strength and courage, you need to be energized by activating hope. This means you need to look ahead; believe that you can do it and that God will make it happen. Knowing God has your back will give you boldness.

3. Don't be a fool. Accountability requires you to commit to choosing the right relationships to influence you. Choose wisely. You won't get to where you want to go without having this level of guidance.

4. Let Christ be seen through your actions. Let Him take the credit, not you. Harmonious passions are created through acts of service to mankind. He's the reason we do these things. If

you're doing them for self-gratification, that's obsession. Serve without taking the credit.

Hope

47When the woman realized that she could not stay hidden, she began to tremble and fell to her knees in front of him. The whole crowd heard her explain why she had touched him and that she had been immediately healed. 48"Daughter," he said to her, "your faith has made you well. Go in peace."

—Luke 8:47-48 NLT

Meditation and Action

The story of the woman healed with the issue of blood is one of hope. As Jesus was passing through the city street, He was surrounded by a great crowd. However, this woman was determined to get to Jesus and touch Him. She believed that this physical connection would heal her and she was determined to make it happen at any cost. She had nothing to lose. Her hope and faith was so strong that she believed that even if she was unable to reach His flesh, if she could just touch His clothing that was connected to His flesh, this would be good enough to heal her. Her hope in being healed was something in the future, something that was yet to happen. In her mind, there was only one outcome. To make hope realized takes a commitment to action. As a result of this woman's faith and determination, she was healed. She fixed her eyes on what was ahead (her healing). Although she could have looked at the crowd and told herself "I'll never make it." "I can't fight through all those people." She refused to let the size of the crowd discourage her and turn away. This is what hope does. It gives you boldness to act on what you believe. What's your issue? Don't focus on the circumstance. Don't allow the crowd to deter your commitment to action in living out your hope. Do it anyway. As the woman was healed based on her faith and commit to act on it, God will honor your faith. It may not be a physical healing but He will give you what you need in that moment. Don't give up.

Commitment

Listen to advice and accept instruction, and in the end you will be wise.
—Proverbs 19:20 NIV

Meditation and Action

Successful people listen before they act. They aren't quick to jump to conclusions and act rashly. However, this takes training in controlling our emotions and behaviors. Emotions can often times override our best judgment and get us into trouble. Learning to listen first and accept instruction can be difficult, particularly when the instruction comes in the form of criticism. In these situations, we're most likely to stop listening and react defensively. This is foolhardy. Listening and learning requires an intentional act, a commitment. Do you have a habit of being reactionary to advice, particularly when it's something you don't want to hear? Wisdom comes from training yourself to listen and accept instruction. Although criticism can be hard to hear, there's usually some amount of truth in it. Think about that. This is why it's hard to hear. If there wasn't any truth in it, we wouldn't care about it and just move on. The fact that it stings is a red flag that something's going on. This is your clue to LISTEN. Have you received criticism lately? What truths are there that need examined? Commit to listening and taking appropriate action. Then go to that person and thank them. This is how commitment and accountability work together.

Accountability

8 Judah said to his father, "Send the boy with me, and we will be on our way. Otherwise we will all die of starvation—and not only we, but you and our little ones. 9I personally guarantee his safety. You may hold me responsible if I don't bring him back to you. Then let me bear the blame forever.

—Genesis 43:8-9 NLT

Meditation and Action

Life's circumstances present in ways to create accountability. We can choose to make the right decision or the wrong one; we see this in the story of Joseph as a ruler in Egypt selling food to his unsuspecting family. Recall that Joseph was sold into slavery by his brothers. Now,

Joseph was in a position of power and his brothers came to him seeking mercy in need of food. However, they did not know that it was Joseph they were dealing with. Before Joseph would give them what they wanted, he demanded that they bring back their brother, Benjamin. Their father, Jacob, was greatly dismayed with this as he feared losing Benjamin as he did Joseph. Judah steps up and takes responsibility for Benjamin's return because he knows what's at stake. Judah does the right thing by taking responsibility and following through. He held himself accountable to his father and if he failed, there was no one to blame but himself. Notice, he says that he will accept the blame forever. How do you deal with life's difficult moments? Do you run and hide, blame? If you have and you're still suffering the effects, take responsibility and make it right. It's never too late to start creating accountability in your life. Accountability creates good character.

Passion

The members of the council were amazed when they saw the
boldness of Peter and John, for they could see that they
were ordinary men with no special training in the Scriptures.
They also recognized them as men who had been with Jesus.
—Acts 4:13 NLT

Meditation and Action

Passion is contagious. People can tell where you've been based on the
passion you have for something. Passion takes the ordinary and makes
it extraordinary. This is what living abundantly is about. Because of
Peter's and John's relationship with Christ and the passion they
exuded to serve Him, they exhibited a boldness and self-confidence
they did not have before. Note that the verse says that they were
recognized as men who had been with Jesus. This was evident from
their passion, hopefulness, committed behaviors they were engaged in,
and the accountable relationships they had with others. In light of this
information, the question for consideration in today's devotion is as
others observe you, is it evident that you had been with Jesus? What
do your passions say about your priorities? If you don't like the
answer, getting back on track will require you to commit yourself to
the right relationships so the faith of others can serve as an
encouragement to you which will increase your hope and commit to
serve others. This will also serve to further your knowledge and

increase your passion for the things of God. As you do these things, your boldness will increase which leads to perseverance and resilience. Make the necessary changes in your behavior today that make it evident to others that you are a believer. You will need to make this an intentional act for it to create passion.

H-CAP Recap

Review the verses for Hope, Commitment, Accountability, and Passion. Hope is for the purpose of providing stamina. It gives you strength to face difficult times. Fix your eyes on your hope and don't give up. Commit to behaviors of following through and living out your hope. This is the only way the goal will be achieved.

Commitment to right behaviors not only applies to giving feet to your hope but also applies to creating accountability and passion. All of the H-CAP traits require committed behaviors to set them into motion. As seen in this week's verse, commitment to listening to advice and taking appropriate action is the mark of a wise person. Although the advice or correction may sting, a commitment to right action regardless of emotion can be a humbling experience. This is the lesson.

People who aren't accountable don't take responsibility for their actions. They blame others or circumstances for their failures. Having such an attitude will prevent you from ever obtaining your goals. You will make mistakes, this isn't the problem. It's what you do when you make mistakes that counts. Develop good character by practicing accountability. Own your decisions and when wrong, make them right.

Our passions are created in the midst of the company we keep. As this week's verse on Passion mentions, they could tell they had been with Jesus because of their boldness (passion). What do your relationships and behaviors reveal about your passion? To increase your passion for godly things, increase your accountable relationships with like-minded people. Let the world see that you've been with Jesus because of your passion.

Intentionally implement the following:

1. Hope doesn't give up. Don't stop believing and allow your hope to drive your behavior.
2. Commit yourself to right action whatever the circumstance. Listen to advice. Don't be quick to discard something just because you don't like it or it doesn't feel right. Right behavior is not about feelings.
3. Take responsibility for your decisions, don't seek someone or something to blame.
4. Allow your passion for Christ to be on display for the world to see. Don't hide it.

Appendix

High Capacity Model of Well-being and Resilience Scale (H-CAP Scale)

Hope

Very true
Frequently true
Occasionally true
Rarely true
Not true

1. I can think of different ways to get the things I want that are most important to me. 1 2 3 4 5

2. When I am faced with a problem, I can think of ways to solve it. 1 2 3 4 5

3. I think I can change the direction of my future. 1 2 3 4 5

4. Once I set my mind to do something, I can achieve it. 1 2 3 4 5

5. I spend a lot of time worrying if things will work out. 1 2 3 4 5

6. I believe I have inner strength.   1   2   3   4   5

7. I think that I might as well give up   1   2   3   4   5
    because I don't see things getting
    any better for me.

8. When things go wrong, I receive   1   2   3   4   5
    some comfort knowing that my
    circumstances can't stay this way
    forever.

9. I can't imagine what my life would   1   2   3   4   5
    be like in 10 years.

10. When I look ahead, I believe that   1   2   3   4   5
    things will get better.

Commitment

| | Very true |
| Frequently true |
| Occasionally true |
| Rarely true |
| Not true |

1. I believe I am a hard worker.   1   2   3   4   5

2. Once I start something, I can finish it.   1   2   3   4   5

3. I usually have to wait for me to "feel   1   2   3   4   5
   like it" before I can get myself going.

4. When I get discouraged, my   1   2   3   4   5
   tendency is to stop trying.

5. The longer it takes me to do   1   2   3   4   5
   something, the less I'm willing to
   carry it out.

6. I carefully plan my actions before   1   2   3   4   5
   committing to them.

7. I can force myself to accomplish a   1   2   3   4   5
   task even though I don't feel like it.

8. Failing at something prevents me   1   2   3   4   5
   from trying.

Tim Barclay, Ph.D.

Accountability

Very true

Frequently true

Occasionally true

Rarely true

Not true

1. I have people in my life I can turn to for advice.   1   2   3   4   5

2. It makes me feel secure to have those I love around me.   1   2   3   4   5

3. Family relationships are important to me.   1   2   3   4   5

4. Most of the people I know can be trusted.   1   2   3   4   5

5. I let those closest to me know how much they mean to me.   1   2   3   4   5

6. It is because of the decisions I made as the reason for my circumstances.   1   2   3   4   5

Passion

	Very true
	Frequently true
	Occasionally true
	Rarely true
	Not true

1. My current role in life is in harmony with the other activities in my life.
    1   2   3   4   5

2. The new things I discover in fulfilling my current role in life allow me to appreciate my role even more.
    1   2   3   4   5

3. My current role in life reflects the qualities I like about myself.
    1   2   3   4   5

4. My current role allows me to live a variety of experiences.
    1   2   3   4   5

5. My current role in life is in harmony with the other things that are part of me.
    1   2   3   4   5

6. My current role in life is so exciting that I sometimes lose control over it.
    1   2   3   4   5

Barclay, T.H. and Barclay, R.D. (2013) The High Capacity Model of Well-being and Resilience Scale

Scoring

Hope Scale: All items are scored 1-5 with the exception of items 5, 7 and 9. These items are reversed scored. For example, if you marked 5 as your answer to any of the reversed scored items, you would calculate it as a 1. If you marked a 1 as your answer, it would be calculated as 5, etc.. The maximum score on the Hope Scale is 50. The clinical population mean is equal to =/<29.63 and the non-clinical population mean is equal to =/> 43.69.

Commitment Scale: All items are scored 1-5 with the exception of items 3, 4, 5, and 8, these items are reversed scored. For example, if you marked 5 as your answer to any of the reversed scored items, you would calculate it as a 1. If you marked a 1 as your answer, it would be calculated as 5, etc.. The maximum score in the Commitment Scale is 40. The clinical population mean is equal to =/<23.98 and the non-clinical population mean is equal to =/> 33.81.

Accountability Scale: All items are scored 1-5. The maximum score in the Accountability Scale is 30. The clinical population mean is equal to =/< 23.15 and the non-clinical population mean is equal to =/> 27.01.

Passion Scale: All items are scored 1-5. The maximum score on the Passion Scale is 30. The clinical population mean is equal to =/< 13.36 and the non-clinical population mean is equal to =/> 20.28.

The overall score means for the clinical population are equal to =/<90.13 and the non-clinical population is equal to =/>124.80.

Tim Barclay, Ph.D.

Interpreting Your H-CAP Score

The H-CAP Questionnaire has been normed on clinical and non-clinical populations. The clinical population consisted of participants with diagnosed mental illnesses from an inpatient unit. Mental illnesses ranged from clinical depression, various forms of anxiety and depression, and dual diagnosis (drug addiction and an accompanying mood disorder). The non-clinical population consisted of graduate students in education in the pursuit of their Master's degree and active duty special operations personnel consisting of Navy Seals, Army Special Forces (Green Berets), and U.S. Air Force Combat Controllers.

Those within the clinical population are expected to have lower degrees of Hope, Commitment, Accountability, and Passion compared to the non-clinical populations. You can use the mean score information for each trait to see where you fall in comparison to the norming groups. You can use this information to assess your individual strengths and weaknesses for each trait as well as your overall score. In applying the H-CAP model to your scores, you can work on your weaknesses by focusing on the devotions for a given trait or you may progress through and work on all of them in order. Either way, you will strengthen each of the traits as they are reciprocal.

Once you have completed the model, you are encouraged to retake the assessment to measure your growth. You can go through the model as many times as you like as well as retaking the assessment to keep track of your growth.

CPSIA information can be obtained at www.ICGtesting.com
Printed in the USA
LVOW10s1829170116

471057LV00001B/228/P